HOW NOT TO BACKPACK

Tips, Tricks and Stories Based on Years of Doing Things the *Wrong* Way

By

David Edwards

Copyright © 2014 David Edwards

All rights reserved.

ISBN: 1505457599
ISBN-13: 978-1505457599

Author Bio

After my initial trip from hell which nearly put me off travel for life, I decided to have a crack at it again and have since made 15 international trips travelling to over 40 countries (some multiple times) in 6 continents. I have dual citizenship (German/Australian) and normally live in Australia, but have also lived in Dalian and Shanghai in China, and San Pedro in Guatemala. In Australia I spent 2.5 years living in a backpacker's hostel while working my normal job of a professional high-voltage electrical engineer in a snazzy office. Why? Why not. It was awesome.

Interests vary by the month, but include photography, travel, writing, skydiving, paragliding, kiteboarding, volcano boarding, flying, surfing, snowboarding, wakeboarding, white-water rafting, boxing, MMA (cage-fighting), weight training, caving, scuba diving, spear fishing, hiking, canyoning, weight training, alcohol distilling, party hosting, performing magic, salsa dancing, nutrition, alternative medicine, massage, Reiki, meditation, yoga, learning languages, being a nerd, building/fixing things, scaring myself and trying new things.

I'm 29.

Foreword

Pfffft! A book on how to backpack? I don't need that! I'm a backpacker – I'm independent, the world is my oyster! Yes, maybe, but have you ever stepped on an oyster barefoot? It *hurts!*

This book is written after years of backpacking.... the wrong way. Not one thing I've written is by common sense. It's all stuff that I've learned through experience.

I know, because I've been... and I've been kicked in the arse by it. Then I did the same again. And again. It sucked each time. I eventually realised I needed to change my carefree, fun-loving ways, ironically enough, to have the most fun.

I've been $0.30 away from stranded in the Sahara Desert, I've been completely out of money four times while travelling, I've even been so stupid as to go overseas without any cash at all and not even any credit cards.

I've had a sword held to my throat, had AK-47's pointed at me, had my nose broken, received 2nd degree burns, been ripped off, been terribly sick, pooped myself in public, been lost in the desert, been pickpocketed, lost a camera 50 hrs after buying it, struggled with 50kg luggage through crowded Tokyo subways with a possibly fractured spine and pneumonia, accidently set off a grass fire next to a Filipino village and camped five days in Iceland without any warm clothes.

I've been stranded, sick and alone, felt like the saddest person in the world and have been in situations that seemed impossible. Many times.

I've had a lot of absolutely incredible times too and have learned a few tricks to make great times awesome times. Want to know how to get free drinks?

Want to know how to make out with a perfect 10/10 girl or boy within two minutes of meeting them (95% success rate)? Want to know how to make money travelling? Want to know how to use your camera properly?

I've now learned some things to ensure a lot more fun times and less shitty times.

I pride myself on the fact that this book isn't researched. If you want to know about something, you can use Google just as well as I can. That's not the purpose of this book. The purpose of this book is to make you think of things that you may not normally think about.

Enjoy and travel smart!

Table of Contents

Author Bio iii
Foreword v
Introduction 1
Chapter 1: Travel Prep 5
    Organisation 6
    Travel Insurance 9
    Money Matters 10
    Know Where You Are 15
    Chapter Summary 16
Chapter 2: Packing 17
Chapter 3: Planning Your Trip 19
    Where to Go When 19
    Alone or With a Friend? 21
    Dangerous Countries 22
    Chapter Summary 24
Chapter 4: Organised Tours 25
    Chapter Summary 28
Chapter 5: Travel 29
    Air Travel 29
    Rail 44
    Road Travel 46
    Boats 48
    Other 48
    Local Transport 49
    Chapter Summary 52
Chapter 6: Accommodation 55
    Staying with Friends 55

Couchsurfing 56
Hostel Accommodation 57
Camping 63
Chapter Summary 65

Chapter 7: Day Trips 67
Exploring 67
Organised Trips 68
Hikes 70
High Altitude 72
Chapter Summary 75

Chapter 8: Partying 77
Where to Go 77
What to Pack 77
Know How to Get Home 79
General Going Out Tips 82
Drinking Laws 82
Magic 83
Being the Life of the Party 83
Picking Up 88
Drugs 90
Safety 91
Chapter Summary 93

Chapter 9: Money Matters - Travelling 95
Location of Cards 95
Cash 95
Border Crossings and Exchange Rate 97
Chapter Summary 98

Chapter 10: Communication 99
Travelling 99
Why You Should Learn the Language 99
Where to Learn the Language 102
Not Necessarily Rejection 103
Fun in Other Languages 104
Australian/English Language 104
Other Language Differences 110
Chapter Summary 111

Chapter 11: Sickness 113
   Preparation 113
   Prevention... 113
   Food Poisoning... 114
   Stomach (Intestinal) Bugs 114
   Different Symptoms.. 116
   Don't Be Scared Off 117
   Funny Experiences 117
   Chapter Summary 124

Chapter 12: Taking Chances, Scams and Beggars 125
   Taking Chances... 125
   Scams 135
   How to Tell if it's a Scam or Not?.................................... 137
   Beggars 138
   Chapter Summary 142

Chapter 13: General 143
   Cultural Experience.. 143
   Fire Safety 146
   Pickpocketing/Theft... 146
   Preventing Pickpocketing.. 149
   Border Crossings 150
   When Shit Goes Down 151
   Changing Location 153
   Trying Different Food 155
   Getting Tailor Made Clothing 158
   Photography 159
   Tropics 164
   Respect the Law.. 166
   Napping.. 168
   Feeling Lonely 169
   Chapter Summary 171

Chapter 14: Getting your Hippy On 175
   Chapter Summary 177

Chapter 15: Making, Saving, Spending Money 179
   Free Flights 179
   Tipping 180

Haggling (Bargaining)	182
Earning Money	184
Saving Money	187
Chapter Summary	190

Chapter 2 and a Bit: **193**
Packing… the rest of it **193**

General Considerations	193
Tourist Refund Scheme	195
When Packing Light Sucks	195
My Packing List	197
Chapter Summary	216

Chapter 16: End of the Journey **219**

Friends and Family Back Home	219

Supplementary material **223**

Getting Time Off	223
Magic	225
Getting Your Hippy on – Experiences	231

Index **247**
Appendix 1: Packing List Summaries **249**

All Items	249
Airplane Ready-Bag	251
Day Trips	252
Nights Out	252

Appendix 2: Checklists **253**

Changing Location	253

Note from the Author **255**
Notes **257**

Introduction

Backpacking, it seems, is only something you learn from experience. There are books everywhere of places to go, but nothing on the subject of the general side of backpacking. This is odd, as whether you see a specific waterfall or not is not as important as the much bigger picture, such as how to avoid being robbed, how to entertain yourself on a plane, how to save money without sacrificing comfort, how to avoid being scammed, how to avoid being stranded with no money, etc.

After many experiences of doing things the wrong way I've learned many things you shouldn't do, as well as picked up some good tips too. Granted, there're a lot of downright stupid things I've done that you'll no doubt shake your head at, but there're some other not-so-obvious things that have tripped me up, as well as cool tricks that I've picked up along the way.

This book can be read in any order. Some chapters are full of useful information but kind of boring; others are less informative but more entertaining. Hopefully together it is both informative and entertaining.

I believe it only makes sense to start this book with the intro to my first trip:

******

My first overseas trip was a bit of a disaster and almost enough to put me off travel for life. It really was. In retrospect, there are some things I could have done better.

Back in the January of 2007 I'm near the end of my university summer break and I hear there are some sale fares to Fiji. I have about $3,000 saved from my summer job and feel like an adventure. It's a Friday afternoon and I go to have a chat to the local travel agent. "Yes," she says, "there are some sale fares, but Fiji is still an expensive place." "You know what," she continues, "you're better off to spend more money on the flight and go to Thailand where everything is much cheaper there." Hmmmm ok. I have a little think then I say:

"Yeah, ok, I'll do that."

"Do what?" she asks.

"Go to Thailand."

"Ok, great! When?"

"Um, when can I go?" I ask.

"Well, the next flight is this Sunday," she replies.

"Righto, I'll take that!"

"What?? *Really?*" she asks incredulously.

"Yeah, why not!"

One hour ago I was just thinking about going to Fiji sometime in the future, now I'm taking the very next flight to Thailand! She sorts me out with travel insurance too, and I leave the shop, tickets in hand, excited to be about to embark on a grand adventure. Suddenly a horrifying thought comes to mind "Oh shit! I need money for it!!" I cycle as fast as possible into town and get to the bank as they're closing the doors. It's Friday afternoon and my flight is Sunday morning. This is my only chance. I plead with them and they let me in, and sort me out with a pre-paid travel card and some Thai Baht. Sweet! All sorted!

Next problem: I'm meant to move house this weekend. I hurry home, pack all my stuff up and spend the next day moving house. Sometime in the morning I get another thought: "Oh no! I need vaccinations, don't I!!" I call a doctor and fortunately they have a spot free, and I get my vaccinations. Phew! I finish the move, go to my new place have a very hurried chat with my new housemates and pack my bags. I head to the airport early the next morning and arrive on time, but my plane to Melbourne is delayed by a few hours. Oh poo. I'm meant to be flying Hobart to Melbourne then Melbourne to

Bangkok. The flights are close together, and with the first flight delayed I realise I'm not going to be able to catch my flight to Thailand. I talk to the airline and after a while they have it sorted; I will fly to Melbourne, then as soon as I land I will need to get a flight to Sydney, where I'll catch a flight with British Airways to Thailand. "Sweet!" I think. I'm booked with a budget airline, so I'm happy to instead be flying with a premium airline for no extra cost. They warn me however that as soon as I arrive in Melbourne I immediately need to get the flight to Sydney as it will be leaving soon after I arrive. No worries!

My flight arrives in Melbourne, and as it's taxiing in, there's an announcement on the plane that I am to see the ground staff immediately as they're holding the plane for me. As soon as the doors open, I'm sternly greeted by a member of the airline staff who whisks me away to the flight that they're holding for me. We're running through the airport for a long time and I'm thinking, bloody hell this airport is big! I ask if my bags will make it too, and she says, "Yeah yeah they're fine, just get on the plane!" On the way I fill out some green form and am pretty much kicked on to the plane.

I sit down. The engines start. The plane immediately starts taxiing away. Jeez, they really were waiting for me huh. I look around. Wow, this is a really big plane for a 1hr flight to Sydney. We taxi to the end of the runway. I look around some more. I notice the flight attendants are all Asian and are all wearing quite floral, tropical-like uniforms. I turn to the person next to me:

"This is the flight to Sydney... right?"

"No, this is the flight to Thailand."

"Oh... shit..."

Yes, due to miscommunication in Melbourne, the silly buggers held the entire plane for over an hour for me, even though a different, better plan was organised. I wasn't the most popular person on that flight.

Fortunately, after walking around the plane to a section where the people didn't know I was the person that delayed them for over an hour, I manage to make friends with some people on the plane... which saves my bum five days later.

Landing in Bangkok, I wait around for a while for my bags, but no luck.

Turns out they're still in Melbourne. I didn't receive my bags until six days into a 13-day trip.

All this; was the highly successful part of my trip. The rest went sharply downhill from there.

Highlights of my misfortune included getting completely lost on the other side of Bangkok and not remembering the street I was staying in (and not even the suburb for that matter), losing my spare bank card and cash, getting tricked and ripped off, accidently letting a travel agent book me accommodation in a place I didn't want to be, running totally out of money, getting food poisoning and not eating for four days (losing 6kg in the process), accidently eating a few mouthfuls of pure chillies as my first bit of food in four days, getting second-degree burns from a failed fire jump, getting the worst sunburn in my life, getting a broken nose, two black eyes and concussion from fighting the heavyweight Tae Kwon-Do champion of Sweden in a packed Thai Kickboxing stadium (with zero fighting experience, leg in bandages, back sunburnt to hell and just a few days after losing 6kg to food poising), and managing the final 36hrs with zero money. All this, in just 13 days.

Of course my following trips were a lot more successful than that, but this first trip provided some pretty substantial experiences and learnings. Read on to hear these stories and more of how you should *not* backpack, plus some tips on things that you *should* do.

Chapter 1: Travel Prep

Note: This chapter is all about preparation, so it is by nature pretty boring. Apologies in advance. If you get bored, just skip forward to another chapter then come back later!

Preparation is super boring and I hate it, but it can certainly pay off later. Many times over.

For long trips I still don't research a thing before I go – for long trips you'll meet people in hostels who want nothing more than to tell you all about a place and give you all the tips. You plan as you go. For short trips however, planning really does make it a lot easier. More than planning it and booking it, the more important part is to actually write the information down and keep it in one place: with you.

I once booked a snowboarding trip to Japan. I felt very organised as I had booked all flights, accommodation and lift passes on the slope, as well as the transfer direct from the airport to the ski lodge. Awesome.

Problem was I didn't print out anything.

I arrived at Narita Airport (Tokyo) with close to 50kg luggage (snowboard, boots, warm clothes and so on, plus all my camera gear; including stupid things such as a 1.8kg telephoto lens). After struggling to go to the toilet with my snowboard bag, backpack, daypack and SLR camera, I then went to get my shuttle, and then thought, shit, which one?!? There was no one standing around with a cardboard sign and my name on it (like I was expecting). I dragged all my crap to the shuttle buses and tried to ask the Japanese drivers if I was on their list.

I wasn't. Bugger. Process was then get out my crappy netbook computer to check my email. Shit! Need to pay for internet. Get out credit card, muck around and pay $5 to use internet. Find number of person I booked through. Drag all my crap to pay phones to call him. Crap. Can't use credit card in it. Dammit. Go to ATM. Get money out. Need change. Drag all my crap to a shop to get some change. They can't take the big note. Shit! Drag all my crap to another store and buy some overpriced food for the change. Drag all my crap to the payphone. Put money in. Wait, how the fooookenhell do you use these Japanese phones? Struggled for a while, but got nowhere. Shit, dammit! Run (limp with my crap) back to the shuttle that's about to leave. Wait, wait, can I borrow your phone? Try the phone but can't get through. Shit, shit, shit! Ask the shuttle driver: Where are you going? Hakuba. Perfect – that's where I need to go… but is this the right bus? The driver has a list of all the people but I'm not on it. How much? $170. Faaaaarrrrkkkk! When is the next bus? In 24 hrs. Shit, shit, shit!

Bugger it, I don't want to spend 24 hrs in this airport, so I take the gamble, pay the $170 and get on the bus extremely frustrated and exhausted, but glad to be sitting down. After a few hours on the bus, they get in touch with guy I booked through. Response, "Oh, yeah, whoops, guess I forgot to put you on the list huh." I was on the right shuttle that I had booked and paid for previously, the idiot just didn't put me on the list. As he didn't tell me the name of the shuttle company when I booked, I didn't know if this was the right one or not. I was expecting to arrive at the airport and see a person holding a bit of cardboard with my name on it, not the complete mess that it ended up being.

Lesson learned (apart from not taking 50kg luggage when travelling alone), before you leave find out the name of the shuttle you're taking, where it's departing from *and print it out!!*

Organisation

Tickets

These days with internet bookings you no longer need paper tickets – just take your passport to the check-in counter, and that's it, right? Wrong.

Catching an internal flight in Cuba from Baracoa to Havana I did the usual of just waltzing in with my passport, got to the front of the queue, handed over my passport and the lady says:

"Ticket, please."

"Erm…. I don't have one. Didn't think I needed one?"

"Oh. Big problem," she responds.

"Why?" I ask.

"No computadora."

Oh bugger. Yes, in the Baracoa airport, there aren't any computers… in the whole airport. Granted, people arrived on horseback or in a horse and cart, and there were goats in the airport complex but I was still expecting a computer at the check-in! Fortunately I had a PDF copy on my laptop which I showed her, resulting in her exiting the whole airport, coming back a few minutes later and handwriting out a paper ticket for me. Without that PDF copy I would have been stuffed, considering this 2hr flight was 12 month's wages for the average Cuban.

Be prepared.

In some airports, more so in third world countries, you need a paper ticket just to enter the airport. No ticket, no entry. This would have caught me out in the Philippines if I didn't have my paper copies.

The Fix

Save a PDF of all bookings on a specific folder on your computer. I have a Travel Folder on my desktop which contains all the info for my trip. In this I have my insurance information and another folder dedicated to flights. I rename these files to the date of the flight so all files are in order of when the flight is. e.g. '2014-04-13 Sydney-LA'. Print these tickets out too!!

For short, busy trips I recommend putting everything in Excel to keep all the condensed information together in the one table. This one-page summary makes things much easier when you have numerous transfers as it's just the one page to refer to for which flight you need to catch at which time. Ensure you include all information, particularly the terminal number as this is the most important part, and not knowing it causes the greatest amount of stress and confusion.

This really helps during booking to see the gaps you might have, as being on the one page in the one format it's easier to see if you've forgotten to book a certain transfer or night's accommodation somewhere. Having the exchange rate listed really helps in the first few days.

And remember to print everything out!

While not necessary, it can help to print out your bank account balances to satisfy immigration that you have sufficient funds for travel. I've only had to show this once, and this was in Montreal (Canada) of all places.

General Considerations

Everything you take with you can be lost or stolen. Therefore, you should take photos of everything you take to make replacement less difficult. As mentioned later, you should make a record of your packing list, but in addition to this you should also scan your passport and give a copy to family, as well as save a copy on Cloud, such as on Google Drive, One Drive, Dropbox, etc.

People tend to take more risks travelling, and while unlikely, there is the chance of dying overseas either from disease, vehicle accident, violence, kidnapping, etc. Therefore, make sure to send all your details to your family members, such as bank account details, life insurance details, superannuation information, etc. A Will is even better.

You should also check with authorities about general information before going to new countries. The Australian Government website Smart Traveller (www.smartraveller.gov.au) is excellent. This gives concise, valuable information on all countries such as safety level, general country-specific warnings, areas to avoid, visa information, health information and so on. It's information rich and concise so it doesn't take long at all to read. Definitely worth a look.

Make sure too, that after you take out insurance to print out and keep the details with you. That is, your policy number and their emergency contact number for the country you're in. Often calling them will necessitate making a reverse charge call, which will be different for each country. Keep this information in a few places such as in your wallet, in your main pack and with your passport. Ensure to note down the emergency numbers of the country you're travelling too, such as police and ambulance.

Travel Insurance

Travel insurance is easily the most boring and frustrating part of travel, yet quite possibly the most important. Unfortunately many people barely give it a second thought. Do not just get the cheapest travel insurance – you really do have to read the Terms and Conditions, particularly the 'General Exclusions'.

Inclusions/Exclusions

I love extreme sports, so travel insurance is particularly hard for me to choose. There might be one provider that covers skydiving, white-water rafting and caving, but not paragliding or kiteboarding, then another that covers paragliding and kiteboarding, but not white-water rafting! I do all these sports, so it's a battle to weigh up which I'm more likely to do, and which I'm more likely to get injured in. Make sure you know what you're covered for.

Biggie here: all insurers have a clause stating you're not covered while under the influence of alcohol or drugs. Get mugged while drunk? Not covered. Go cliff jumping and land on the rocks while booze-cruising? Not covered. Get stabbed while walking home after a night out? Not covered. If you have to get a medical evacuation due to bad injuries, you can spend the rest of your life paying off the bills.

Motorbikes. Let's face it, when you're travelling in a third world country, guaranteed you will hire a scooter. Problem is most insurers won't cover you unless you have a motorbike license. Be careful. In Corfu, Greece, I went on a quad bike adventure with a few people. Five bikes went out; three came back. First was the guide that flipped his bike a few times at 60km/h after a bee went in his goggles. I thought he was dead, but luckily he was ok. We then got a new guide and bike and continued on. After telling horror stories of the Corfu hospital, we continued along till one part where a guy and his girlfriend go off a 5m cliff and the bike lands on top of the girl, breaking her arm and collar bone. Seeing a girl stuck under a quad bike not moving sticks with you. I have also lost count of how many people I saw in Thailand and Bali covered in bandages after a motorbike accident. Like swimming and getting a tan on a tropical island? Doesn't work with a broken leg. You'll be sitting on the beach watching jealously as your friends go swimming. You'll get a great tan though.... except for the worst tan line ever where your leg is in bandages. I'm assuming it's not yet in fashion to be brown all over, and one white leg! I don't want to sound like a kill-joy (I still do all those stupid things), I'm just saying be careful and know what you're covered for.

Excess

For a long trip, if you can get $0 excess, go for it. Just think, in one year, how many times do you go to the doctor? Guaranteed it will be more while travelling. If you do manage to get $0 excess it also stops the avoidance to go to the doctor. If it's going to be $80 to go to the doctor you might think 'It's ok, I'll just tough it out'. Every time I've put off going to the doctor I later wished I went much sooner. The sooner you get things seen to, the better.

Claiming

Insurance is great… as long as you can make a claim. Some insurers are better than others. They'd rather keep money than give it out, so make sure you make it as simple as possible for them. Some insurers require receipts for all items lost or stolen. This can be extremely difficult. This is where buying online can come in handy as you will have email copies of all receipts. If you don't have receipts of all your possessions, make sure to take a photo of everything you have in your pack. This way, both you and the insurer know exactly what you have with you. Make sure of course too to write down the serial numbers of all electronic items you have.

Store all these photos and information on Cloud. There's not much point having all this information recorded on your computer if that gets stolen!

Money Matters

I first started travelling with a prepaid travel card. *Don't ever use these!!!* They are so bad in so many ways. First of all the fees are very expensive. That is, you pay to load money on, you pay each time you withdraw money from an ATM, and you get a crap exchange rate too. The worst part though, is that you have to load money onto them. Not an issue before you leave home, but once you're on the road and realise you're out of money, it's a three day wait between doing the transfer and having the money. I've been stuck in Thailand, Germany and Morocco waiting for the bloody transfer to go through. Having zero money for three days *really* sucks.

Also *make sure you actually have your card before you leave home!!* For a while I was living and working in China where I had a week's holiday anywhere in the world every four weeks. Pretty sweet. Travelling once a month it became a bit of a routine so I'd only pack just before leaving. I normally take more crap than I need, so I decided to go light this time. This was all good until I arrived in Kuala Lumpur (Malaysia), went to the airport ATM to take some cash out and realised, "Ooohhhhhh. Shhiiiiiiiit!" No card in my wallet. No cash either. Nothing... absolutely nothing. Somehow I travelled so light I didn't bring any cash or credit cards. Other than my Shanghai metro card and some receipts I had a completely empty wallet. I couldn't even leave the airport!! Not a good way to start a trip!

Beware too with MasterCard International. If you think you can lose your card and get a replacement Fed-X'ed to you the next day, think again. MasterCard International only appears to hire the stupidest people possible. I have never dealt with any company as useless as them. It really is like they are purposely acting stupid. I'm not exaggerating at all. Losing a card in Mexico, I had to wait *four months* to get a replacement card! First step was an extremely frustrating call where I gave them my friend's address in Guatemala. Even though it was an English-speaking call centre, they misheard almost every letter, so it took almost 10 frustrating minutes until they had it right. That obviously didn't help, as a month later it still hadn't arrived. Fortunately I had another three spare cards in the meantime so I was ok. I then had to go back to Australia for my brother's wedding and ordered another card. Another frustrating call and they say it will be there in two weeks.

"Are you sure?" I ask.

"Oh yes sir. In two weeks. Definitely sir," the dumb-arse phone operator responds.

I ask again, "Are you sure you have the right address? The last card didn't come."

"Oh yes sir, I have all the information."

Still not convinced, I ask again, "Are you sure? What makes you different from the last person that obviously got it wrong?"

"Oh no sir, you can guarantee it will be there in two weeks."

Three weeks later: nothing.

A frustrated me then makes another phone call. After a long time on hold I manage to talk to a guy and do the frustrating process of telling him my address again. After this he says:

"So what's your billing address?"

"What?" I ask, surprised.

"What's your billing address please?"

Somewhat annoyed, I respond, "It doesn't matter, because I'm obviously not there. I'm travelling. I asked it to be sent to this address where I am right now."

"Please sir, tell me your billing address."

"It's irrelevant."

"Please sir, your billing address."

"It's all very irrelevant, because last phone call I spent 30 minutes spelling out my current address where I wanted the card sent… because that's where I am. You realise this is a Travel Card, right?"

"Please sir, your billing address."

"Well it doesn't matter, but it's Unit 1/1 ##, ####### St, Wollongong."

"Yes, that's where it was sent."

"ARE YOU F#@&ING KIDDING ME?!?"

After some deep breaths, I try again, "Phfffffwww. Ok, let's try this again."

I then spent the next 15 minutes telling him the address of the next place I'll be, this time in Canada.

"Right, so are you sure you have the address correct?" I dubiously ask.

Operator calls out the address correctly (finally).

Unconvinced I respond, "Yes, *this is the exact same thing that happened the last two times.* They had the correct address, yet sent it to the wrong one. How can you guarantee me you won't do the same? You have the correct address now. Please send it there…. but you're just going to send it to my billing address just to piss me off, aren't you?"

"Oh no sir, I'm different. I apologise for the last operators. You can be guaranteed it will be sent to the address in Canada."

"You're definitely sure? ...because this is the exact same thing that happened the last two times."

"Oh no sir, I personally guarantee it."

Feeling relieved after all this mucking around I respond, "Ah great. Thank you so much. This has been so frustrating and I'm so glad someone is finally looking after it properly."

Take your best guess what happened? Yup, it didn't arrive. Dickhead sent it to my billing address again, just like the last two. After Canada I'm back in Guatemala and I try for the fourth time, going through the half-hour frustrating process again. This time the person says, "Oh no, replacement cards will always be sent to your billing address. I need to issue you a new card to send it to a different address. I don't know why the last three people didn't do that." Two weeks later, my card actually did arrive!

How is it possible that 75% of the staff in Lost and Stolen Cards aren't aware of this? I mean seriously, this is their job right? Isn't this all they do?

Long winded explanation I know, but each time it seemed like it was dealt with, but wasn't; resulting in a four-month process. For important things like that, ensure it is a *new* card, not a replacement, and that it isn't going to your billing address. Also make sure to get the operator's name, ID number and calling centre location. Two days after the call, call up again to see what address the card is being sent to – it may still be your billing address.

Make sure as well to record the card numbers and issuing banks of all your cards, such that if your cards get stolen, you know which to cancel. If you have multiple cards and all get stolen, it can be difficult to remember which ones you had with you.

While relevant in only one country, note that MasterCard doesn't work in Cuba, only Visa. I knew this before going so I just took out a lot of cash in Mexico, though it wasn't enough and I had to rely on a friend of a friend to borrow money. Embarrassing, and not something you want to rely on. In Nicaragua it's pretty hard to find a Mastercard ATM too. Always travel with at least one Visa and one Mastercard.

The Fix

Apologies, I can only offer specific advice for Australians at this point. It's too hard to write the best card for all nationalities, although the general advice is helpful to all.

For Australians, get a Citibank Visa debit card. I cannot recommend it more – it is amazing! 28Degrees used to be my card of choice, but as of January 2014, they have added fees to ATM cash withdrawals. Citibank however, at the time of writing, is completely free. As it's a debit card, it also links with the option of a high-interest savings account. It's perfect – I keep all my money in the high-interest account, earning 2.9%, and only keep max $500 in my account linked to the card. Therefore, if my card gets skimmed or stolen somewhere, they can only get a maximum of $500 or less, plus I'm earning maximum interest. Great thing too is as it's a linked account; funds transfer is instant; none of this three day wait crap. It's also completely free. No fees even to withdraw cash from ATM's anywhere in the world. Exchange rate is better than all too. Plus, it's Visa, not MasterCard, so it can be used in Cuba too. The other benefit is that as it's a debit card not a credit card, all transactions appear on your account immediately, whereas it normally takes three days between making a purchase and seeing it on your statement for a credit card. This instant reporting is good for budgeting and knowing how much you've spent.

Get a 28Degrees credit card too though. It was almost as good as Citibank, but now not so much due to the new fees. Get one anyway as a backup card is *essential*. There's no annual fee, so there's no reason not to. If using a credit card, a handy trick is to keep your card topped up. That is, overpay your credit card such that you are in credit. This means you're using your own money, so there's no interest to pay. Before they started implementing fees, I had taken out over $20,000 from international ATM's using my 28Degrees card without paying a cent of interest or fees. I'm probably part of the reason for the change!

Be warned with credit cards with a large limit as losing it can mean someone stealing money you don't have. Your card should have insurance so hopefully you'll get that back, *however* the insurance does not cover any money you have topped on it. Therefore, if you keep your card topped up, it's better not to have too much on it. Better to have a card with 55 day's interest-free for cash withdrawals, if possible. Since moving to Citibank now, I'm using a debit card, not a credit card, so the above no longer relates to me.

While not a money issue, I also take a backup drivers licence with me. Simplest way to do that is to go to the motor registry, say you've lost your ID and they send you a replacement. It's that easy.

Know Where You Are

If you're travelling in just the one country, chances are you'll get a phone with a data plan, yet even so, it will probably take you a few days to get this organised. Until then you'll have no internet in your pocket. If travelling through lots of countries it's almost guaranteed you won't have internet on your phone. This means you have to be organised beforehand. One great trick that few people seem to know about is the 'Store map for offline use' function in Google Maps on your phone. When you have an internet connection, search for the city you're going to, and you should see an option at the bottom of the screen 'Save map to use offline' and simply download the map of the city you're travelling to. You can do this with multiple cities. You can then use the map as per normal even without an internet connection. Note though that you cannot use the Search function. This still requires internet.

As you can't search offline, be sure to make use of the other great tool; 'place markers' while you still have an internet connection. How this is awesome is that once you've booked a hostel, just search for it on Google Maps, click on it, and then click the 'star'. This will create a pinpoint place marker on the attraction such that you can easily see it, plus it will automatically sync to your phone too. I tend to do this for both the hostel as well as the train or bus station that I will arrive at. These two steps are pretty much essential whenever changing location such that you can find your hostel.

Chapter Summary

- Print out all tickets and hotel confirmation
- Make copies of all your documents (passport, travel insurance information), send a copy to family and store on Cloud
- Write your Will, or at least give all your details to your family, such as bank account numbers, superannuation information and so on to your family in case you die while overseas
- Check information about the country you're travelling, such as with www.smartraveller.gov.au
- Ensure you are aware of your travel insurance exclusions
- Try to get travel insurance with $0 excess for long trips
- Keep insurance information with you, including emergency phone numbers for the country you're in
- Keep receipts (at home) for all items that you take with you. Scan these (or take a photo) such that you have an electronic copy too
- Store photos and serial numbers of all relevant pack items on Cloud
- Research the best travel card that gives you no fees to withdraw money from ATM's. Ensure you travel with multiple spare cards in case you lose a card
- Ensure you know which cards you're travelling with so you know which cards to block or cancel if your wallet or pack is stolen
- If you do lose your card and order another one, call them up two days later to confirm it's being sent to the correct address
- Pre-cache the maps on your phone with the city that you're travelling to
- Create place markers on the map with important items such as your hostel and point of arrival

Chapter 2: Packing

Urgh, I hate packing. I mean, how do you know what you'll need over the next year? Should you take those fancy going-out shoes or not? Hiking boots? What about one of those waterproof pack covers?

Packing is horrible, and you're never going to get it perfect... but after years of doing it wrong I've learned a few things.

Actually, you know what.... while very important, this chapter is really boring, so I'm moving it to the end of the book.

Chapter 3: Planning Your Trip

Where to Go When

So, you want to travel? Great! …but where? There are a lot of places in the world, so I'll just focus on the main places, but I think everywhere has its time.

Where you go of course depends on where you live. I'm writing this from the perspective of an Australian but will try to make it general. Your first trip when you're young should be somewhere cheap, where other young people go. For Australia, this equals Bali and South East Asia, such as Thailand, Cambodia, Vietnam, etc. Be prepared for a huge culture shock. Expect to be ripped off, scammed and have a difficult time… but also the best time of your life. Just be careful of the temptation to go 'troppo'; that is, being in such a different place that you become a very different person and do things you normally wouldn't. If you want to ease yourself into it there's the South Pacific like Vanuatu or Fiji, but be warned – it's just as expensive as Australia. New Zealand rocks as the adventure place.

For Europeans, there're a whole host of options on your doorstep. For a cheap party place; Greece springs to mind.

For Americans, I recommend Mexico. I love the rest of Central America but it doesn't have the same party scene as Mexico. Make Mexico your first trip, but DON'T do the all-inclusive Cancun thing though! Go somewhere cool like Playa del Carmen. It's certainly not as dangerous as the media would have you think and no more dangerous than any other American city.

After having a great time and learning things about yourself, it's time to work for a few years and save up for your Big Trip. For Australians and Americans, this is of course Europe, and for Europeans it's Australia. (Sorry, I don't include the USA for the backpacking trip as, while it's an amazing country, it doesn't have much of a backpacking culture. It is best done as a road trip with some friends and a car.) This Big Trip is the sort of trip where you want to have a good $15,000 saved before you go, and may well come back with an additional $5,000 in debt. For travellers going to Australia, make sure to get a working visa. Australia is not so much about the sights and attractions; it is all about the lifestyle. The longer you stay, the more you will get out of it. Get a working visa and pick up some good cash. You may return home with more money than you started with!

Many Aussies get a working visa for the UK expecting that each weekend they'll make a trip to somewhere in Europe… but they never do. When you're living and working somewhere you get stuck in your routine, plus the time and mucking around to get to Prague for example barely seems to make it worthwhile just to be able to spend a day there. General consensus is that it's better to save up then travel properly. Of course to work in the UK would be a great experience and everyone loves it, just don't expect to be exploring a different country every weekend.

Europe is an absolutely amazing place and is perfect for the 22-26 year-old demographic, plus of course others that have slipped through the cracks. Not many 18-21 year-old backpackers there due to the cost. There's culture, amazing landscapes, so, so many fun things to do, and of course, amazing nightlife. There's something for everyone and it's extremely easy to travel around. With enough money, you could just keep travelling around Europe. You can never see it all!

There are of course other places you want to see however, particularly Central and South America. Interestingly enough, the traveller age demographic here is typically 26-30 as the backpackers tend to go here after they've done Australia and Europe. Central America is great for different reasons. It's a lot less touristy than South East Asia, so it's cheap but without all the street hawkers and scammers. In my view it's much easier and more pleasant to travel here. The only problem is that this therefore equates to less nightlife. Of course it's still there, just certainly not on the same level as South East Asia or Europe. This is why I recommend to do it in this order – go to the crazy places when you're young, go to Europe when you have a bit more money but still want to party, then when a bit older and a bit more cultured and partying is no longer such a priority go to Central/South America or

Africa.

I recommend doing the USA after you've done a few travels and amassed a few American friends. This is because there's not much of a backpacking scene, so having friends that you can visit will save you lots on accommodation and will take you to some really cool places where you get to see the *real* America. Of course after this, you'll want to go to Europe again as it's so awesome.

Alone or With a Friend?

Depends. In my view, the biggest factor is whether there's a backpacker scene or not. Europe is the birthplace of backpacking so of course there's a huge backpacking scene. For sure you'll be fine doing it yourself. In fact, I recommend it as it makes you more flexible and means you have a greater chance of getting Couchsurfing hosts. Even without trying, you're making new friends every few minutes. In 4.5 months in Europe, the longest I went alone was about 1.5hrs in a train (in which I was happy to be alone for a while), then at a stop a few Aussie girls piled onto the seat next to mine, thereby ending my 90 minutes of alone time. Backpacking is just so easy in Europe too, with English everywhere, good transport and minimal scams. There's not much that can go wrong.

In countries without a backpacking scene, I recommend going with a friend. I don't know if it has changed by now, but when I travelled Thailand, Bali and Morocco there weren't any hostels, only hotels. This meant it was a lot harder to meet people, so you have to put yourself out there more. Of course there're other people in your position that want to meet people and band together too, but it's just harder to find and takes a bit more approaching of people.

Shit tends to go down a lot more often in third world countries and that's where it can help *so* much to have someone else with you, both to lend you money if you have your money stolen, or for mental support when everything goes wrong. It can also really help to have the other sounding board to discuss if some offer sounds dodgy or not.

In Central America I was surprised just how well setup it was for backpacking. It's so easy; it's just like Europe! There are many hostels with quite a defined backpacker route, so meeting people is no problem at all.

For the USA there's not so much of a hostel culture and transport can be pretty bad too. The USA is awesome though, so I recommend going with a friend, buying a car and doing a huge road trip.

Dangerous Countries

Speak to the average person in the USA and they'll say sure as hell don't go to Mexico as it's super dangerous, and they'll try all they can to try and convince you not to go. To the uninitiated, this can seem quite alarming… until you ask the question, "Have you been?" Of course the answer will be a solid, "Hell no! I ain't crazy!" I've now learned to only take advice from people that have actually been. Turn on international news and yes, you will always see lots of stories about drug-related gang violence in Mexico. We've all heard about the public beheadings and so on. Sounds very dangerous right? Interestingly enough, after Japan and China, Mexico is for sure the safest feeling place that I've ever travelled to. The towns are just beautiful and the people are great. Note the keyword, that it's 'drug-related gang violence'. If you're not part of a cartel, then you'll be fine. If someone is dealing with exports of drugs worth millions, they probably aren't interested in mugging a backpacker for some soiled underwear and an iPod. Read news stories about the US however, and it's full of violence to innocent people; drive by shootings, massacres in cinemas, muggings, etc. Much of the violence is non-provoked. That's the real scary stuff.

Of course there are still dangerous parts (a friend of mine was kidnapped, beaten and mugged at knife-point in Mexico), so just make sure to keep your wits about you. Recommendation, as always, is to check out Smart Traveller to see the safety warnings, and places to avoid. This will still however paint a bleaker picture than it is for most people but the warnings are very useful. I find Trip Advisor very good to hear people's personal experiences. My family didn't want me to go to El Salvador due to all the bad publicity about the place, but I went regardless and felt very safe. The people were very friendly and not out to scam you in the slightest. Don't listen to people that haven't been.

Smaller towns tend to be a lot safer as it's unlikely there'll be gangs there, and as everyone knows one another, people can't get away with crime so well. It tends to be a much nicer laid-back, friendly atmosphere. Big cities can be quite dangerous though. In big cities don't walk around by yourself at night. In fact, try to avoid being outside at night full stop. Avoid pulling your phone or camera out in public and avoid the back streets. Keep your wits about you and listen to your instinct.

Chapter Summary

• Different countries can better suit different stages of your life (though this depends on the person too)

• If doing a working holiday in the UK, don't expect to see much of Europe while working

• In Europe it's simple and easy to travel alone. Making friends is super easy

• In third world countries without a backpacker scene or places known for scams it is better to travel with a friend

• Don't take advice of people that haven't been. In many 'dangerous' countries, the violence is only targeted at drug gangs. Tourists are normally safe (however precautions need to be taken). Refer to Smart Traveller for government issued warnings, and Trip Advisor for personal experiences. Make your own mind up

Chapter 4: Organised Tours

I'm not such a huge fan of organised trips, yet they certainly have their place.

The Good:
- You can see and do a huge amount in a short amount of time
- Everything is taken care of
- You can see and do a huge amount in a short amount of time

The Bad
- You can see and do a huge amount in a short amount of time… but you won't properly experience the country
- You might have a shitty group of people that you don't like and have to spend the next three weeks with them
- You spend such a short amount of time in each place, so you have to go back to experience it properly
- Despite what they say, it will end up costing you quite a lot more than if you did it yourself

I did a 17-day Contiki trip when I first got to Europe. It was great. We saw 10 or so countries in 17 days, which was a great way to get a taste for Europe so I could see which countries I wanted to go back to and spend more time in. The only problem was you just skim over the places and don't get to *know* a place. For example, I thought Italy was a bit of a shithole…. which everyone else considers to be absolutely slanderous words. I saw Venice and Rome, but I certainly didn't experience Italy. As everyone says, Italy is about the experience, not the sights. Throwing a coin in the Trevi Fountain does not mean you've seen Italy. You need to get out there and Couchsurf in the small villages and then no doubt you will experience Italy and have the time of your life. The organised bus tours are much like a school trip – you are somewhat shrouded from the place you're going to. In the group I went with, the vast majority of the people in the group didn't meet any other person. Most people on the tour were groups of friends who didn't socialise with anyone else other than the people they came with. You can meet some cool people on these trips, but be warned there will also be a lot of rich whiney kids with no personality.

All tour companies will try to tell you that it'll be cheaper to do a tour than to do it yourself, but this is so untrue it's unbelievable. In El Salvador I did a canyoning day trip run by a local company. On this were also a bunch of people that were doing a Central America tour with a very popular international tour company. I asked how much it was costing them; a staggering $90/day. I was running on closer to $40. I thought, well, maybe if they're travelling in their own bus and doing activities every day it's possible. Here's the scary part: that absurd $90/day doesn't include activities or food. All that gets you is the guide, basic accommodation and transport *on local buses*. To put that into perspective interstate buses in El Salvador cost only 70 cents. If that's not enough, instead of getting a cheaper group price for the activities, *they pay more* (as our canyoning guide laughingly told me in quiet). Therefore, their cost would be more like $130/day, compared to doing it yourself for $40/day. That, my friends, is nuts.

When time is short however, particularly when going to a third world country by yourself, or to a country that does not have a backpacker scene, then they can be a great idea. I did half a trip in China with a tour company before my visa ran out. It was great. It was run by a small independent company so it was nearly half the price of the main tour groups, and instead of bussing around in our own fancy bus we did it all using local transport. It was more like backpacking but with a guide to get us the tickets and show us which train to get on. Ok, so I know what I'm describing here is exactly what I was laughing about the other guys doing in El Salvador, but I had only two weeks in China before my visa expired so this was the best way to see the most stuff. As I say, it all depends on the circumstances – if time is short then for sure they're great. I also like the more down and dirty tours where you use local transport as opposed to busing around in your big fancy bus as it gets you closer to the culture of the country, plus of course it's cheaper too.

There'll generally be a few different companies offering more or less the same trip. When comparing them make sure to ask what *isn't* included. Asking this is more important that what is included such that you can get a more correct idea of what you really will be paying. That is, check for things such as breakfasts, lunches, dinners, activities included, entry fees, tax, whether tips are expected and so on. From what I've seen, tours tend to include most breakfasts, half your dinners and no lunches. There will generally be a few basic activities included, but none of the expensive activities. The tour guides typically will get a commission from the activities too, so they will try to get everyone on all the trips. If 90% of the group gets convinced to do an activity, then you will probably want to do it too so you don't feel left out. Therefore, you'll probably find yourself doing all the optional activities. Make sure to add all these things when weighing up how much the trip will really cost you. Don't forget partying too. Depending which tour company you go with, it might be a drinking session with a little bit of country exploring between beers. This can add considerable cost. If the tour cost is, say, $130 per day, you probably have to double that number to get a true figure.

Chapter Summary

• Organised multi-week trips are good in places with no backpacking scene, if time is short, or to get a quick overview of a continent before doing a more in-depth trip

• In larger tour companies like Contiki expect many of the people to be not very independent or interesting. No doubt there will be great people there too, but expect a number to be spoiled, whinging kids

• Expect the cost to be much greater than doing it yourself, contrary to what they try to tell you

• Check what's not included when looking at tours. Remember that your final cost per day will end up being far more than the advertised price

Chapter 5: Travel

Air Travel

Backpacking tends to rely on air travel to get you to remote locations. Only problem is a number of people are scared of flying. Here're a few considerations if you're one of those unlucky people:

1. Air travel is about the safest thing you can do. In the *bottom* 39 major airlines, the chance of being killed on a flight is one in 2 million. Each flight tends to be pretty long too, so once you take the distance in to account, it's one fatality for every 3 billion person-kilometres. It's 40,000km to go around the world once, so this means you'd have to travel around the world 75,000 times to statistically die in an aircraft accident. You've probably got more chance dying in the taxi on the way to the airport. (Ok, so I lied in the Foreword – I did research these stats. How geek would I be if I knew that!).

2. You're not 30,000ft above the ground – you are on top of 30,000ft of (slightly) compressed air. Imagine you have a few hundred thousand balloons of air between you and the ground. Just because you can't see air, doesn't mean it's not there. Other than 4-seater aircraft, all aeroplanes have at least two engines and can run fine on one. If for some reason both stopped working, the plane won't plummet out of the sky – it will still maintain a glide ratio of about 15:1. That is, for every meter it will drop, it will go forward 15. At 30,000 ft high it can travel 150km on zero power, which is generally enough to get to any safe landing area. This actually happened once before to a Boeing 767 in the 1980's, in which the silly Canadians got confused when going from imperial to metric... and put in only half the fuel needed. All engines stopped yet they managed to glide to a safe landing with zero power. This became known as the 'Gimli Glider'. Google the story if bored!

3. Turbulence. If you're in turbulent air it can feel unsettling when you drop, but even if you drop 100m you're still only dropping 1% of your height. For example you may be at cruising altitude, then you drop down to 99% of cruising altitude, then go back to 100%. You're still 30,000ft high in the air; there's nothing to hit.

4. Landing. Sometimes when you land it can feel a bit rough. Stop your whinging and get over it. To understand what I mean, go for a drive to airport and watch all the landings. It's actually a heck of a lot smoother than you think. It's incredible watching them land actually. Just think how much it hurts if you fall off a chair onto concrete at home. A lot. The jolt from a plane is nothing like that. In fact you pretty much can't even feel it. Even with a hard landing the plane isn't going to veer off course and fall to bits. Planes are incredible. You're safe.

Booking the Flight

Different websites are good for different places. Skyscanner is awesome for Europe, especially if you have no plans, as you can be as vague as you want. For example, you can search flights leaving Germany for the month of November. You might see – oh, in two weeks there's a cheap flight going from Stuttgart to Greece. Hmmm, sounds fun! I might do that! I like it for reverse searches too. For example, once I wanted to go to Iceland but was in Ireland at the time. Searching from Ireland was horrendously expensive. Instead I did a search: Iceland to Anywhere for Next Month. I saw really cheap flights going to Germany on the airline German Wings. I then went to the German Wings website and realised they did flights Cologne to Iceland for a ridiculously low price of $79. I then made my own way over to Germany to catch the flight from there; seeing friends in Belgium, Holland and Germany along the way.

For the America's however, I've found Skyscanner doesn't seem to work. Instead, I use Kayak. I find it much better than Expedia as you can search for three days either side of your intended date. This is extremely important as one day might be $500 and the next only $100. If you're researching lots of different routes, this function is vital. I tend to use this to find which airlines are cheap for that route, then go to their own website to find the best day to fly. I should add as well that I only tend to use these sites for direct routes. That is, if I want to go to a place that will necessitate making a few stopovers, your own research will get you a much better price than letting Kayak or one of the others take care of it. To do this, the first step I do is to find which flights fly direct to the place I want to go. Simple go to Google and type in 'flights departing xxxx', where 'xxxx' is the airport name. It is very important to type in 'departing' not some other word like 'leaving'. Doing this will show directly in the results page all the flights departing that specific airport. All you need to do then is to search the list for a budget airline that flies to the airport closest to yourself, or to another budget hub-airport. Then just do the same for the airport you're leaving from to see which budget hubs it flies to. Hopefully it matches up for just one stopover. It may well take you a few hours to find the best route, but you can easily save hundreds that way. Even if it takes you six hours to find a route $150 cheaper, it means you're essentially earning $25/hr. Bloody well worth it I reckon!

Beware with some of the budget airlines though, such as Ryan Air in Europe. Appears cheap, but you can be caught out. I thought I was in luck when I found a flight from Porto (Portugal) to London for just $0.01. Cheap, huh? Cost me $200 in the end. The flight was $0.01, but then you have to pay for baggage, credit card fee, booking fee, tax, fuel surcharge and so on, and it's soon a $150 flight. It also went to Ryan Air's version of London, in the form of Stansted airport. It's still considered London but is a few hours away and cost me $50 for the train. Sometimes it's cheaper to pay more.

Also, depending on the airline sometimes return tickets can be *cheaper* than one-way. Often a one way flight will be around 70% the cost of a return ticket, and sales are generally only for return airfares. Therefore if there's a sale on you may well save money by buying a return ticket. If you need to travel on specific dates note too that sometimes *first or business class can be cheaper than economy*, or more correctly, sometimes economy can be more expensive than first class. Sounds strange I know, but prices are set according to demand and most people will only be looking at economy. If everyone wants to fly on a certain day, it can push the price up past that of business class. In my experience in the US, if you book last minute, business class will often be cheaper... though still really expensive. You're generally better off to wait for a few days, but if you do need to fly on a specific date and money is no object, check out first or business class.

Never pay extra for an extra legroom seat – you can often get this for free at check-in.

Visa Considerations

If you're going to the USA, make sure to get an ESTA (Visa Waiver program) if you are from one of the 37 applicable countries. If you don't have a visa or the ESTA, you cannot fly to the US (not even for a stopover to another country). The process is pretty simple. Simply go to the website https://esta.cbp.dhs.gov/esta/, fill in your details, don't admit to being a terrorist, pay your $14 or so and it's done. Make sure to do all this as soon as you book your flight. Don't wait till you get to the airport to do this. My dad discovered it's pretty stressful to do all this in the minutes before the check-in desk closes!

When flying you generally will need an exit ticket from the country you're flying to, to prove you will leave. I don't understand how this makes a difference as *you don't have to actually get on the flight*. It's just annoying really. This doesn't seem to be an issue when going around Europe, but most other places it can be. This caught me out when I was flying New York to Guatemala. I had previously caught a bus from Belize to Guatemala in which there was no requirement to have onward travel booked. I was therefore quite surprised that when flying in that the rules seemed to be different. As I was not aware of this requirement I obviously had no onward travel booked. It was pretty stressful to be at the airport check-in and the girl not allowing me to check in. Fortunately I had arrived early at the airport (always get there early!!) so I was able to get on the internet and book a bus from Guatemala to El Salvador.

Note that you don't need a flight out of the country; it can be a bus or train too. Just find the cheapest bus leaving the country and book that. If possible, find a company where you can get a refund. That is book your bus out of the country to satisfy the check-in counter (make sure you have the details printed off), and then cancel the booking when you arrive.

The country of Panama is particularly strict; even catching the bus in you need an exit ticket booked. This catches out many unaware people. I managed to get in with the deposit that I'd paid for a sailing trip to Colombia. Many of my friends have done it with a fake plane ticket; photo-shopping a ticket to make it look like they had a flight booked. Currently that seems to be working, but with the amount of people doing it, they might clamp down on it soon. Forgery and immigration don't often combine to be your friend!

Connecting Flights

If you have connecting flights in China, make sure you have a minimum of 3 hrs between flights, if not more. *More than 80%* of flights in Beijing are delayed, and over 40% delayed for 45 minutes or more. The Chinese culturally don't like to break news, so even when they know your flight will be delayed, they get you on board the plane, depart 25m from the terminal, say there's air traffic congestion and then make you wait in the stuffy plane on the hot tarmac for 2hrs, even though they knew it would be delayed.

I once went on a day trip from Dalian to Shanghai just to renew a visa. Arrived ok, got my visa renewed, went to the airport, checked in and… 38hrs later the plane leaves. Fortunately we were able to wait in the airport not sitting in the plane, but they would say the plane will leave in the next hour or so, then just when it's nearly time to board, they delay it by another hour or two and continue to do that for 1.5 days. Somewhat frustrating! It's for this reason that I always travel with my laptop charger and a book in my carry-on so at least I'll have something to do.

Even out of China, leave plenty of time between connecting flights. If you're going international to domestic, often you'll have to change airports which can take considerable time. What's even worse is international travel with a stopover in another country. This is no issue if the stopover is part of the ticket (such as Sydney to London which includes a short re-fuel stop along the way) but if you're booking the legs yourself you will have to pass through immigration even if you have a connecting flight. For example I once flew Guatemala to Australia. This involved flying Guatemala to Mexico (where I had to pass through immigration in Mexico), hurry to my next flight to LA (where I had to go through immigration again), then walk across to a different terminal in LAX, fly to Australia (and go through immigration), then catch another two flights to finally get to Tasmania. Ensuring you have sufficient time between flights is essential. If these were all close together and I missed the first, I would have had to re-book and pay for all following flights. Not something you want to do!

Make sure too, that you know which airport and terminal you've booked. Often one city will have numerous airports, particularly if transferring international to domestic. Budget airlines will often use a separate budget airport. Ensure your next flight isn't 50km away, or at least ensure you have sufficient time to make the transfer.

Getting to the Airport

Get there early! It's not that bloody hard! What else are you doing beforehand anyway? Get to the airport early and relax. Rushing to the airport ain't fun!

Fortunately I've never missed a flight but I have been close. I was flying Atlanta (Georgia) to Austin (Texas) once. I checked with the airline – only need to check in 30mins before departure. Sweet as! If I leave Atlanta one hour and a quarter before departure, that should give me plenty of time as the airport is only 20mins from Atlanta.

Famous last words.

We have plenty of time driving in, so my friend and I stop for some take away along the way and get to the airport easily enough. At check-in there's not even a queue. If we didn't stop for takeaway, it would be less than 25 mins from the heart of Atlanta to being all checked in. Sa-weet! All to do now is the security check and walk to the gate. Ooooohhhhh, shiiiiiiiiiiiiit!!!! Walking around the corner from the almost-deserted check-in counter, I'm greeted by a huge line for security check of over 1000 people, which takes *half an hour* to get through, even with 20 different bag screen lines. It takes longer to get through this than immigration in LAX! After 20mins, I'm starting to get worried I may not make it to my gate in time. Finally I get to the bag screening, and as always, my bag has something in it that they want a closer look at. Bugger bugger bugger! Hurry hurry hurry! They ask me to come around to a counter and say, "Before we start going through your bag, please be advised that you shall not touch any item in your bag as we are going through it." "Yep, no worries, just be mindful that I'm late for a flight, so please be quick about it."

TSA guy looks at the x-ray screen and says, "Ah, looks like a can of drink."

"Oh yeah, sorry, I totally forgot – that's an energy drink from the weekend. Chuck it out."

TSA guy fumbles with bag.

"Yep, it's just right down the very bottom," I said, hoping to speed up the process.

TSA guy looks confused and asks if it's in front pocket.

"No, it's in the main pocket," I respond. "The one you're in now. Just right down the very bottom."

TSA guy starts to open front pocket.

Somewhat agitated I say, "No, it's in the pocket you have open now. Not the front pocket. Just right down the bottom."

"Oh, in the side pocket?" he asks.

"No! No, not in the side pocket. IN THE POCKET YOU HAVE OPEN NOW. It's down the very bottom.

TSA guy looks confused.

"Just start taking stuff out, and reach ALL THE WAY DOWN TO THE BOTTOM. That is where the can of drink is. It's in a white plastic bag, right down the very bottom of the main pocket; the one you have open now."

TSA guy feels bottom of bag. Gives it a good feel and asks, "It's in the side pocket?" Note, my bag does not even have a side pocket. He then starts to open the front pocket.

"Listen, I'm quite late for a flight. Can I just pull it out for you? Ah jeez, listen, it's not in the front pocket, it's not in the side pocket. IT IS IN THE MAIN COMPARTMENT – THE ONE YOU HAVE OPEN NOW WITH YOUR HAND INSIDE. PULL OUT EVERYTHING. IT. IS. RIGHT. DOWN. THE. BOTTOM."

TSA guy looks confused, but at least he starts taking an item painfully slowly out of my bag. Pauses. Takes out another. Reaches in. Looks confused.

"Yes! Yes! Just reach further. It's definitely there. Just RIGHT DOWN THE BOTTOM. All the way down the bottom! It's in a plastic bag."

TSA guy looks confused, but still proceeds, reaches *RIGHT DOWN* with both hands, feels around for a while, then suddenly he triumphantly pulls out a can of energy drink, in a white plastic bag as described.

Me (quietly under by breath, "Oh thank fuck."

The TSA guy innocently asks, "Did you want to drink it sir?"

"No, I want to get on the plane I'm late for."

"Are you sure? You can drink it."

"No, really. Thank you for my bag. I just want to catch my flight. Thank you." In my head, "#@%&!!"

I then run out of security, run down the escalator, pushing past some people to the ga-aate oh whatthefuck! Turns out you have to catch a train to get to the gates.

Stuff it, I don't have time to frig around waiting for a train, so I take the option of just running instead. After running for a fair distance, I reach Gate Section A. Shit, I still need to get all the way to Gate Section D! I can now hear the train, so I wait for this and jump on for the next three stops for Gate Section D and run to my gate. The gate should have closed 2 minutes ago, but fortunately they let me on, close the doors and very soon after takeoff. Phew!!

Make sure you know which airport too. I've been in Avalon Airport (Jetstar's idea of Melbourne) where I saw a Swedish girl bawling her eyes out when she realised she was at the wrong airport. Yep, she was on her last dollar, the flight was her way out, and she was 50km away from the airport she needed to be. She was, unfortunately, totally stuffed.

Organising Bags

Organise your bags before you join the check-in queue. Trying to take things out of your backpack to put in your daypack while shuffling forward every 15 seconds isn't much fun. Here're a few considerations for what goes where:

I always fly wearing shorts, thongs (flip-flops) and a t-shirt. It's the most comfortable thing to wear, and it's always hot in a plane before you take off, especially if the plane gets delayed on the tarmac. For short flights, it's generally fine the whole fight, but for long flights it can get pretty cold when you reaching cruising altitude. That's why I always bring along with me a pair of jeans, socks and a jumper (sweater). If you're flying somewhere cold make sure to get changed into your warm clothes *before* you land, even if you're warm enough on the plane. Once you land you're rushing to beat everyone through immigration, and once you have your main pack, it's generally too difficult to take that into the change rooms. Maybe I'm less intelligent than others but failure to prepare in the past has resulted in me walking around the city of Reykjavik (Iceland) at 1am looking for my hostel in nothing other than shorts, thongs and a singlet. If that wasn't enough, I've also been in Dalian (China) in *-13C* wearing shorts and thongs. Shorts and thongs in -13C is not much fun. Another time flying from Malaysia back to China, I had to wait over one hour in the taxi line in shorts and thongs while it was snowing on me. Funniest thing was this little kid that said innocently to his dad, "Daaaad. Why is that man not wearing shoes? And, and why is he only wearing shorts?" I could only laugh.

I even flew to Japan for a snowboarding holiday in shorts and thongs, not thinking that, just perhaps, the rest of the country is cold too; not just the ski field. Funnily enough, when the shuttle bus to the mountain stopped halfway for a toilet break, half the bus (all Australians) rushed through the snow in shorts and thongs to the toilets to change into some warm clothes. I had quite a chuckle to myself that maybe it's just an Australian thing to wear shorts, thongs and a singlet to the snow!! More than that though, I think it's a case of when you fly to a different hemisphere it's too hard to get your head around that it was summer when you got on the plane, but is winter when you get off.

Oh, I should reinforce... 'thongs' is Aussie for flip-flops. We don't all wear sexy underwear to the snow!!

Make sure to remove all your sharp items from your carry-on. Normally I keep my pocket knife in my daypack, so make sure to put that in your backpack to avoid having your beloved knife confiscated. Americans: make sure to put your gun in your checked in luggage, not your carry-on.

As mentioned in my Packing Tips in Chapter 2 and a Bit, I strongly recommend *against* using the TSA approved locks on your bags. Instead, what I do is to secure them by untwisting a paperclip and using that to secure the zippers. I hear of people using cable-ties, but seeing as you can't travel with a knife, I'm not understanding how you can easily take them off on the other side. Stick with paperclips!

You should take all your essentials in your carry-on. As mentioned in the Introduction, my first ever trip was to Thailand in which the airline left my bags in Melbourne. I didn't get my pack until six days into a 13-day trip. At the time, I thought, "Woo! I've got travel insurance – I can get 'emergency' items for free!" Good in theory, crap in practice. There were markets outside my hostel selling cool clothes… but no receipts; can't claim on insurance. This meant I spent the entire day while terribly sick with food poising roaming the city to find a clothes shop that gave receipts. After probably five frustrating hours in the heat, I finally found one; the Calvin Klein store. Cheapest t-shirt I found was $300. No thank you. I ended up just buying some underpants from the market outside my hotel. Here's another tip – if you're a size medium in Australia, you sure as hell aren't a medium in Thailand! It was like wearing underpants made for an 8-year-old!

For a long flight it can help to have some moisturising lip balm and saline nasal spray. For newer planes it's not an issue, but the air-conditioning systems on older aircraft can cause you to have your nose completely blocked up for the entire trip, as is what happened to me once. As the air is very dry inside too, you can also get cracked lips, so that's where the lip balm can come in handy. Best thing about the lip balm though is that it's the secret to my best magic trick that leaves the audience absolutely stunned every time. More on that later.

When getting on a plane I always have both my daypack and another bag, such as a shopping bag. I keep all my essentials in my daypack which I put in the overhead bin, and everything I need for the flight I put in the smaller bag which I keep with me at my seat. Saves having to root around in the overhead bins later on.

For the flight, I always have in my ready-bag:

- Quality in-ear headphones, with an airplane adaptor. You can buy the adaptor in electronics stores, or in the over-priced airport stores. I see this as a must on long flights as airplane headphones are terribly uncomfortable and bad quality (until recently, the Qantas headphones were made in a prison camp in China, where the inmates were beaten and given electric shocks if they didn't make the unrealistic targets. This is true.)
- Earplugs (two pairs as you'll probably lose one)
- Laptop. If flying on an A380 I take my charger too as they include power points
- Notepad and pen. Notepad for playing Mr Squiggle with the person I'm sitting next to, and you always need a pen for the immigration arrival cards too
- Book

- Water bottle. This is important as often you just get juice served in cups which you always spill. Bring a water bottle on and fill that up
- Jumper (sweater)
- Socks

Note, I keep my jeans in my day bag in the overhead bin not my personal bag as you need to get up to put them on anyway.

Checking In

As mentioned previously, it's a good idea to have your itinerary printed, particularly in third world countries. Make sure too that you have printed evidence of your exit flight/bus/train/boat out of the country. Simply saying you have something booked is not sufficient – they need to have the details to put in their computer. An exit ticket isn't always required, but if check-in closes in 15 minutes and they won't let you check-in without an onward flight it can be very stressful. It can be a good idea to research a bus company that does refundable international trips out of the country, such that you can book this quickly if required by the check-in desk.

When checking in, ask if you can get an exit row seat. Often you can get the extra leg room for no additional cost. If not, for short flights I go for a window seat for the view but anything longer than 2hrs I always ask for an aisle seat. Aisle seats give you a lot more freedom to get up and move around, go to the toilet, etc. For long haul flights, you're above the tops of the clouds so you can't see anything anyway.

I once had a friend that thought he was lucky – he was in the window seat, he had a free seat next to him and the plane was just about to take off…. until he sees a 100-year-old woman being helped up the aisle and sat next to him…. in the aisle seat. As it was an intercontinental flight, after a while my friend needed to go to the toilet. Problem was it took the old dear a good two minutes to sit down the first time, so he couldn't exactly get her to stand up, nor could he clamber over her. Just gonna have to wait till she needs to go. She didn't. The entire intercontinental flight she didn't go once, leaving my friend in absolute agony. Don't be this person!!

Security

The security check is where wearing thongs comes in handy too. They don't seem to do it anywhere else, but in the US you have to remove your shoes.

Thongs are a lot easier to take on and off than hiking boots.

I also make sure to take everything out of my pockets and put them into my daypack before I get to security. It's then a simple process of thongs and laptop in one tray, day bag in another and that's it. No mucking around trying to juggle all your things.

If carrying liquids and aerosols it can pay to have your own clear bags to put them in. I've been in airports in Europe where they charge you money for the clear plastic bags that you have to put your items in. Total scam!

The Flight

Make sure to say hello to the person sitting next to you as soon as you sit down. If you don't say it immediately, it becomes more awkward when you eventually do say hello. You can meet some highly interesting people on flights. I've met Olympic swimmers, numerous company CEO's, a judge, a stripper and a whole host of other interesting people on flights.

After the usual hello you can always start conversation by the "coming or going?" question. That is, are they starting their journey or going home. If they respond that they're going home, you can ask them about local tips about the place. If you get on sufficiently well on the plane, who knows, they may even invite you around! Keep in mind though, they might be starting work again the next morning and may be tired and unable to have visitors. Conversely if they are just starting their journey, with a bit of luck they may have researched the place you're going to and may have some tips for you too. By making friends on the plane means you may also be able to share a taxi with them when you land.

If I'm sitting next to a fun person, I like to play Mr Squiggle. If you're not familiar with this game meant for young children, it's pretty simple to learn. Use a small notepad, or a large piece of paper folded into 8 or so sections. Get one person to put some squiggles (lines, shapes and so on) on the paper, change pen colour, then use your imagination to change these squiggles into a picture. It's a lot of fun and get's that child out in you. I once caught a flight with an attractive girl, played Mr Squiggle and years later she told me she still had the drawings!

After the meal is served, there always seems to be a spare meal. Ask for it. Works almost every time. Airport food is always expensive so it makes sense to eat as much free food as possible. Hahaha, funnily enough flying from Sydney to London, on the bus from the airport into the city I got chatting to another Aussie. Turns out he was on the same flight as me. He was excited to be in London, but a bit upset as he was hungry as hell – he was asleep when the food came around so he missed out. I made sure to thank him for his meal without smirking *too* much!

Avoid sleeping tablets unless you're used to them. I once took a sleeping tablet on a flight, then woke up *completely* paralysed. One of the scariest experiences of my life. I mentally awoke but couldn't even open my eyes. After a while I could open my eyelids but nothing more. Couldn't even move my eyes. Here I was, mentally 100% alert sitting slumped in the chair, head down, 100% conscious but totally paralysed, just being able to look where my eyeballs were fixed. I was so scared I wanted to scream, but couldn't open my mouth. Unbelievably scary! This is what they used for torture back in the 50's. I could see my finger, so I just concentrated on that really, really hard. After a while I managed to twitch it and after a lot more concentrating could start to move it, and then finally got movement back in my body. After experiencing the scariest thing ever to happen to me, I obviously wanted to tell someone. Telling the person next to me probably wasn't the most tactful move as I think I really freaked her out!! ("Whoaaa! That was so crazy! I was, like, sleeping, but woke up completely paralysed, and I was like totally scared, and totally paralysed and wanted to scream but couldn't so I was just shit scared and then just looked at my finger till I could wiggle it and now I can move it, woohoo! So scary!"). Yeah, she didn't talk to me again.

Touchdown

Go to the toilet *before* you pick up your backpack. Taking all your luggage into the stalls is very difficult, as is peeing while wearing a backpack and daypack.

Immigration

Immigration is not as scary as it sounds and doesn't take as long in LAX as most people say it does. Most times I've been through LAX immigration in around 10 minutes. Still, some people say they're in line for 1.5 hours, so make sure you allow enough time for transfers.

When you get to immigration there'll typically be a minimum of three lines to get everyone through. Which do you take? The very sad, unfair and unfortunate fact of life is…. don't take the line with black African's in it. This is so unfair and I feel so sorry for them, but time and time again I notice that if I take the line that's three times as long but has only white people in it, it will move through faster than the short line with two black African's in it. Totally unfair, but not much I can do about it. Same goes for Chinese too. If there's a big group of Chinese looking lost and confused and unable to speak English, this is going to hold up the line. Go in the other queue.

Make sure to keep every bit of paper the immigration official gives you. In most countries they just stamp your passport and give you the paper slip you need when you exit the country. They always have these exit slips at the airport, so I often chuck mine out. Just make sure this is the piece you chuck out, not your visa… like I nearly did in Mexico. In Mexico, your visa card is a piece of paper that is not attached to your passport and looks just like the disembarkation slip. I chucked mine in the bin where I was staying, but luckily my friends mentioned something about the card so I could rescue it in time!

Baggage Pickup and Customs

If travelling with delicate items such as a guitar or surfboard, *check it before you exit the airport*. A good friend of mine from England came to Australia, took up surfing and became really good. He wanted to bring his board back home to Mother England, but went via South America for four months on the way home. He spent the next four months backpacking around South America, schlepping this frigging surfboard around with him everywhere, including mountain tops of Bolivia, jungles in Colombia, etc. Didn't get to use it once. After all this care and hassle, he flies from South America to London, gets home, opens his surfboard bag only to find it in three pieces. Enough to make you cry. Really. He then calls the airport to get them to pay for the damages, where he hears the really bad news – once you leave the airport they no longer cover you, as they claim the damage may have occurred in the taxi. For someone whose surfboard had so much sentimental value, the effort he took to carry it everywhere, arriving back home with no money, just to find that some lazy person has destroyed his expensive board; it really does break your heart. Check your items before you leave the airport!

Declare all. I've come in with three controlled or illegal substances into Australia, including Xanax, Ephedrine and Yohimbine. I just tick the box for illegal substances and keep my questionable items at the top of my bag. Conversation:

"What's this?" asks the Customs officer.

"Xanax. It's a sleeping tablet," I reply.

"Oh. ok. And this?"

I decide to be completely honest. "Ephedrine."

"Is that like the thing for your nose?"

Not believing my ears, I reply, "Umm... Yep. Yeah, spose so!"

"Righto, no worries then. Come straight through!" comes the very unexpected reply from Customs.

Probably all fine in the US, but Xanax is a tightly controlled drug in Australia, and Ephedrine and Yohimbine are illegal. If in doubt, declare and never ever try and smuggle drugs in. Only thing that they actually have ever confiscated from me is Sichuan pepper from China.

Transfers

Most flights only allow you to check in 3hrs before your flight. Sucks if you have a long time between non-connected flights. Carrying your bags all that time is not fun, particularly when you need to go to the toilet. This is where a bit of charm can go a long way. Sometimes if the airline operator is open for another earlier flight and it's not too busy, with a bit of luck you may be able to check in early. In LAX I managed to check in 10hrs before my flight instead of the usual 2 or 3. That's 7 hours less of carrying your backpack. Worthwhile I reckon!

If you can't do this, most airports will include overpriced baggage storage to allow you to go into town while leaving your backpack in storage... except for LAX. With all the concerns about terrorism, there's nowhere to leave your bags. Very annoying. I was once in LA for a 10hr layover and decided to do what any other tourist in LA would do – go to downtown Compton. Of course, this meant walking around the infamously dangerous black-only suburb dressed in surfy-style boardshorts, thongs and a singlet; complete with my backpack on back and daypack on front. Pretty sure I stood out. This hunch was made all the more evident as I exited the train station and walked past a bunch of huge black guys smoking a joint, complete with homie clothes, gold chains and NWA caps who looked at me, squinted their eyes, screwed up their noses and said "Ay yo, you don't belong here. Deeze are da *streetz*!" I then did what anyone else in my position would do; smiled, laughed and continued on my way deeper into Compton, hoping to see Dr. Dre, a drive-by shooting or thugz rollin' dice. Unfortunately I saw neither, but on the plus side, I didn't get stabbed either.

Red-Eye Flights and Overnight Transfers

Sleeping in airports is definitely a viable option. Check www.sleepinginairports.net for reviews of the sleep-ability of many airports. Depending how you've packed it can be really pleasant. With a sleeping bag, pillow, earplugs and eye mask, it's really good. I absolutely hate eye masks, but you'll have lights shining directly into your eyes, so they're essential. For security you can clip your bag strap around some fixed chairs, or even better, thread the bag straps through it. I leave mine there while going to the toilet for a pee, but be careful with this as it may be seen as 'an unaccompanied suspicious package and destroyed'.

Make sure, of course, that you buy food before you arrive in the airport as it will be horrendously expensive there. I'm a massive fan of flatbread and peanut butter as it's compact, filling and keeps well. Other winners for me are nuts and crisps.

At Arrival

Never get a taxi that someone offers you, no matter how genuine they sound. Guaranteed they'll rip you off. Just go to the taxi rank. There'll be taxi's there.

Rail

Rail Passes

Awesome or crap? Depends.

In Europe, in my experience, rail passes are a total waste of money and they limit you too. The only people that say rail passes are great are people that went to Europe before the proliferation of cheap air travel. Go on Skyscanner.com and you'll be rewarded by a plethora of cheap flights. Make sure to check stand-alone train tickets too. For example, I once took a train from Bruges (Belgium) to Cologne (Germany), booking on the day at the train station. As it turned out there was a sale on, and a first-class ticket was cheaper than a normal ticket. Yes please! Another time I needed to get from Copenhagen (Denmark) to Munich (Germany). Normal ticket price $179, but as luck would have it, there was a sale on, so I did it for $49. Rail passes suck, but trains are still awesome.

I'm a huge fan of trains. As a paragliding pilot, I love flying and even look forward to turbulence, yet I'd still rather get a train. No security mucking around to go through, no long check-in lines, no need to arrive an hour before leaving – just rock up at the train station five minutes beforehand, get on the train and be rewarded with a huge amount of legroom. Also, trains always take you into the city centre, saving having to pay for transfers. For short distances, trains are faster and a lot less tiring than a plane.

For Japan, a rail pass is a must if you plan to cover a lot of distance as trains are horrendously expensive there. The trains are downright amazing in Japan but unless you have a rail pass they're just too expensive to catch.

Metro Card

Metro cards are generally awesome everywhere in the world... except for Montreal (Canada). Don't get a weekly card there unless you want an expensive surprise!

I arrived in Montreal on a Thursday with the intent to stay for ten days, so it made sense to get a week long card... or so I thought. I used it a bit here and there, but come Monday my card wouldn't work anymore. I tried a few times until the staff came to help me out. Here came the following conversation:

"Have you got a weekly card?" asks the Metro staff member.

"Yeah, I just bought it last Thursday," I reply.

"Well today's Monday – it's expired," she says in a 'like, duh' tone.

"Huh?? I bought it Thursday."

"Yes, and today is Monday.... which means it's expired."

"But I paid for a weekly ticket... on Thursday.... so it should expire on Thursday, right? As in, a weekly ticket should last a week... right?!?"

"No. All weekly tickets expire Monday. Did you want to want to get another?"

"Hahahaha, wow. No, no thanks. Stuff this, I'm walking!"

As it turns out if you get a weekly ticket on a Sunday, you still pay full weekly price but it only lasts one day. Figure that out! It gets worse though… all monthly passes expire on the first of the month. This means on the first of every month at 8am you have tens of thousands of regular commuters whose metro card is expired, all trying to buy tickets at the same time. I'm yet to understand the logic of this one.

Road Travel

Bus

I used to think buses were slow and uncomfortable… until I got to Mexico. In Mexico the buses are great. Bucket loads of legroom and seats that recline a huge amount. Believe it or not, you can get a really good sleep on them. If there're night buses available, take one for sure! In addition to saving the cost of a night's accommodation, it means you're not wasting your day time travelling either.

When travelling with your backpack in the under-bus bin, try to get your bag as far back as possible so everyone else's bag is in front and on top of yours. Makes it difficult to remove; thereby reducing the chance of someone stealing it at a stop along the way. If you can't do that, make sure to get a seat with a view of the luggage compartment. If there are stops along the way, you want to be able to see the luggage compartment to ensure no one walks off with your bag en-route.

Ride Share

Brilliant. So far I've only rideshared in Quebec (Canada) but it was great. The bus from Montreal to Quebec City was $54, whereas through rideshare it was only $14. Just jump on the website www.kangaride.com and input where you want to travel to and when. This works for all of the USA and Canada. There is a list of people that regularly drive certain routes, and you can just book to ride with them. It's just like an intercity bus, with a timetable of all the rides and the departure and arrival points. Most drivers on this are people that perhaps live in one city and their partner in another and therefore drive up each weekend. They're happy for a bit of extra company and contribution to the fuel. It's set for specific times, so you won't be waiting around wondering where the hell your ride is. It really is just like a bus, but 1/3 the price and the added bonus of meeting cool people on the way.

I'm sure there's an equivalent in many countries.

Hitchhiking

Avoid it.

A friend of mine was travelling Mexico on the cheap. After trying to do a trek on his own accord in the Copper Canyon, which, among other things involved running from a dodgy house and seeing freshly dug graves next to a marijuana crop close by, he decided to be a bit safer and took a bus to the next town. Problem was the bus didn't go there. It dropped him off at the side of the road in BF nowhere. He therefore had to hitchhike, and got picked up by a dodgy car filled with muscular scary-looking Mexicans. All good for a while, until he thought, "Wait... I don't think this is the right direction." This instinct came more apparent when the car took a turn down a small path and continued into the bush, in the middle of nowhere. Oh shit. The car stopped and they started beating the shit out of him. They then put a sack over his head and held a knife to his stomach. Ohhhhhhhhhh sshhhhhiiiiiiiiiiiiitt! He thought that was it – in the middle of nowhere with a sack on his head and four guys holding a knife to his stomach. Fortunately they let him go, but took all his stuff. Now he was totally stranded in the middle of nowhere, with nothing, and having just almost been killed. Problem was, he had to get to a town.... and the only way to do that was by hitchhiking again! Can you imagine that!?! He made it into town and saw the cops who said he was very, very lucky. If he were Mexican, they would have killed him for sure. He was only spared because, being a tourist, if they killed him there would be a bigger police investigation.

If you can't afford the transport, you should probably save a bit longer before going travelling... though guaranteed if you do hitchhike you will have much better stories to tell!

Boats

Check the condition of your bag straps before getting on boats. Carrying my daypack with $8,000 of camera gear in it, I was climbing up a boat in Fiji, thinking, "Wouldn't it suck if my bag strap broke now"... and at that exact moment my strap broke, nearly sending all my gear into the sea. Luckily dad was behind me. Very. Lucky.

On small boats for day trips, I still take my camera, but I carry it in a waterproof bag. If I'm going kayaking or doing something where there's a chance of the camera dropping in the water, I clip the bag to a lifejacket. Makes it float!

Other

Camels

They're shit.

The idea of riding a camel through the Sahara Desert sounds all very romantic and awesome... until you get on the bloody thing.

In Morocco I booked a tour which included a 2.5hr camel ride into the Sahara Desert where you camp for the night. Booking it, I thought, "What, only 2.5hrs? That's a bit wussy. I want to ride right into the middle like the next Laurance of Arabia!" That was, until I got on the thing and discovered just how amazingly uncomfortable they really are. I used to always wonder why you see pictures of Bedouins and Berbers walking through the desert leading six camels behind them. I'd always think, "Why don't you ride the animal ya silly drongo!"... but now I know why. It's not the hump that makes them uncomfortable, it's how they walk, which they seem to do in such a way as to cause the maximum amount of back pain. You can almost hear them giggling to themselves, in Camel Talk going, "Hey dudes. Ha, haha, hey dudes. Seriously check this out... watch this.... I take a big step then stop suddenly, then take another big step and stop suddenly again just to piss this guy off on top of me. Check out the face of that silly tourist! Ahhahaha, man he's hating it! Just a bit more and I reckon he'll get off me! Mwahahaha!"

We survived the ride into the Berber camp, but on the way back I had a heck of an amount of back pain. This other guy in the group was obviously feeling the same as he couldn't take it anymore, got off and actually walked the whole way back, walking for multiple hours through the sand in the desert heat, up and down towering sand dunes at a fast walk to keep up with the camels. He was really struggling and hating it, yet somehow that was still a better option for him than riding a camel. *That's* how bad they are!

Moral: If you're going to the Middle East, let's face it, you haven't really been unless you ride a camel. It's a Must Do, but just try the 2hr ride before you go signing up for a 10 day camel trek!

Local Transport

You always have to try the local transport. This doesn't mean you must take the local transport every single time to call yourself a backpacker, but you should always try the local transport at least once. It will always be loud, crowded, slow and uncomfortable, but the experience will make it worthwhile. I like it because you get to see how the locals travel, and realise this is what they have to do each day. It makes you feel a lot more fortunate for your cushy lifestyle. Remember too, that the crapper the experience, the more of an experience you've gained! Exp +1!

For big trips where I have time, I pretty much solely use the local transport. Why pay $25 for a direct hostel-to-hostel shuttle when you can pay $10 to catch three overcrowded old buses and two taxis to get to the same place? Haha, ok, so that may sound ludicrous to some, but the more you do it, the more you get used to it and before long you catch yourself saying, "The trip was pretty easy." when referring to taking three buses, two taxis and a boat, taking over 6hrs just to cover 60km. You may ask 'why bother', but this training will help you for the rest of your life – never again will you bitch about a three-hour bus ride or a 10hr plane trip.

Of course the natural temptation is to take the direct, easy transport option that's advertised in your hostel. I know for myself at the start of my Central America trip I just took the shuttles without even considering the local buses. The thought of getting on a local bus when speaking extremely limited Spanish is quite daunting, but once you sum up the courage and actually do it, you realise it's not actually scary or difficult at all. Generally Wikitravel has all the information you need, telling you exactly which buses you need to catch to get to a certain place. Buses always have a sign on them saying their final destination, so it's pretty easy. Even if you get stuck and lost somewhere (which is unlikely), what's the worst thing that can happen? There's no situation you won't get out of, and the more you test yourself getting out of your comfort zone, the easier everything else becomes.

Sometimes the ludicrousness of it can make it fun. While in Thailand, after getting the worst ever sunburn on my back, I travelled from the island of Koh Tao to Surat-Thani in an overnight local boat. Problem was the ceiling was just 1.2m high and people were packed in, so if you had to get up for a pee, you had to try and crawl over all these people lying down shoulder to shoulder. Of course, this also meant me scraping my burnt back on the wooden beams when accidently standing up too far, then spending the rest of the night on an unforgiving straw mat. I actually really enjoyed it. Even catching the local buses in El Salvador where they pack close to 100 people into old American school buses... I really enjoyed it for some reason. It's when you stop fighting it that you enjoy it. I remember once being jammed in so tightly that I couldn't move at all, plus the escape hatch above me was broken, letting in a torrential tropical downpour straight on my head, but I just stood there and meditated. I can never meditate alone in the quietest room in the world, but in this packed bus, it just worked for some reason! The other plus side is that as you're all so tightly packed in, no one can even move their arms so you can't get pick-pocketed!

A different trip that was not so fun was going from Kuta (Bali, Indonesia) to the Gili Islands, off Lombok. What we thought would be a 4hr journey turned out to be 14. To make it even worse, we paid for return tickets the first time, but there was no way in hell we were making the return journey witthe same way, so in the end we didn't save any money either! This so-awful-it-was-funny trip is further described in the Sickness section in Chapter 11.

Other times, shit can just get weird. Central America is well known for its Chicken Buses; that is, old American school buses pimped out with mag wheels (yes, fancy chrome wheels on a bus), chrome decorations everywhere on the exterior, pumping sound systems, neon lights throughout and a sick paint job. Some even sport big 32" LCD TV's inside. They're freakin' awesome yet are the cheap local transport. They are known as Chicken Buses due to the likelihood of there being live chickens in the bus. Sounds like bullshit, huh? I've actually had to step over a bunch of chickens sitting next to the driver to get on a bus once, and even my first trip I was sitting next to a woman with a chicken in her handbag. Awesome. Actually this first trip would be my most interesting chicken bus trip too. After doing the hellish 140km swamp trek in Guatemala, we had to catch a bus the last 50km through the jungle to the town we were staying in. Even in a direct bus, this 50km took a ridiculous six hours! This 'road' was more of a 4x4 track, being a dirt track with huge potholes and deep puddles to cross. After tackling this for a while, we got stopped by the military, in which the soldiers carrying AK-47's, Uzi's and M16's, plus side arms of large handguns and large knives ordered all males off the bus. They looked more like a guerrilla army than a proper army due to each person carrying a different type of gun. It felt pretty sketchy. We were shitting ourselves slightly as it was just the males ordered off, and we were in the middle of nowhere, but they just searched the bus for an hour while we waited outside in the rain. Finally, they let us back on. We continued on for a few hours, then *the same military vehicle* stops us again. Fa-ark. This time everyone gets ordered off and they go through absolutely everything. We're all standing outside waiting, very bored, until one hour later they triumphantly plonk down some cardboard boxes on the ground. We all gather around. Intrigue mounts. They slice open up the box.

A few slimy fish slide out.

Huh?

They then open the next box. Inside is the skinned carcass of some animal, resembling a small pig. The mood becomes very serious. We (the tourists) wonder what the hell is going on. The lead man shouts to the crowd "Six years prison!" while pointing at the carcass. Whoa, bloody hell! We're guessing it's some protected, endangered animal. He repeats; "Six years prison!" He then looks around at the crowd and says, "Whose is this?"

Oddly enough; silence.

He asks again whose it is. Once again, no one owns up. Perhaps he would have been better off asking whose it was *before* saying it's a six-year jail term. I'm now thinking, oh crap, we're all going to have to go to the police station and get interrogated until someone admits. Faa-aaark. I've just finished a 140km hike through mud, and this is the last thing I want to do. Fortunately however, after asking again they just give up and take the carcass with them, letting us get on the bus and continue on our way. What the hell was that all about?!?

Chapter Summary

Air Travel

• Air travel is extremely safe

• Use Skyscanner to find the cheapest flights in Europe and Kayak or Expedia for the Americas

• Check with budget airlines if their airport is way out of the city, particularly if you have a flight transfer

• If you need a one-way ticket, check the return ticket price. It may be cheaper

• Close to the date of the flight, first or business class may be cheaper than economy

• Make sure to get an ESTA if flying to the USA. Do this straight after you book your ticket

• Book a refundable bus ticket out of a country if flying one-way into a country with no exit air ticket

• Make sure you have enough time for transfers, taking into consideration immigration and whether you need to travel do a different airport (particularly if flying one leg with a standard carrier, and the other with a budget airline)

• Get to the airport on time

• Take sharps out of your carry-on and put them in your backpack

• Secure your pack zippers with an unfolded paper clip, some wire or string

• Put all your essentials in your carry-on in case your main bag gets lost

• Dress appropriately for the country you're flying to (warm clothes for cold countries)

• Consider taking along some nose spray or lip balm for long flights if you are easily affected

• Have a plastic ready-bag containing the items you will use during the flight and keep the rest of your things in the overhead bin. See the recommended list in the chapter and the Appendix

• Have your itinerary printed

• Have a copy of your exit ticket printed

• Ask for an exit row seat at check-in

• Get a window seat for short flights and an aisle seat for long flights

• Organise your stuff before security – take things out of your pockets and put them in your bag

- Say hello to the person sitting next to you as soon as you sit down. It's a lot more awkward to say it one hour into a flight
- Play Mr Squiggle on the plane with the person sitting next to you
- Ask for a spare meal (if meals are included)
- Avoid sleeping tablets unless you're used to them
- Go to the toilet before picking up your luggage
- Assess which immigration line to take. Avoid the line with the most amount of people not speaking English or the local language
- Keep every bit of paper Immigration gives you
- Check the condition of fragile items before you leave the airport
- Declare all items
- See if you can check in early if you have a long time between transfers (be charming). Otherwise, see if there's bag storage available
- Airports can be good to sleep in. Check the reviews first on www.sleepinginairports.net
- Only ever get taxis from the taxi rank

Rail

- Avoid rail passes in Europe – get flights or sale train rides instead
- Get a rail pass if travelling in Japan
- Don't get a weekly metro card in Montreal unless arriving at the start of the week

Road Travel

- Buses can be great, particularly night buses
- Put your bags as far back as possible in the undercarriage luggage compartment
- Sit where you have a view of the luggage compartment so you can see if someone takes your bag
- Consider Ride Share in lieu of buses
- Avoid hitchhiking

Boats

- Ensure your bag straps aren't about to fall off
- If using a kayak or something similar, put your valuables in a waterproof bag and clip it to a lifejacket so it floats

Other
- Camels are uncomfortable. Try them before committing to a long journey
- Make sure to experience the local transport

Chapter 6: Accommodation

Staying with Friends

The best option without doubt is to stay with friends when travelling. Over time, as you travel more and get more friends around the globe, this gets easier and easier. I've now got so many friends in Amsterdam that I probably have more friends there than I do in Australia! Staying with friends will get you the 'true' experience. Even though Amsterdam (Holland) is a tourist Mecca, I managed to spend over a week there without meeting a single tourist. I just did all the Dutch things with my Dutch friends and had an absolutely amazing time. The same goes for Georgia, USA. If I just travelled through there I would think the place was a bit of a shithole, but staying with my friends for three weeks, I had some of the best times of my life there. I truly had more fun there than just about anywhere else I've been. There's nothing quite like staying with boys from the south (who talk like Forrest Gump), drinking Budweiser while shooting shotguns off the jetty in the warm afternoon sun. Friendliest people there too – within moments of meeting the friends of my friends, I felt so welcomed that I felt part of their group – as if we had all been friends since early childhood. I've also been fortunate to stay with friends in Ireland, England, Germany, Denmark, Canada, New York, Guatemala, Malaysia, Panama, Colombia, and of course, all over Australia. Since then I've also made a lot more friends in Europe, the USA and Canada, which I plan to meet up with next time I'm there.

It can be uncomfortable to ask to stay at someone's house though. Here's where you can use Facebook to your advantage. For example, I was staying with a friend in Ireland and was booked to fly to Amsterdam. I wanted to stay with my friends, but of course you always feel intrusive asking if you can stay. Instead, I just went on Facebook and changed my status to, "Just booked my flights to Amsterdam. Woohoo!!" Within minutes, I had offers of accommodation from multiple friends. It's pretty funny how you can turn it around, so they are inviting *you*! While this may seem like you're using your friends, it's not. It's an open way of finding out who is able and most excited to host you. No use asking someone that doesn't have time if you have a different friend that wants nothing more than for you to stay at their house. Of course, repay the favour by cleaning their house, cooking them dinner, paying for their drinks, etc.

Couchsurfing

Couchsurfing is awesome. Get on it. Make sure you don't leave this until you start travelling though. I used to host travellers a lot when I lived in China, but as I had so many requests all the time, I would only host people that had references. Generally any less than three references and I wouldn't host them. Therefore, if you just join Couchsurfing with intent to get free accommodation when you travel; you may find this exceptionally difficult to do until you get your first few references. Best way of course to get references is to start hosting. I can understand your hesitation to let strangers into your house while you're busy working, but really, it's awesome and a lot of fun! While living in Shanghai I was working 50hr weeks and I had a girlfriend so I didn't have much spare time, but I really, really enjoyed hosting. I loved the honesty of it too. I lived in an absolutely *piiiimping* apartment. Multi-billion dollar complex including a few fitness centres with full size indoor pools, sauna's, steam rooms, tennis courts, squash courts, a golf putting green, swan lake, mazes, bowling alley (yes, a bowling alley), and believe it or not, a waterpark-size man-made beach and large wave pool, complete with sandy beach, palm trees and all. All in the middle of Shanghai.

I don't want to brag (my company was the one paying for it anyway), but I'm just here to paint the picture that this of all places is not the place you want to invite strangers if you have security concerns. I would however make a colour map to get to my place, leave my office to meet them at the metro station, give them my keys, access card and map, show them how to get to my place and tell them I won't be there for another six hours. I'm basically telling them they can steal whatever they want, and they can get away with it as I won't be home for another six hours. Of course there was never any trouble – only great experiences.

Many people I hosted came to stay for a night or two but ended up staying over a week. They certainly weren't uninvited guests – I had so much fun with many of them that I didn't want them to leave! Having Couchsurfers at your house makes you get out and do more things too. When was the last time you did a touristy thing in your city? Chances are you stopped doing the touristy things in your city two weeks after moving there. Get out and explore your own place!! You can discover lots of new things about your town through tourists oddly enough.

Hosting will pay you back too. I was in New York recently and finding a Couchsurfing host was almost impossible. All the cool places get requests all the time and get sick of it, and all that're left are weird people. I sent off a heap of requests but couldn't get anything. It was then that I remembered that while in China I hosted a guy from New York. I sent him a message which of course he couldn't refuse, so I saved $50/night for four nights (hostels in New York are *expensive!*).

Hostel Accommodation

Having spent more than 1200 nights in hostels, I've picked up a few tips along the way.

Choosing your Hostel

I always seem to use Hostelworld and Hostelz to find hostels. Generally I don't even read the hostel introduction or what facilities are included – I just go straight to the 'reviews' section. After all, this is what counts. If it says 'we stayed here and it was really clean and the owner was lovely, but the showers need to be fixed', I would avoid this place at all costs as it's probably nice, but stale and boring. If it however says 'I stayed here and had a great time!! Good common room and easy to meet people,' then I would definitely stay there, even if the rating was bad. Generally the highest rating hostel would be the more boring place as this is where the people who want hotel-style accommodation go. Look out for 'I' versus 'we' in the reviews. If there're lots of 'I's', then it will attract single travellers and no doubt you'll meet a lot more people.

Things that put me off hostels are:

- Biggest in town
- Key card access
- Bar included

Why Biggest in Town sucks: It just means it'll be packed full of people and impersonal. Expect it to be like a hospital; modern, super clean and sterile. Generally there'll be too many people there to meet people. Yes, the smaller the hostel, the more people you will meet. Go to a huge hostel and you'll probably only meet two people. Also, the people that go to these places are typically the more boring and uptight type that doesn't want to socialise with other people and just want a cheap but clean room to stay.

The smaller hostels are pretty much always a lot more fun. When they're smaller, you'll meet everyone there, and probably do everything together too. It's great when it's an owner-operator as the owner will generally be really cool and hang out with everyone. It's more like hanging out with friends as opposed to just being a bed for the night.

Why Key Card Access sucks: Key card access generally means a new, renovated place without character (see above). It also means when you get up in the middle of the night for a pee, the door will close behind you, leaving you outside your room at 3am in just your boxer shorts. One of the best hostels I ever stayed in was in Cologne, Germany where there weren't any locks at all!! The owner just recognised who stayed there, so that would get you through the front door, then all rooms had no lock. It was strange at first, but it meant that everyone just felt more open and the entire hostel would just hang out together like a bunch of friends each night. It was awesome!

Why Bar Included sucks: A bar is the single biggest thing that puts me off a hostel. The reason I love hostels so much is that people all hang out and drink, talk and party together. Go to a small hostel with a cool common room or garden and you'll see everyone sitting together socialising. If there's a bar however, it's like any other bar – people hardly approach each other. People stick with the people they know, holding their beer to their chest like a shield of protection. Also, it means you're paying expensive bar prices which quickly exceeds the cost of your room. If a hostel has a bar, it means you cannot drink your own alcohol there. Hugely annoying. Much better are the places with no bar where you sit with everyone, everyone shares cheap drinks and all people socialise with each other, and then once sufficiently tanked, you go with your new bunch of 15 friends to the town and have a great old time. Most times however, you are having so much fun at the hostel that you never leave! Even if you're a non-drinker (or perhaps especially if you're a non-drinker) I'd avoid the hostel with the bar included too as this means the people will be hanging around in the common rooms socialising, not in the noisy bar where you can't hear each other. Make your friends in the hostel, then go out on the town.

When location is more important than vibe, such as when using it for a transfer, I select 'Map View' on Hostelworld to find one closer to the airport.

Booking Your Hostel

While I pretty much exclusively use Hostelworld to find hostels, I don't always use it to book them as sometimes you can save 10% by contacting the hostel directly. That's because that 10% deposit you pay on Hostelworld goes to Hostelworld. For many places they will charge the same price as if you paid through Hostelworld, though others will give it cheaper.

Note too, if it says on Hostelworld that it's full but the hostel looks awesome, still give them a call. Once when I was in Portugal, I booked a hostel where it said I got the last bed, but when I arrived it was almost completely empty. Similarly in Central America if you do a search for hostels the next night it will say they are all full even when they're not. The reason for this is that hostels will only allocate a number of beds to Hostelworld such that it leaves space for walk-ins. If a place says it's booked out on Hostelworld, it does not necessarily mean it's booked out.

In some places there may be nothing advertised on the hostel websites at all. Therefore, it pays to check Wikitravel as well as this will generally list many of the hostels in the town that may not be listed elsewhere. If there's nothing cool there, do a Google search too. Classic example is Puerto Viejo in Costa Rica. Everything on Hostelworld and Wikitravel looks crap and expensive, but a Google search shows some great hostels.

Finding your Hostel

As mentioned in the 'Know Where You Are' section of Chapter 1, ensure to pre-cache the maps on your phone and put a place marker on your hostel before you go. Make sure to have the phone number of your hostel in case you get lost trying to find it.

Which Room to Take?

Get the mid-sized dorm – if a hostel has options for 4, 8 and 12-bed dorms, go for the 8. People who want privacy will always go for the 4, so that will always be full, those that want to save every penny will always go for the 12, so that will always be full, or near full too. Most people think, why save $2 for the 8 bed dorm when I can have the 4, so often there're actually less people in the 8 bed dorm than the 4, plus you've saved money too! It's often a better crowd too – the people in the 12 bed are often stingy hippies, and with so many people in it, you feel less secure about your stuff. The people in the mid dorm are the mid type – probably experienced travellers with a lot of good stories that know how to save money, yet are keen for a good time too.

Top or Bottom Bunk?

Personally I always go for the bottom bunk as it saves having to climb in and out of bed when you need to pee, plus you can sit on it when you need to organise your things. There are a few bad points to the bottom bunk though… like almost getting killed or pissed on.

Yes, while staying at a hostel in Hobart (Australia), I decided just to have a quiet night, and watched the hostel movie 'Step Brothers'. You know, the movie where they make the bunk beds "…because it will create so much extra space for activities! Think of all the extra activities we could do!" but then in the movie the bunk beds collapse, almost crushing the guy underneath.

I think you can see where I'm going with this story.

I hop into bed early one night and fortunately didn't drink anything. Sometime around 3:30am, while sound asleep I hear this loud 'CRACK!!'. In the space of microseconds I wake up, and with the reflexes of a mountain lion, roll out of bed *as the whole bunk above comes crashing down to where I was sound asleep just microseconds before*!! I don't mean that just the bed slats broke – the entire bed frame collapsed. I still have no idea how I managed to jump out so fast. The scary part was that the wooden beams of the bed above punctured right through the mattress that I was just sleeping on. If I had just one or two drinks that night, I no doubt wouldn't have had the same reflexes and those beams would have stuck into me. It must have been quite a shock for the girl sleeping above too!! Hahaha, I wonder if she had a dream that she was falling? Well, we all survived so we thought it was pretty funny. Of course, me being the arsehole I am, I made sure the next day to send my girlfriend at the time a message saying, "Hey, how's it going? I ended up with a cute American girl in my bed last night. How's your day been?" Hehehe, I'm bad.

Another reason why bottom bunk can suck, is if you have an old drunk passed out in the bunk above, and you awake to a watery dripping noise. In slumber-state you ponder what that noise is for a moment, till you realise.... "SHIT!! The guy above is pissing himself in his sleep!!"

Hostel Etiquette

You will always find stereotypes in hostels, and it always seems to ring true. For example there's always the Asian that never talks to anyone, never leaves the room and just spends the entire day sleeping, then is up all night playing computer games in bed when everyone else is trying to sleep. Then of course there's the arsehole that comes into the room in the middle of the night while everyone is asleep, turns the light on and starts looking for their toothbrush; totally oblivious to the fact that other people are trying to sleep. And of course the Aussies that party on till morning keeping everyone awake.

There're a few things you can do to *not* be the arsehole in the room. First starts with a bit of prep work. Before bed organise the stuff you need, like your boxer shorts, toothbrush and earplugs. Keep your earplugs under your pillow so they are easy to find in the dark. Same with your room key – when you go to bed put it in an easy to find location, such as under your pillow or tucked into the waistband of your boxer shorts. While staying in Guatemala, there was a magnitude 7.1 earthquake just 100km away. For whatever reason I was already awake, so I was just lying in bed enjoying it, but then it got a lot stronger the story above me was shaking a huge amount. Figuring it's best to be in the open outside in case the building collapsed, I ran outside, only to have the door close and lock behind me, trapping me outside in my boxer shorts at 5am. This particularly sucked as there was no one else in my room, *and there was no spare key*! After trying all options, the staff finally managed to break open the lock.

If someone in your room snores, wake them up. If you do nothing about it and just lie in bed unable to sleep and angry at the person, you'll be angry at them the whole next day and that's unfair to them. It's your problem. Guaranteed all snorers would rather be woken up then have everyone in the room pissed off at them the whole next day. The best way to stop someone snoring is to pinch their nostrils together gently for three seconds. This forces them to breathe differently, and they will stop snoring without even waking up. Only problem is this can be, well, a little bit creepy. Imagine sleeping peacefully, then waking up to see some stranger holding your nose in the dark. Less controversial option is just to gently shake them. Waking them up should give you and everyone else enough time to fall asleep before the person starts snoring again. It's your problem, deal with it.

Actually while on the subject of snoring, due to having my nose broken a few times I was a snorer but now largely am not anymore. First trick I did was a very low carb diet. This is an intense diet I once did for two months in order to get six pack abs. Got the six pack (now gone of course) and it came with the side effect of a large reduction in snoring. Yay! I noticed the reduction (well my girlfriend did), so I Googled it, and many people were saying the same thing. I don't know why, but I don't really care either! Sidenote – if interested in getting a six-pack, check out the books by Lyle McDonald. It's actually possible to go from nothing to a visible six pack in four days by following the right techniques. This is how long it took me to get 80% of the results. I wouldn't believe it if it didn't happen to me personally. It's all about diet and Lyle covers it like no other. Natural, yes. Healthy, no. Works, yes. Of course there're a few tricks you can do, such as pushing on your thighs when flexing your abs as it makes them stick out twice as far! Anyway, going back to stopping snoring, the other thing that helped was learning to play the didgeridoo. How this helps is that to play didgeridoo you need to do circular breathing. That is, a technique where you breathe both in and out at the same time. It's actually a lot easier than it sounds. Anyway, apparently this strengthens the nasal passages or something like that and stops you snoring. Going on any more about the above is out of the scope of this book, so if you want any more info on the above, just shoot me an email at LiveTheAdventureLife@gmail.com. Don't worry, I'm not going to sell you some shit, I'm just stoked I found something that worked!!!

Make sure if you have an early departure that you organise all your stuff the night before. That is, pack up all that you can, and leave out the clothes you will wear the next day. Of course there're still some things you will have to muck around with, such as boxer shorts, towel and so on. Best to just chuck all those last items into your pack, and then organise all your stuff outside of the room.

Getting a Warm Shower

Hot water systems are rare in third world countries. Instead what is more common is to have an electric shower head that heats the water as it passes. Great theory as it saves energy, however rarely are these any more than lukewarm at best. Typically these output a constant heat value, so the more water pressure you want, the colder the shower. The problem is that the water heater only turns on when there is a specific amount of water going through. To ensure you get the hottest shower possible, turn the bathroom light on. This is your indicator. Starting with the shower off, very slowly turn the tap until the light goes dimmer – this is your indicator that the shower heater has switched on as the high current draw of the shower will cause a voltage drop on the light, causing it to go dimmer. Turning the tap on to just this point means you will have the shower heater on with the least water pressure, and therefore the warmest shower possible.

If you're lucky enough, your hostel may have a gas system. As distributed gas systems are rare, this is more likely to be powered by a large BBQ cylinder. These run out. There's no way the hostel will know unless you tell them. I've been in hostels where people were having very unpleasant cold showers all morning, feeling very upset. Come my turn, I realised the gas was out, told the staff, got the cylinder swapped over and had a fantastic warm shower.

Camping

I haven't done that much camping while travelling, other than in Iceland, Mexico and Australia. It's definitely got a few pros and cons. Personally I'm a huge fan of car-camping, but not so much tent-camping. Car-camping is awesome as you can have the best adventure ever; go wherever you want, park wherever the hell you want, wake up in paradise and not pay a cent for accommodation. The best trip of my life was car-camping in Iceland. Some friends of mine exclusively car-camp when travelling. In the US they spent most nights at Wal-Mart as the chain actually allows it, and they provide security for safe sleeping. Possibly Wal-Mart car parks are not the most romantic places to spend the night, but they're everywhere, are safe, and include toilets.

I joined up with them in Mexico, but as they were a couple obviously they'd stay in the car and I'd stay outside in a tent. Admittedly it did feel pretty sketchy to be sleeping in a tent at the side of the road in the middle of nowhere in Mexico. Scary part is unless you have windows in your tent, people can see you, but you can't see them, only hear them. Of course, most people are good but it does make it hard to relax and sleep. In Mexico, I'd often pitch the tent at the petrol (gas) stations as it's about the safest place you can do it. Just go to the security and ask if you can pitch the tent. When they invariably say no, just give them 20 pesos and start pitching your tent anyway. I have a great video where I'm in my tent and you can hear birds absolutely everywhere. Sounds like I'm in paradise somewhere. I then open the tent door to show I'm camped in a petrol station at the side of the highway. Pretty funny.

If worried about security, there are many campgrounds, however these often don't cost much less than a hostel. Not a fan of these as generally the only people you'll meet are 65-year-old German couples. Fun at first, though still not the same as a hostel full of young people.

If doing a long camping trip I highly recommend spending the money to buy a camping guide. That is, a book listing all the campsites around. The money you save in petrol not having to look around for sites will quickly pay the book off. In some countries there are specific Free Camping books, listing all free campgrounds. This can save you a huge amount of money, particularly in Australia where camp fees are really high and there're large fines for sleeping in the car in certain places too.

A lot of hostels will let you pitch a tent which will cost you less than a dorm, plus you get your own private room too. Pretty awesome. Only problem is your things aren't so secure. My view; sleep in the car, or sleep in a hostel.

Chapter Summary

- Try and stay with friends while travelling (make sure to keep in contact with cool people you meet everywhere and visit them on their home turf)

- If shy about asking someone straight up if you can stay at their house, or if you have multiple friends in the one place, you can put a post on Facebook saying you're going to that specific place. Watch for invitations of who is most able to host you

- Repay the favour by cooking dinner, cleaning the house, paying for their drinks, etc.

- Start hosting people on Couchsurfing. You'll start to make friends overseas, as well as get references so you can surf yourself while overseas

- Use a website such as Hostelworld or Hostelz or one of the many others to find hostels. In small remote areas check out Wikitravel too

- Avoid the large modern hostels, particularly if they have a bar. Generally the smaller the hostel, the more people you'll meet. Bar Included normally means you can't drink your own alcohol. It takes away the close-knit hostel feeling and makes it more like a normal bar where it's hard to meet people. Stay at a small place with character, make friends there, then hit the town with them

- See if you can book directly with the hostel. You may be able to save 10%

- If Hostelworld says they're full but you really want to stay at a particular place, give them a call anyway. They may have space

- Go for the mid-sized dorm generally

- Bottom bunk is more convenient, but comes with the possibilities of the top bunk crashing down, or someone pissing themself above you

- Organise all your stuff before nighttime, such as boxer shorts, toothbrush, ear plugs or anything else you may need

- If you're in a key-card room, or another that locks automatically, keep the key tucked into the waistband of your boxers, or under your pillow

- If someone in your room snores, wake them

- Consider a low carb diet or learning to play didgeridoo if you suffer from snoring... or more correctly, if other people suffer from your snoring!

- Organise and pack your stuff the night before if you have an early departure

- Use the 'light' trick to get a warm shower in places with heating shower heads

- For gas systems, notify the hostel staff if there's no hot water

- Car camping is totally awesome, tent camping not so much. Buy a camping guide if planning on doing a lot of camping

Chapter 7: Day Trips

Exploring

Chances are, if you're travelling you want to see and do some stuff too. I pretty much always use Wikitravel to see what's about. Surprisingly few people know about Wikitravel, which is a shame as it's fantastic. It's in the same style as Wikipedia, but instead of being about the history, climate and so on of a town, it deals with how to get there, things to see and do, where to eat, accommodation, etc. It's like the Lonely Planet, but with the bonus of being free, more comprehensive and up to date. Other times I just like to go for a walk and purposely get lost and see the *real* town. I often like to go to a souvenir store and look at the postcards as this tends to showcase the most photogenic parts of the city. I then go on a mission to find those places.

What to Bring

I always take my Ultra Sil daypack (see Chapter 2 and a Bit). In this I tend to carry my:

- Camera
- Jumper
- Water bottle
- Peanut butter and flatbread
- Spork

Taking your own water can save you a lot of money by not having to buy bottled water. I'm also a huge fan of peanut butter and flat bread. Keeps well, tastes great, compact and non-messy. Of course you can just use the flatbread to scoop out the peanut butter, but if you're civilised you can use a spork. A spork is a combination spoon, knife and fork. They're pretty awesome.

Available from all outdoor stores. In tropical places I also carry a pocket knife for mangos. Be warned, even small pocket knives are illegal in some counties, such as China.

Always leave your backpack in the hostel if you can. Unless they're real arseholes, pretty much all hostels will let you leave your bags there for the afternoon after you've checked out. One day however I was in Bruges (Belgium) and for whatever reason I had all my bags with me. I went to go up the famous bell tower, expecting there to be bag storage there. There wasn't. If you have seen the movie 'In Bruges', this is the same bell tower where the fat American has a heart attack climbing it. I'm not surprised! With backpack on the back, daypack on the front, I climb the 366 stairs, up the staircase so narrow that both my packs were rubbing against the walls and I often got a bit stuck. Other than being bloody difficult, it was quite a workout too! This was particularly bad coming down as I couldn't see where I was putting my feet, which is a real issue on a narrow spiral staircase. I was shitting myself that I'd fall down. Avoid taking your packs into ancient, narrow buildings.

Organised Trips

Most hostels will have information about all the tours and activities about. In general, in first world countries their prices will be better than tourist agencies, however in third world countries it seems to be the opposite. Hard to generalise, so just go out and price hunt.

There're always gung-ho people that want to be independent and do it all themself instead of a tour, however this of course has its pro's and con's. In cities I tend to avoid tours as guaranteed it will be full of stupid people, and the tour will probably visit 'authentic places' where, for example, clothes are supposedly handmade (there's one person that demonstrates weaving for about 2 minutes), and the rest of the shop is, well, a shop that sells the exact same factory-made stuff as in the markets, but at twice the price, yet the silly tourists still buy everything. As a general rule, *never* buy from a shop that someone takes you to. In backpacker towns however I often prefer to do the tour as it supports the local community and can save a lot of mucking around and confusion that comes by doing it yourself. You can generally tell how good a tour will be by the cost; the cheaper the better. If it's expensive and in a touristy area it will attract stupid unadventurous people; people that prefer luxury over experience, families and so on. The cheap backpacker tours tend to be *much* different than the expensive tours in touristy areas. That is, they are fun, have good fun people on them and don't treat you like an idiot. They can also be cheaper and less dangerous than doing it yourself too.

For example, I was in San Pedro (Guatemala) and wanted to climb a certain nearby mountain. I found someone that wanted to go too, so I went to the tourist agency and found a tour for Q70 ($9.80) including transport, guide and entrance fee. Sounds reasonable to me for a 7hr trip! I was keen to book, but she wanted to be adventurous. I thought it would be a shit fight, as I'd heard about troubles with the entrance fee on the top but she was adamant, and seeing as I tend to live by the motto of 'If you have two options…. take the crazy one', I had to go with that option! We plan it for the next morning, and after a night out, I wake up with super bad kidney pain. I figure I'm just dehydrated, and it will be all good in an hour. It wasn't. We find the correct chicken bus to take us there and get there ok, but two hours later, I'm still in a lot of pain. If I'd have known it would be this bad I would not have gone. It's so bad I can barely walk, but we're in the base town now, so I don't want to turn back. We hike up the mountain, me at a total snail's pace in a lot of pain. Eveeeeentually we make it to 20m from the top, where we're stopped with a guy wielding a machete. Q70 entry fee each he demands (it should be Q30). This is the same price as the full organised tour would have been (including entry price). We argue for a while, where it becomes quite heated. He's got a machete and I'm barely standing as it is, so we're at his mercy. Rather than support extortion, we just turn around and head back down, having not seen any of the view. Back in town I'm in so much pain, I can barely walk or do anything at all. See the doctor and find out I have salmonella. Had I done the tour it would have been cheaper and I would have seen the view after all the effort I'd gone to to get there.

Interestingly enough, the same girl the next day wanted to see the Chichi markets. Rather than take an organised trip, she spent 3hrs on local boats and chicken buses to get there; then came to the horrific realisation… it's closed today! Bugger. Turned around and spent the next 3hrs coming back.

While the above was still amusing rather than irritating, a friend of mine has a much better story. The same crazy cat that nearly got killed hitchhiking in Mexico decided to do a hike by himself. I don't mean a normal hike either, I mean an 80km hike (carrying all his gear) across a mountain range in one of the most dangerous parts of Mexico. After getting very lost and being stuck in monsoon rains, he came across a house full of *super* drunk people. The house was right on the path so there was no way to avoid it. They invited him in which he kind of had to accept, then kind of had to try one of the homemade spirits they offered him. They also offered him to stay there, but considering the guy had a gun in his pants, everyone was absolutely shitfaced, and this was the place well known for being rife with criminals, this was not an offer he was too keen on. He managed to leave but not far from the house he saw a huge marijuana crop, complete with a few ditches dug just the right size for bodies. Damn. The trip didn't get any better either, with the monsoon rain soaking everything in his pack, including his food and camera, only to be followed by immense heat the following day, resulting in severe dehydration complete with hallucinations and a feeling of spinning and being separated from his body. Following this was other interesting things, like seeing people in a car moving drugs, climbing over an unfinished bridge while utterly exhausted, waking up covered in frogs, etc.

Some adventures, particularly in dangerous places, are best done with a guide.

Hikes

Hikes are an awesome way to experience a place… just make sure you know what you're getting yourself in for. Once in Guatemala I saw a sign in the hostel, 'Five-Day Jungle Hike – Sign up at Reception!' So I did.

The guy at reception clearly knew nothing about it. I booked knowing nothing other than it would be a trek to some remote ruins, it would be six days, not five, and all that I should bring is some snacks and a towel. I had expectations it would be around 60km or so through beautiful luscious jungle.

It wasn't.

Early next morning I met up with the rest of the group. They all had gumboots (rain boots). Apparently they were all told to bring boots. I only had my Lacoste fancy shoes. We take a minivan on a 4x4 track for a few hours till we get to the departure point. The guide tells me I need boots. I think, "Nah, it's fine – I'll just put some plastic bags over my shoes for the wet bits." *Fooortunately* they had one spare pair of boots at the departure point, and *fooortunately* they eventually convinced me that I'll need the boots. We set off and are greeted by a muddy swamp. It was such thick mud that your feet get stuck with each step. Oh shit, now I see why we need the boots. Well there's probably just a bit of mud at the start. A few km later we ask the guide, "Soooo, so how far does this mud actually go for?" Response from the guide is an embarrassed laugh. Oh, that's not good. Turns out this is it. Instead of being the 60km hike I was expecting, it ended up being a 140km trek, of which 115km was thick sticky mud. I don't mean it was just a bit of mud that gets your shoes dirty – it was deep, thick, sticky mud that you get stuck in with each step, plus sections of swamp that you have to wade through. Being a swamp, the whole trail was completely flat with no change in elevation. This means no view, no change in scenery and no change in vegetation – just boring swamp plants. Certainly nothing not like the luscious jungles of Cuba and Belize I was expecting. Swamp also means mosquitoes – lots of them. We still managed to see some largely untouched ancient pyramids deep in the jungle, but overall, we didn't consider the trip worthwhile!

Also make sure never to leave the group. I nearly became cat food the first night. In our group was a girl that had hurt her knee previously and couldn't walk fast. Therefore after stopping for lunch on the first day, we split into a fast group and a slow group. I joined the fast group for a while, then thought, "Bugger it, why rush. I'll walk with the slow guys." Bad idea. I left the fast group to trudge back through the mud to the slow group. After a while walking back alone, I got that 'Oh shit' feeling. I should have met up with the slow group by now. Bugger, bugger, bugger! If it was flat ground I could have sprinted to catch up with the fast group, but in sticky mud it's impossible. Shit, shit, shit! Continuing walking back, I know for sure I should have met up with the slow group by now. I'm nearly at the lunch spot feeling alone and worried when I catch a glimpse of the guide ducking into a side path. I yell out and he's surprised to see me. He motions me to follow him, as he walks through the swamp, using his machete to cut through the overgrown track. I'm trying to ask where the others are, but I speak almost zero Spanish, and he speaks zero English. I follow him for quite some time until we see the others in the slow group. They are *very* surprised to see me. As it turns out, instead of taking the main path, they took a shortcut; which wasn't really a path at all – just the guide hacking through the jungle with his machete. Fortunately after walking for a while, Dionne thought she left her jacket at the lunch spot, so the guide went back to look for it. After not finding it, he comes back, at which point I caught the glimpse of him. I was *amazingly* lucky. As it turned out, Dionne didn't actually lose her jacket after all – it was in the bottom of her pack where she didn't see it. If she hadn't thought it was at the camp, and if the guide hadn't gone back, and if I was 4 seconds later… I wouldn't have seen them, and I would have been totally lost in the Guatemalan jungle swamp. It would have meant climbing a tree and sitting outside for the night alone in a place full of deadly snakes, tarantulas, pumas and jaguars (we saw plenty of fresh Big Cat tracks on the walk as well as a tarantula and deadly snake). The guide would have been seriously pissed off too, as it was still another 7hrs walk to the campsite. They would have all arrived, cooked dinner then realised, "Wait… where's Dave?" The guide would then have to walk the 7hrs back to find me (not knowing where I was either), finally find me, then walk all the way back. It probably would have been the end of the trip. Don't ever leave the group!

High Altitude

Beware of hiking, or even just hanging around at altitude. One of the biggest things that not many people think of, is sunburn. For every 1000m the UV rays are 10% stronger. I was in Shangri-La in China, just 110km from Tibet at 3,300m altitude. I banded with a few people in a hostel and we set off for a bike ride. We all took sunscreen and reapplied regularly, but still underestimated the effect of the sun. The ride ended up being a lot longer than expect too, so pretty much everyone returned burnt to a crisp. With no natural aloe vera in the area and a very limited pharmacy there would have been very little reprieve, but luckily I had some after-sun cream with me. Popularity +1!

In case anyone is wondering, the reason for the increased sunburn is that there's less atmosphere, not because you're closer to the sun. We're sitting 150 million km from the sun, so 2km more ain't shit. If this is something you didn't realise, I should probably also take this opportunity to say that putting on the air-conditioner or opening the fridge doesn't help make the world cooler either. Air-conditioners make more heat than cool it's just that they put the cool inside and the heat outside. Same as leaving a fan on in a room when you're not there does not make it cooler. In fact it will probably make it slightly warmer due to the heat produced by the motor.

The other obvious effect of altitude is altitude sickness, and no, this is not something that's just confined to Mt Everest. I have a friend that owns a ski shop in Utah at 2000m, and she said even there many people get altitude sickness. This is especially if coming directly from the coast, or a low altitude area. It can be a thing that's pretty easy to deny as many people (particularly fit young males) see admitting to it as a sign of weakness. The issue is that it is completely random who it affects. At 4000m an 80 year old fat smoker may not feel a difference, yet a fit young athlete may be gasping for air just standing. You can imagine a fit person going for an extreme ski holiday would not want to admit to altitude sickness and definitely wouldn't leave the mountain to reduce their altitude for a few days. The problem is amplified when people drink lots of alcohol as it makes it worse, plus people would think the headaches and general feeling like shit are from the alcohol, not the altitude. Take note of how your body is feeling and realise it's not a sign of weakness if you get altitude sickness. I recommend checking out the website www.altitude.org. There's great information and cool calculators on it. You should definitely arm yourself with some knowledge before going to high altitude places.

The term 'altitude sickness' is a bit of a misnomer too as altitude sickness doesn't necessarily mean getting 'sick' (which is normally associated with nausea). 'Altitude affected' might be a better them. I climbed a 4500m peak in Mexico before knowing anything about altitude sickness. I just thought that there was the greater chance of sunburn, plus I would get out of breath more (there's 40% less oxygen available at 4500 m). The altitude made it bloody difficult, but still we managed to go from 3100m to 4500m in a decent 3.5hrs. Pretty soon into it I developed the headache from hell. Of course there was no stopping and going back though; there's a mountain to climb! We made it to the top but had to deal with a splitting headache all the way down. Worst headache I've ever had. I made the obvious assumption that this was due to the altitude and knew that descent really was the only cure, yet I wouldn't have considered myself to have 'altitude sickness', which I thought only hardcore mountain climbers got. As such, I didn't give it much more thought. I spent the night camping at 3100m which was a lot less than the summit, but still 950m higher than where I was staying previously, so my headache continued throughout the night. Note they say you should only increase altitude by 300m per day. Some headache tablets later and I was able to get to sleep, though as the sun dropped, so too did the temperature. Before long the *inside* of my $35 Walmart tent was covered in glistening ice caused from my breath freezing. And I thought Mexico was just horses, deserts and cacti! Yes, with every 100m the temperature drops an average of 0.65°C. If you do the maths this equates to the campsite being 23° cooler than nearby land at sea level. If it's say, 18°C during the night at sea level, it'd be -5°C at night at the camp site, and -12°C at the summit.

Chapter Summary

• Use Wikitravel to see what activities are around

• Look at postcards to see the most photogenic parts of the town

• Take lunch with you in your daypack. Consider taking a spork with you

• Leave your backpack in hostel storage

• In touristy places organised tours will tend to be expensive and terrible. Avoid these. In backpacker places however they are often a better option

• Know what you're getting yourself into before you sign up to a long hike

• Never leave the group when hiking

• Beware of the increased UV rays at altitude

• Be prepared for cold temperatures at altitude

• Altitude sickness doesn't necessarily mean feeling sick. Getting altitude sickness is not a sign of being weak. Reduce altitude for a few days if you become affected

Chapter 8: Partying

Sheesh, no doubt there're whole books on partying. I'll see if I can summarise it somewhat.

Where to Go

Well if you read my advice on which hostel to stay in, no doubt you're at a cool place where you can drink your own booze and meet cool people, so this means you've found where to go. The first place is the most important, the rest you'll figure out with the more you drink.

What to Pack

When I go out I tend to take:

- Phone (only if I have an active SIM card)
- Wallet (cash only, no card, no ID)
- Crap camera
- Two decks of cards, set of foam hearts, permanent marker and stick of lip balm (for magic)
- Umbrella (when cold and raining)

If you're in a place where you don't have a SIM card, then there's no point taking your phone. Turns out if you want to know the time, you can ask someone, and if you need to write down some info or a phone number, turns out you can borrow a pen and paper too. Going without your phone means it also stops you playing with your phone and lets you talk to people instead.

Wallet is pretty important. I avoid taking my ID or credit card because once

I've got a few drinks in me there's a fair old chance I'll lose it. I take enough cash I'm willing to spend. Going without a credit card saves waking up the next day, going, "Shiiiiiitttt! How did I spend all that money last night?!?" If you only take cash it saves you overspending and buying drinks that you really don't need at 3am. Places where they card you I take my ID, otherwise I leave it in my hostel. I'd prefer not to lose it. I recommend keeping an emergency $50 in the zipped up section of your wallet for a taxi home… though no doubt, this will just be spent on alcohol. *Try* to keep it as your emergency cash!

I don't think I need to mention it, but make sure you have condoms with you too. This doesn't necessarily mean you're going out with the intention of getting laid – it just means you're prepared if it does happen.

Phones suck for taking pictures at night. Maybe it's just because I have a crap phone, but I like to record the memories of a fun night and a phone just doesn't cut it for me. I tend to take a cheap, compact camera. I've found the Canon's to be awesome… for the simple reason that they include the Movie Digest function. Perhaps other brands have it too, not sure. Either way, this function means that every time you take a photo it simultaneously records video too and stitches all these short clips together to make a video of the night. Brilliant. I only wish I had this while in Iceland. After a particularly huge night, I was going through my photos the next day and was totally stumped by one photo… a photo taken from behind the drum kit. How the hell did I even get there??! Did I become the drummer in an Icelandic band last night?!? I would love to have seen the video with it!

I still do recommend however to take a crap camera not a good camera so you're not too upset if you lose it. If you don't have a crap one, tie a long piece of string to your shorts and to the camera. Can use clear fishing line if you want to avoid looking like *too* much of an idiot.

I always take my basic magic tricks with me when I go out. Yeah, I know that sounds really nerdy… and it is… but it's awesome too. Actually carrying the permanent marker has helped me out numerous times as per the following semi-regular scenario. You can do the same. You may be out with a girl somewhere who's disappointed to discover she has a hole in her black tights. Being the amazing gentleman you are, you just nonchalantly take the black marker out of your pocket and casually colour-in their skin where the hole is. She'll be surprised and delighted that like a modern day MacGyver you've just saved the day without even saying a word. See the chapter on the magic tricks for more info why else you should carry these props.

Yes, coming from a small country town, I know carrying an umbrella (apparently) makes you gay, but knowing my track record with losing jumpers and jackets I'd prefer to use a $2 umbrella than a good jacket. In fact, I'm so bad with losing jumpers, that in Hawaii whilst seeing the police to fill out a report about losing my camera; I lost my jumper in the process. What makes it even worse is that the cops came to my hotel. Yes, somehow, somewhere in between my room and the front entrance I lost my jumper while seeing the cops about a camera I lost.

Know How to Get Home

My first trip was to Thailand where shortly after landing and checking into my hostel, I met some people and had an epic night out. After a misunderstanding with a masseuse (yes, I really did just want a massage), I ended up on the other side of the city of Bangkok alone and quite inebriated. 5am I start stumbling home then think… wait… which direction do I need to walk? Actually, what's my hotel even called… Oh shit!! What suburb am I even staying in?!? That's a terrible thought when you're just 9 hours into your first overseas trip, and you're already hopelessly lost. I also had zero money left with me. I tried to ask passerby's how to get home, but without even knowing which *suburb* I wanted to go to, this was completely fruitless, not to mention frustrating! I kept on walking, though feeling terribly sick (turns out I picked up food poising in the first hour or two of travelling) and very lost and alone. I just kept on walking and believe it or not, found my suburb, my road, then my hotel. Not something you want to repeat… though of course I did somewhat.

I flew to Montreal (Canada) to see a girl I was briefly with on a previous trip. Unfortunately, after I arrived she said she met someone else just a few days beforehand. Bugger hey. Fortunately I have a few other friends in Montreal, so I called up another friend and she says she's having a party tonight. Super! I go to her house and have a great time, and as it turns out, she has a very attractive friend too. She lives in the clubbing district, so we hit the town. Everyone thinks I'm crazy for not wearing a jacket out, just a jumper, as it's minus whatever it is and all the footpaths and roads are covered in snow. I figure if I take a jacket and gloves I'll just lose them. Aussie mentality, "Yeah nah, all good. I'll be fine." We hit the town and perhaps because I'm little upset about the fail with the girl I came over to see, I drink a bit more than I should. I lose the others, so I head home (to the house of the original girl I came to see). I start walking, but unfortunately I'm a bit inebriated and can't focus my eyes on the map on my phone. Dammit. I don't know which direction to take, so I choose a direction and just start walking.

Turns out her house was 3km away, which doesn't seem too much, but that's over 30 blocks! More than enough to be horrendously confused where you are. This would suck enough during a warm day, but when it's nighttime and you're walking through snow in nothing more than jeans and a jumper, it's downright scary. I remember being so cold and lost that I was scared. When you're drunk and yet still feel so cold to the point of scared… you know you're *really* cold. I just kept on walking, walking, walking; looking for landmarks. I was ecstatic when I found the bridge near her place, but still needed to find her short 100m long street. I must have found it as that's where I woke up. Next morning I phone my other friend.

"Where the hell are you?" she asks.

"I'm at Jen's," I reply. *<name changed for privacy reasons>*

"Why didn't you stay here?" she asks.

"Huh?"

"I gave you keys to stay at mine."

"Nah. You didn't."

"Yeah, I did."

"Huh?" I check my pocket and find a key… presumably to her house. "Oh… shit."

"Yeah," she says. "I gave you my keys, confirmed you knew my address, and you said you'd come here," she continues.

"Oh."

Turns out instead of being lost for hours in the snow to walk to the house of a person I didn't particularly want to see, I could have just walked just a few hundred meters to my friends house where I would have been sharing the futon with her really attractive friend. Know where you're going!

On a different trip, I was on a Contiki 17-day tour through Europe, which included going to the beautiful city of Florence in Italy. Of course come nighttime the whole Contiki group just wanted to party at the Contiki clubs with other Contiki bus groups. Fudge doing that *every single night*! I wanted to party with the locals, so I banded with another mate and hit the town square. Well, we knew zero Italian and the people we met knew zero English, but after a few drinks we became fluent in Italian (apparently) and had all sorts of drunken conversations all night. Great night!! Only problem was getting back home; the campsite we were staying at was 40 minutes away; by car.

Of course we were too stingy to pay for a cab ride, so we decided to walk the 15km back, even though we had absolutely no idea where it was, other than the general direction. Fortunately, at the start of the trip I took a photo of the hotel list, so we had the address. Lucky!! We drunkenly flag down a car that takes us some of the way, then drops us off, still a long way away. We then keep walking, but I'm so tired and drunk that each step is a huge effort. Our bus is leaving to Switzerland (600km away) at 8am the next morning, yet I barely care even though I know trying to get there on our own accord the next day will be horrendously difficult and expensive. I'm about to have a sleep at the side of the main road when we successfully flag down a cop car. We chat to them for a while in our new-found Italian skills and are feeling pretty confident that we can get home in the cop car, until they say (in Italian accent, complete with hand motions), "We-a are-a not-a a taxi!" and drive off. Dammit. More walking and we manage to flag down another car that takes us further. More walking and we meet some council workers and get some more directions off them. We continue on foot, then of all things, we flag down an empty off-duty full-size bus which takes us the rest of the way to the campground. Phew!! We jump the 2m tall spiked fence and manage 1.5hrs sleep before leaving for Switzerland. Epic adventure!

General Going Out Tips

Break big bills at the start of the night. Once pissed you won't realise if they didn't give you enough change. This is particularly relevant in Indonesia where the 10,000 note is an orangey-pink colour, and the 100,000 is a pinky-orange colour… or is it the other way around? They both look pretty much the same, and after you've had a few drinks, you sure as hell aren't recognising the difference between four and five zero's. 100,000 IDR is still only $9, but still a bit annoying when you realise the next day that you got your notes mixed up and accidently handed over 10 times the note you intended to a few times!

Drink of Choice

My drink of choice is a Long Island Ice Tea. Yes, it appears to be expensive, but realise it includes a shot of vodka, tequila, gin, white rum and triple sec. It's all alcohol, with a touch of coke for the colour. Dollar for alcohol, it's often cheaper than beer. I'm also quite a fan of mojitos, but make sure not to have too many due to the sugar content.

Make sure though to order a water every second or third drink. You'll feel much better for it the next day.

Some hostels really annoy me when they include a bar as they don't let you drink your own drinks. I discovered a great solution however; order a beer that comes in a dark bottle. Finish this, then go back to your dorm and fill it with your own rum and coke or whatever you like. No one will be any the wiser as the dark glass will disguise whatever you have in it. Looks like you're buying from the bar yet you're drinking for a fraction of the price. Gold.

Drinking Laws

Most countries have laws about drinking in public. In some places it matters; in other places it clearly does not.

I arrived in Dublin, Ireland and didn't know the laws there. To avoid getting a big fine I went to one of the cops and asked, "Is it legal to drink in the street here?" Here came the reply (in a jolly Irish accent), "Oh no, certainly not! …but just don't let us catch you alright!" said with a smile and a wink. Hahaha, you gotta love the Irish!

Magic

Magic is something that sounds really geeky… well that's because it is.

Fortunately however the geekiness of it all is cancelled out by the Awesomeness Factor. It's an incredible weapon to have in the arsenal of having a great night out. I've performed numerous impromptu shows at hostels where I've had an audience of around 40 people (just start doing a few tricks, then suddenly everyone is watching). Everyone loves to see good magic and if they don't want to watch it, they don't have to (unlike the person that plays the guitar at the hostel all night long, stealing all the vibe). Other than at bars and common rooms, it's great at the dinner table too. While travelling you're always meeting people and having dinner together and it's so much fun to surprise them by suddenly swallowing your knife, tearing up your napkin and having it suddenly restore itself, pushing a glass through the table, etc. This will be a dinner they won't forget!

Not only that, it can also be used for free drinks and if your Couchsurfing profile says you can do a magic show for them, for sure you'll be getting free accommodation.

It is also one of the best things to do for cold-approaches for meeting people. No need for corny pickup lines, no awkward conversation starters, no 'waiting for a reason/right time to approach' or anything like that. Just walk up to someone and say, "Hey, do you want to see some magic?" and no matter whether they say yes or no, just start doing a trick anyway. After the first they'll be hooked. I've even been at a bar where there was this *unbelievably* attractive girl (honestly, one of the hottest girls I've ever seen in my life). Within less than five minutes of first noticing her I was making out with her; tongue and all.

This, my friend, is magic.

As this is somewhat of a section in itself though, I have moved this to the Supplementary Material section at the back of the book. Read it.

Being the Life of the Party

Being a Leo, I tend to like being the centre of attention. Being the centre of attention doesn't mean being a dick, and it doesn't even require that much confidence either. I'm an introvert by nature, though I've become famous on many an occasion. Thinking back, almost everything involved some costume piece. A costume piece is a great substitute for charm!

Falls Festival – Tree Trunk Man

The first claim to fame I had was at a 3-day music festival in Tasmania, Australia. This was at a very scenic location, some 3km from the beach. Near the beach I found a short, hollowed out tree trunk that I thought would be funny to wear on my head as a Ned Kelly helmet. The people around me thought it was surprisingly funny, so I kept it on, and walked the 3km back to the campsite in 38C heat with a 10kg hollow tree trunk over my head. Thinking I would just ditch it when I got to the campsite, I was surprised to see people swarm over to me as everyone thought it was so funny. I didn't really have time to chat with them though, as there was a comedian I wanted to see at the second stage that was about to start. It was a packed audience, so I was walking around with a tree trunk on my head, trying to find a place to sit. The comedian comes on stage, and before he's able to say his first joke, he looks out and sees me walking around with a tree trunk over my head. He's too surprised to even say his first joke, laughs and gets me to come up onstage. He, and everyone else is laughing and he says, "Hahaha, mate, just… hahaha, what the hell?!? You gotta explain yourself on this one!" I get the microphone, look out to the audience and say, "Well you see, I've got a bit of a dilemma – I've got the tree trunk, but no roots. Anyone in the audience wanna give me a root?" (note, 'root' is Australian for sex). This gets a lot of laughs. "No need to be nervous – my bark is worse than my bite!" More laughs.

The comedian is now looking stunned. Here he has a full festival stage with a large audience, he hasn't even said a single joke, yet some other random dude has got the mike telling jokes to the audience. He gets the mike back from me and says "Whoa, whoa, I'm the comedian, I'm the one meant to be telling the jokes!" I got the mike back off him and said "Settle down mate, you've had your go, it's my stage now!" The whole audience started cheering and laughing so much now! Well I didn't have any more jokes, so I said, "Just kidding," gave the mike back and jumped off stage. Yes, I'd just upstaged a famed comedian.

Fortunately the rest of the show was really good and funny, so I didn't feel bad for my stunt at the start, and he even invited me over for a beer afterwards.

After this, with a following of people, I went to the main stage where people were now swarming to take my photo. I even went into the mosh pit, jumping around with a 10kg tree trunk on my head in the 38C heat. After leaving the mosh pit I still had a crowd around me, but while waiting for a girl to change her camera film for a photo, with the heat and exhaustion of it all I very nearly fainted and ended it there. For the next few years I would meet people where we got into conversation about the Falls Festival, and the 'tree trunk man' would always come up every time. Only sad thing is this was in 2003, before digital cameras. I, unfortunately, have zero photo evidence of it.

College Ball – Seedy Mexican Drug Dealer

In my third year of university, there was a ball on held by one of the accommodation colleges. It was just before exam time so none of my friends wanted to go. Dammit, it was $10 for an 18-hour ball. How could you pass that up?!? Unfortunately that meant I was going to go to a ball alone where I knew no one. Solution? Be grand.

From years ago I had a 5-sizes-too-small grey suit with tails. Awesome. I decided to go as a seedy 70's Mexican drug dealer... whatever that is! In the preceding days I dyed my hair black and put on loads of fake tan in preparation. Come the night I put on the suit with a white shirt buttoned only halfway up, then got permanent marker and drew hair all over my arms and chest. I then drew myself a monobrow and a big seedy moustache, plus smudged the pen all over my face... ya know, to be dark and handsome. I then topped it off with a big gold chain around my neck, some gold-framed brown aviator sunglasses and snakeskin shoes. I enter the ball, where everyone else is wearing nice cocktail dresses and nice fancy suits and polished shoes. They see me, and it's instant fame. All the guys' faces drop as suddenly they want to be the cool guy dressed as the seedy Mexican, not the average guy in a smart suit.

Would you believe it however, there's only one other guy not dressed in a suave suit... and what is he wearing? Yep, he's dressed as a Mexican too! Of course, we become great friends from that night on!

Oktoberfest – Irish Hat

Years later, I'm in Munich (Germany) for Oktoberfest. This Mecca for

Australians is an awesome 16-day beer fest attended by *6 million* people. All the beers are sold in huge tents, each with a capacity of up to 8,000 people (and they are all totally full). Everyone is either seated at picnic benches, or jumping up and down on them, partying to classics such as 'Country Roads' and 'Hey Baby' performed by a 20 piece traditional band. It is *amazingly* good fun. Anyway, I want to do something a bit different, so I decide to wear my leprechaun hat which I bought previously in Ireland. It's a huge green leprechaun felt hat, complete with big orange beard. Catching the bus there, the Aussies are giving me shit about it, saying, "It's not fucken St Pat's day ya wanka. Whaddya doin' ya dickhead?" I started to feel a bit self-conscious about it, so I start to second-guess whether I should take it or not.

I take it.

I'm there for opening day and I'm at the main rowdy tent, the famed Hofbrauhaus. You have to arrive *early* to get a seat, but the beers aren't served until 12 noon when the mayor cracks the first keg. Everyone is thirsty, sober and impatient, so its time has not yet come. Once first beers are consumed, out I pull my hat; to be greeted by instant fame. *Everyone* wants their photo with the leprechaun. It was awesome! Everyone is dressed in the traditional Bavarian dirndls and lederhosen; then there's this leprechaun getting around with a bad Irish accent. So much fun to go up to people and say, "Excuse me ma'am. I've lost my pot of gold. Have you seen my pot of gold around here?" Of course, everyone wanted a photo with the leprechaun. I even got interviewed by some German TV crew too! Greeeaaat day!

Fuzzy Koala T-Shirt

Years ago in the Melbourne Markets I found a t-shirt with a smiling koala face on the chest; the face being made out of furry material so you could pat it. Awesome. These t-shirts were of course however, only made for 6-year-old children. I get the largest size there which still is so small it exposes my belly button… but I don't care – I have a fuzzy koala T-shirt!

This fuzzy koala then became my travelling companion and best ever wingman. That little fuzzy koala and I went everywhere to all the best parties; because *you can pat it!* Girls will always fall for a cute child's t-shirt that you can pat. After many war wounds of spilled drinks, he eventually had to go into retirement in storage, where he is a highly cherished part of the few possessions I have.

Wolf Hat

While in Japan I bought a very cute looking beanie with the head of a plush toy wolf on it. Very cute. Taking a weekend trip to South Korea in winter, it was very cold so I wore my hat out. I didn't need to say a word. Entering the club, the Korean girls are attracted to the cute hat like Dutch are to a free BBQ. Fantastic night.

Looking at all the above, I don't think that I need to point out that just some interesting costume piece is all it takes. You don't need any special looks or even a witty line – all you need is something to make you stand out from the crowd.

Aussie Flag

I always travel with an Aussie flag or towel. Not to be a wanker, but at festivals it's great. I was in Georgia, in the Deep South of the USA to see some friends. This is the place where it's all about hog hunting, shooting off shotguns, flying the Confederate flag and of course the nicest, most hospitable people… unless you're Black, Mexican or gay. I happened to be there for a trifecta of awesome days – Halloween, followed by the Georgia-Florida game pre-party, and the game itself. While expecting the local girls to resemble Swamp People; playing banjo, front teeth missing and wearing homemade alligator boots, I was pleasantly surprised to see all the girls were, in fact, stunning. I went out wearing just some boardshorts and an Aussie flag and had a fantastic time.

Typical scenario over the next three days:

Beautiful girl would come up to me, looked stunned and say:

"Oh my God! Are you, like…. Australian?!?"

"Yeah."

"Oh my God! No way!!"

Learning that there's an actual Australian in town (*and he's talking to her!*) she'd get excited until her friend would then come up to her and say to her, "Don't be stupid. It's Halloween. He's putting the accent on!" and she'd pull the girl away. This same situation continued to happen time and time again. They just did not believe there was a real life Australian in their town!

Picking Up

For picking up, I'm not that great on it so I recommend the book 'Conquer Foreign Women' written by a friend of mine, Ruben Russo. There's also the companion book 'The Wingman-Bible'. You can find these on Amazon. Yes, the title 'Conquer' is a bit out of taste but there's some good info in the book!

There is however one great success story I had that I think I should share. I was in the awesome city of Barcelona in Spain. The city is right next to the beach, which is full of stunning women, half of them sunbathing topless. I've still seen nowhere like it. I was at the beach with a cool Brazilian dude I met in the hostel. We were looking around, mouths open, at the beauty that surrounded us. I tend to dislike beaches full of beautiful girls as it's just a tease – you see all these stunning girls almost naked, yet they just want to lie down and sun bake undisturbed. What made it even worse was that a lot of the girls were topless. Looking around I knew that meeting a girl would be almost impossible.

Almost. But today I woke up with an unexplained shot of confidence.

Looking around, I noticed that there were a number of old Asian women walking around trying to sell people massages. I thought, "I can do this!" so I went with my friend up to these two beautiful girls and said:

"You like a massage, you like a massage? My friend here, he does an amazing massage. Just this morning I was feeling very stiff all over, but after a massage from him, I felt brilliant. Look – shoulders, hips and ankles; all in alignment! You're lucky today too. Why's that? Because it's the first Sunday of the month! And what do we do on the first Sunday of the month? That's right, first minute free!"

We'd then proceed to give these beautiful girls massages while talking some bullshit about tension in their backs. I'd make a big deal of timing it to exactly 60 seconds, no more. I had my phone out, timing it and giving 15, 10 and 5 second warnings. This was an important step because it stops them worrying that you're going to stay for a long time like a weirdo. The one minute is enough however to build up enough rapport to keep chatting once finished. This would typically result in a phone number, then off to the next. Success rate was huge! Before long we'd amassed multiple phone numbers; all from stunning girls, some even topless. Impossible just became possible.

We continued on until we met an Ecuadorian girl and her Ukrainian friend. Once we'd finished the one minute, she surprised us by saying;

"How much for a full massage?"

Straight away I replied, "30 minutes, €30," which is of course incredibly expensive even for a professional. (Note at this point I hadn't yet learned how to give a massage and was, well, terrible at it.)

She said "Hmmm, that's too much. How much for 5 minutes?"

"5 minutes, €5."

"Ok."

Not quite believing this was happening, I then gave her a massage which was pretty much just me playing with her arse for five minutes. She then actually paid me five Euros and gave me her number. I almost couldn't take the money as the whole thing was a joke anyway, but hey, *I just got paid the equivalent of $8 for walking up to a good looking girl on the beach and playing with her arse!!* She then followed up by giving me her phone number and an enjoyable following two nights.

There're a few reasons why this ploy worked. First, we had a reason to approach them (even if ridiculous). Next is that we just kept on talking at the start. If you approach a girl and just say one line, it's typically not enough time for her to get over her surprise and to size you up. If you keep talking, it gives her time to relax, get over her surprise and think of something to say back to you. It avoids that awkward silence. You notice at first that they look surprised and confused, but just keep talking and you can see their expression change. As mentioned earlier too, we also timed the 60 seconds exactly such that they would reduce their shield. Let's be honest, if someone starts talking to you out of the blue you don't know in the first 10 seconds if they're weird or not. If you're not rude at the start you may never be able to get rid of them if they're a weirdo. By stating at the start that you'll be gone in 60 seconds it lets them relax more. Of course after that 60 seconds you've both had enough time to size each other up and see whether you want to continue conversation.

Finding a Place

I'm not a fan of one night stands as I'd rather get to know the person, but it does happen from time to time. There're places to go, and places not to go. In some places such as Australia, it is very safe to go to the beach, whereas places such as Playa del Carmen (Mexico) can be quite dangerous. Other places can be safe but illegal, such as Hawaii and San Diego (USA). You're not even allowed to be on the beach at night there for some reason.

I was once staying in Pacific Beach in San Diego and was making out with a girl on the beach. The hostel I was staying at was right on the beach too, with the bar area overlooking the beach. A cop car drove up the beach, then for whatever reason shone its spotlight on the hostel, which grabbed everyone's attention, then the pricks shone the spotlight on me and the girl; causing the entire hostel to first look at the cop car, then look at us and laugh and cheer. Best to avoid that!

You can sleep with a girl in your dorm, as long as you know the people in your room, you've discussed it and arranged a time. It's pretty rude otherwise! Ok, let's be honest… it is pretty rude but at 2am the two of you probably really don't care!! If the dorm is empty, go for it! If not, check somewhere quiet in the hostel. Hostel rooftops can be pretty secluded yet safe. If you have to use the dorm, get a bottom bunk and put a towel hanging down from the top bunk. This should give you enough (visual) privacy. I had a girlfriend in a dorm for ten weeks once and it was never an issue; we just timed it when there was no one else there.

If you meet a girl out one night and can't take her anywhere, it really doesn't matter. Saves a night of bad drunken sex and if you're a good enough at making out with clothes on she'll be even more horny the next day. Avoid drinking and you'll perform a heck of a lot better.

Drugs

Best to avoid it in foreign countries as penalties can be very harsh.

If you do, *thou shalt know where thy drugs are*. A good friend was in South Africa, bought a bag a pot and had a great night, though he had an international flight early the next morning. Come the next morning he couldn't for the life of him remember where he put the weed! He also slept-in so he didn't have much time, resulting in him frantically having to go through his pack to see where he put it, though couldn't find it anywhere. He was shitting himself going through airport security in case it was down the bottom of his bag somewhere! Fortunately it never showed up.

Of course I don't condone taking drugs (particularly in a book!) but I can't control what other people want to do. If you do want to buy drugs, then make sure you know the person selling is legit. Don't buy from someone on the street that offers you as you don't know what you're getting yourself into. Best to ask around at the hostel. You should be able to find someone easy enough that either has what you want or knows someone that does. If it's difficult, then no problem – you don't want to be the only person in the group on pot/coke/ecstasy or whatever.

Definitely don't go walking around with drugs on your body. I've been searched numerous times by armed police in Guatemala. One time I even had to kneel on a dock for almost an hour as they searched us all. Someone was found with 18g of coke on them (worth about $6,000 in Australia) and we were told we all were arrested (shitting ourselves), but we were all clean so eventually we were let go.

Safety

Don't get hammered in unfamiliar or dangerous locations. Have drinks yes, but don't get shitfaced. In dangerous countries in South and Central America particularly, you're inviting yourself to be a target for a mugging. A Gringo stumbling home alone at 3am in a deserted street is a pretty easy target.

A great tip I've learned is to walk in the middle of the street at night when walking down quiet dodgy-looking streets. This has a few purposes. First people cannot surprise you from shadows, hidden doorways, alleyways and so on. Also, if there's a dodgy person walking towards you on the footpath, it saves the awkward feeling of crossing the road to avoid passing them. Stay in the middle and you avoid everyone… just don't do it when there are cars obviously.

If you do get mugged, don't fight back. In Barcelona I met a dude that got stabbed after he tried to fight back when people robbed him. I always thought that to be stabbed was like a bit of a puncture. It's not. He showed me the photos before he got patched up. His entire belly was open, looking like shark gills. It looked horrific! Don't get yourself stabbed.

Funnily enough, he surprised us all by coming out with us the next night, even though his stomach was covered in patches and bandages. We go a club, and soon after entering he becomes really excited, points to a spot on the floor and says "Hey look, my blood's still there! That's my blood!" Crazy guy!!

Chapter Summary

- If you don't have a SIM card, leave your phone in the hostel
- Avoid going out with your license and bank card. Wallet and cash (with $50 emergency cash in zip-up section) is normally the best way to go
- Take along a crap camera. Try to get one with Movie Digest function to record the night's photos
- Learn magic (see the Supplementary Material section). Take out sponge hearts and two decks of cards (one modified for the Magic Kissing Trick), a permanent marker and some lip balm
- Better to take a $2 umbrella than a good jacket that you may lose
- Know how to get home
- Break big bills at the start of the night
- Beer isn't necessarily the cheapest drink. Consider Long Island Ice Teas
- Drink a water every second drink
- If you're not allowed to have your own drinks at a hostel, order a dark glass bottle of beer and refill it with whatever you want
- Find some accessory (such as a funny hat) to make you the life of the festival, party, club, etc
- Avoid drugs. Drugs are not condoned in this book, but if you do want something, only buy through a legit person. Don't walk around with drugs on you, and know where all remnants are
- Don't get hammered in dangerous locations
- Walk in the middle of the road at night (in places with no car traffic)
- Don't fight back if you get robbed

Chapter 9: Money Matters – Travelling

Location of Cards

I always travel with my Citibank card, 28Degrees card, Commonwealth Bank card and Jetstar Platinum credit card. The more the better! I keep two in my daypack (with my passport) and two in my backpack. If one bag is stolen, I still have the others. I don't carry any cards in my wallet. I only need cash once per week, so there's only a need to carry my card when I need to do an ATM run. I keep the weekly cash with my passport. Passport is kept safe, so my cash is too.

The exception to this is first world countries where EFTPOS transactions are common. I will commonly carry my card with me there.

I have photos of my cards stored in Cloud in my Dropbox such that if my bags are stolen, I know which cards were stolen, and their numbers too so I can easily cancel them.

Cash

Cards don't always work in all countries, and you only tend to use your card when you're out of cash and it's too late. Also, in some countries like Guatemala, it's common that the ATMs are empty 20% of the time. For this reason, I always travel with $400 cash in a major commodity, such as Euro's in Europe or US dollars in Central/South America. Of course half in my daypack, half in my main pack.

In Guatemala, you can only withdraw a maximum of Q2000 ($280) per day, even if you try eight different ATM's, as I once did in desperation. If you're taking an expensive tour, start taking out money in the days prior.

Keep in mind too that many small towns do not have ATM's. This caught some girls out staying in Lanquin where the hostel had a tab system. Come check-out time, they didn't have enough cash. This involved taking a shuttle 3hrs to the next town, however even so they couldn't withdraw enough cash. This would mean withdrawing all the money they could, then taking the shuttle all the way back, staying the night in Lanquin, then 3hrs back to Coban the next day to withdraw the rest, going back to Lanquin to pay, then finally leaving the next morning; taking two nights and over 12hrs in an uncomfortable shuttle, just to pay a bill. Fortunately for them I lent them the rest of the money and caught up with them a few days later. When someone's in the shit, help them out.

If you are in the situation where for some reason your card does not work in a particular country, use it to your advantage. In one of my first travels I had a Travel Card that didn't work in Amsterdam. Fortunately I had a backup card, but I complained to the card company with some sob story and asked for compensation. Got $200 back!

I always buy wallets with a zip-up section. In poor countries, I use this to keep all my big notes. That is; I may have $60 in my wallet, but only $10 showing in the main compartment. If you haggle someone down, only to open your wallet to have a week's wages showing, you look pretty arrogant. Hide it so you don't make them jealous. It's the right thing to do. In Europe or the US the zip-up compartment is great too – I always keep a $50 emergency note. This is meant for when shit hits the fan, yet somehow always seems to get spent on alcohol on nights out. Meh.

Many people also carry money in socks, yet I can't remember the last time I wore socks and shoes out (it's all shorts and thongs in backpacker places), so that doesn't work for me.

Border Crossings and Exchange Rate

Thou shalt know the exchange rate before crossing the border.

Let's face it – you probably don't know the exchange rate as you cross the border, yet those on the other side do, and they're watching you come. Until you find your first ATM you're at their mercy – you have money from the last country that's no longer useful to you, and everything in the new country is in a new currency. Some conversion has to take place. Know thy conversion before thee cross the border!

Best to find the exchange rate on the internet beforehand and write down a few common amounts, such as 10, 20 and 50, and the other way around. Also the amount you want to change. If you're caught on the spot, they will confuse you so it seems like a good deal at the time, then after five steps you realise you've been totally ripped off. Best off to be prepared.

E.g. Going from Belize to Guatemala:

BZD	**GTQ**
10	39
20	78
50	194
170	661

GTQ	**BZD**
10	2.60
20	5.15
50	12.85

I tend to write this down in the notepad of my phone. Paper works too though. Note, I've included the amount of '170' as that's how much I want to change. This way I know I should receive at least 600 or so. Anything less than that is a total rip-off and not worth doing.

Also, before you cross the border go through all your bags and find all coins you've accumulated. After a few months in a country you may well have accumulated near a kilo of coins. Get rid of these before crossing over. Of course save a few of your best ones for memento's to show your kids, but no one needs to carry around 30 five peso coins for the rest of their trip.

Chapter Summary

- Travel with multiple credit/debit cards
- Keep half your cards in your main pack and half in your daypack
- Always have a wad of emergency cash in US Dollars or Euro's or a major currency to account for possible card problems. Spread this between your backpack and daypack
- Withdraw sufficient cash in third world countries and only carry your card when withdrawing cash
- Know the exchange rate before crossing borders. Write it down, along with how much you should receive for common denominations
- Get rid of coins before crossing the border

Chapter 10: Communication

Travelling

If you don't have a phone plan with internet, check the name of the place you're going to before you leave your hostel. Travelling around Japan, I just went on Wikipedia and typed in the cities I was going to, for example, Nagasaki, and it would give the name in Japanese characters (長崎市). All I then had to do was to go to the train station and look for the train with the same characters. Easy. I wish I had the foresight to do this on a previous trip in Greece, as I was getting a bus from Corfu to Athens. I was expecting this to be easy, however absolutely no one there spoke English, and all signs were in Greek. There were about 15 buses lined up, so I just took the one that started with an 'A' (Αθήνα). Right choice fortunately!

Avoid asking buses if they are going to the place you want to go to. For example, if you ask, "Hangzhou?" for example, they will probably nod even if they're going somewhere else, either from not understanding you or cultural reasons. This is particularly a cultural issue in China where they will always say yes even if they mean no. It is much better to ask in the language of the place you're in, "Where are you going?" This cannot be answered with a yes/no response. They will have to respond by saying where they're going, giving you confirmation that it is in fact the right destination.

Why You Should Learn the Language

You really don't need to know much language to travel; however learning the language will give you a much richer experience. If you're happy to just to go to a place, take photos during the day and get plastered at night, then really, you don't need to know anything more than about seven phrases (Hi. Bye. How much is this? I want that one. Thank you. Please. Excuse me.).

To be honest, I love taking photos during the day and partying at night, but you will have so much more fun if you speak the language too. You will feel like you are *experiencing* a place rather than just seeing it from a bubble. I feel very invasive and rude if I go to a country and don't speak the language… Having said this, I *did* live in China for 1.5 years knowing not much more than ten phrases. Pretty embarrassed about that. I blame having a bilingual Chinese girlfriend!

Before embarking on my Central America trip, I had learned some Spanish using an online course and then continued learning a bit more on my trip with Google Translate as the need arose. I had enough to scrape by, but not enough for conversation. Come Cuba, it tore my heart not to know Spanish.

Along with Iceland, Cuba is my favourite travel destination. It is a truly amazing place. Considering my travel diary of Cuba took 40 pages for just a 13-day trip, I think I'll just leave it at that without going into detail; but one experience was particularly special to me, as below.

I was in the beautiful small town of Trinidad and one afternoon I decided to go for a walk along the train tracks for sunset. Coming to a large shed, I saw plumes of black smoke rising behind it. My heart quickened. Could it be? No, no way…. or could it be? I had boyhood hopes that behind this shed may be a steam engine. I hurried around the side and all my hopes materialised in an instant – yes, there, on the tracks was a beautiful 1914 steam engine in perfect condition, with boilers raging and steam and smoke pouring out of the chimney! I was super stoked! There were some Cubans at the maintenance shed, so I had a quick chat with them in extremely broken Spanish. They say that it will be ready to go in half an hour. Cool, I think, and hang around and check out this wonderful piece of machinery. As an engineer I'm very interested how it all works, but with my extremely limited Spanish it is not possible to ask the questions I want to ask. I hang around for half an hour, at which it reverses a bit up the track, then starts moving forward. I think it's cool, and go to walk away, but the guy says, "Arriba, arriba!" and motions for me to jump on. "Whoa!! Are you serious!?!" This is too cool! I jump on the moving train and ride it through the town – just me and three Cuban train engineers. What makes it even better is that there are no carriages; it's just the engine and water tank. I'm standing right behind the 100-year-old boiler getting blasted by heat and steam. It's absolutely brilliant. We chug through the town, with everyone stopping their bicycle or horse to watch us go by. I even got to pull the steam-whistle as we crossed the roads! Already it's one of the best experiences of my life just because of the randomness of it all. We keep chugging along in the dusk light and soon we have exited the town and are now in the beautiful Cuban countryside, complete with beautiful rolling hills and mountains covered in the beautiful Cuban palms. It's incredible. I then get on top, now standing on top of the train having the time of my life. It gets better. Coming up is a huge wooden train bridge, like the ones you see in old Western movies. Still standing on top of the train, we go over the bridge, the whole bridge and train noticeably swaying as we go over. Brilliant! We continue on into the night and stop at another bridge where we need to refill the water tanks (for the steam). All four of us are now sitting on the train, parked on the middle of a rickety wooden bridge overlooking the beautiful Cuban countryside under a warm Caribbean night sky, with the black smoke of the boiler reaching up into the night sky, passing by the almost-full moon.

It was such an amazing experience, made better by the fact it was just such a random, unplanned encounter. I don't even know what the guys were doing with this train, but I was just so glad to be part of it! It takes a long time for the tanks to fill, so we sit on the tank in this amazing setting and try to talk, but my extremely limited Spanish prevents this. I can't begin to explain how frustrating this was; to be sharing such a moment with these very kind guys, but not to be able to talk to them. It was at this point that I vowed to learn Spanish.

The ride back was great too, as it was now completely nighttime, with the only light coming from the flames of the boiler. It really is amazing to be riding a train at night – just the roaring sound of the boiler, the sound of the steam pistons going psssh... psssh... psssh, the orange flames lighting up the ground next to the track and the sparks and red embers intermingled in the black smoke reaching up into the sky. Best part was going through a tunnel where the orange glow lit up the inside of the tunnel and all sounds were amplified. Amazing experience. Would have been so much better if I could speak Spanish too.

If the above was not enough to convince you, then the Argentinean and Colombian girls should be (or men, if you're a girl or homosexual). Everyone I've met has been stunning. Learn Spanish, broaden your selection pool.

Basic Phrases

Going through Europe however, it is not possible to do this as there are so many languages. At least make sure to learn the basics though.

While in Paris I went to see the Eiffel Tower (obviously). Catching the metro back to our hostel in a distant suburb, my friend jumped on without a ticket and I just paid for the cheaper local city ticket. This was all good until a few stops before ours four French train police, or more correctly, four scary-as-fuck French train *commandos* board. They much more resembled SWAT team members, wearing all black combat fatigues and all carrying automatic machine guns. Our stop comes so my friend runs off and jumps over the exit gate. I try with my ticket which doesn't work, so I'm about to jump the gate too, when these four heavily armed commandos come running behind, stop me and start yelling at me in French. Shit! These guys are seriously scary looking and we've all heard stories about arrogant French, particularly when stupid English-speaking tourists are involved. I mumble a feeble, "Parlez-vous anglais?" and the whole situation changes. The lead commando immediately changes his composure and explains to me very politely in impeccable English that I've got the wrong ticket and it would be a €50 fine, but today he would let me off. Phew!! Knowing that one basic phrase meant I had at least gone to *some* effort which possibly was the reason for saving me the €50.

The first thing most people want to learn in another language tends to be all the swear words. Don't be this person. When my dad was a young lad, he went to Sweden. Before going, he learned how to say "Hello" and "Fuck you". All very well indeed… but the poor bugger couldn't remember which was which. I don't imagine saying "Fuck you" to anyone would go down too well, no matter how much you sincerely smile as you say it!

Where to Learn the Language

Of course starting at home before you leave is a good place to start. I'd say as a minimum download some app on your phone, so you can at least learn the basic phrases while doing a poo or waiting for the bus. One program that I really like, especially as you don't need an internet connection to use it, is AnkiDroid. It's a flashcard program, so it's great for increasing your vocab. It's fairly useless if you're a total beginner, but for building your vocab after you have a reasonable foundation in the language it's great. There's a huge amount of pre-prepared flashcard sets you can download from within the app. There are many other good programs for total beginners. Many people recommend DuoLingo. I haven't used it so I can't comment.

For German, Japanese and Spanish, I bought the Rocket Language programs. I haven't purchased other programs so I don't know how it compares to others, but I found the series to be very good. It includes audio lessons so it's great to use it while walking to work. All you do is listen to it while walking to work, so it's like learning the language without going to any effort. Be warned though, for difficult languages such as Japanese or Mandarin it can be very hard to concentrate properly and take it in unless you're giving it 100% attention.

These packages will get you to some level, but pales in comparison to taking some lessons in the country itself. For Spanish, I highly recommend Guatemala. I was paying US$160 per week which included 20 hours one-on-one Spanish lessons and a home stay including private room and three cooked meals per day. Unbelievable! Not only that, the location was incredible, at the base of a dormant volcano, directly overlooking a beautiful lake, plus there were hummingbirds flying 2m from where you're sitting. I studied at 'Orbita Spanish School' in San Pedro. I highly, highly recommend this place. In one week you'll learn more than you would in months of mucking around with computer programs.

Not Necessarily Rejection

If you say something to someone that catches your eye, but their response is a confused look and an "I don't speak English", it can be easy to assume they're just saying that to brush you off… but it's not necessarily the case. In Belgium I met a Spanish girl where I got that response, assumed it was rejection, but then she said, "Wait… my friend… she speak English", and dashed off to find her friend. Her friend then became translator and we have a great evening together. A few weeks later I even stayed with her at her house in Spain, plus she then took me on a small trip around the south of Spain too. Conversations were extremely limited, but we still had a great time together!

Fun in Other Languages

A little trick that I love and have done no less than 40 times is below.

When you meet a Dutch girl, (which you'll meet lots of!!), say to them:

"I learned some Dutch once, but can't remember how to say it now. Can you please tell me how to say 'Choose my side', in Dutch please?"

As it turns out, 'choose my side' in Dutch is more-or-less pronounced "Kiss my cunt". When they say that, look shocked and say, "Whoa, you move quickly! I mean, I like you and all… but don't you think you should take me out to dinner, or at least buy me a drink first?!?" They'll look confused for a moment, then will realise what they've just said and burst out laughing. Guaranteed they'll laugh. No Dutch girl I've tried this on has *ever* heard of it before. It's original as all hell and guaranteed to get them laughing. Save this for when there're lots of people around that can all hear it and it's a lot funnier. If you say that when there's just the two of you then it's a bit creepy.

Sometimes they may be a little confused as to which context you mean the phrase in. If this happens, say, "Choose my side, as in if you're in a group argument and you want someone to choose your side." Note, if you're not aware, a Dutchy is someone from Holland, which is part of The Netherlands.

Australian/English Language

The more I travel, the more I realise that words that I think are words… turn out not to be real words at all. The curse of being Australian.

In my first lot of travels, I had American friends that said they couldn't understand me. I thought they were joking. They weren't.

This, I only realised after years of travelling more and realising that Americans don't seem to grasp the concept of slang, or shortening words; which Australians appear to be masters of. It seems all the time I'm discovering words that I think are proper English, are not proper at all.

The first foray I had into this confusing field was in Venice, where I was on a tour with some Aussies and Americans. Note to the Americans, it's pronounced 'Ozzie'. Please stop saying 'Aussie' with an 's' sound. Anyway,

I'm there with a bunch of Aussies and Americans. Someone makes a comment about the mozzies. The Americans reply:

"The what?"

"The mozzies."

"The what?"

"Ya know, the mozzies."

"The *what??*"

Silence. We all think the Americans are retarded. The Americans think we're all retarded. We try again:

"Ya know, the *mozzies*!!" (slightly exasperated)

It's no use. This continues on for a few more minutes. We're stunned. How could they be this stupid? Have they not been getting bitten? How could they not have seen the mozzies? They're everywhere on this campsite. *Finally*, after a few minutes of getting nowhere, one of the Aussies says:

"Ya know, the *mosquitoes*!"

"Oh yeah! There're so many huh! I've been bitten so many times by them!"

The Aussies all go into a shocked, paralysed silence. In everyone's unmoving, expressionless faces it is clear what we're all thinking: "Oh…so… mozzie isn't *actually* the word for mosquito. Whoa… "

Our whole lives were turned upside down by this. You go your whole life thinking you're speaking normal English… then you realise it's not. The poor Americans were thinking we were talking about Mexican Aussies!!

We shorten basically anything three syllables or longer. I think surfing is a good spot to start. Let's look at the following description of surfing:

When you go surfing, you wear boardies and a rashie if it's warm. If it's cool you wear your springie, and if cold you wear your wettie. If it's really cold, you wear your wettie with your hoodie and booties. You are attached to your board with your leggie. If there's no surf, then you sit on the beach wearing your sunnies. If it's cold, you'd wear your hoodie and beanie.

This, we consider, is all normal speak.

To get more confusing though, it's not always "chop the end off and add 'ie'". Sometimes it's an 'o', such as bottlo (bottle shop, or liquor store), servo (service station, or gas station), or druggo (drug user).

There is no rule as to why sometimes it's an 'ie' and sometimes it's an 'o'. You just know from birth. *Never* attempt to make your own shortening. It's not like accidently using 'le' instead of a 'la' in French where you'd look stupid but they'd understand; using an 'ie' where there should be an 'o' is an unforgivable offence.

Sometimes, it's all very different. For example, the capital city of Queensland is Brisbane. We shorten (shorten??) this to Brisvegas. I honestly don't know why. Devonport becomes Devrock, Wollongong becomes 'the Gong' and Wagga Wagga becomes just Wagga. Woy Woy however stays as Woy Woy, not Woy. Woolloomooloo remains as Woolloomooloo. If you try and find a pattern in this madness you'll just end up crazy.

I thought it was funny when I had a Swedish housemate in Australia that bought a car. One day she comes in and says, "You Australians.... you guys are unbelievable... you shorten *everything*!" She then thrusts out some official looking paper at me. "Look at that!" she says, pointing. I look where she's pointing, but I have no idea what she's talking about.

"Rego," she says.

"Huh?" I reply.

"It says, on the official sticker, 'rego'."

"Uh-huh," I reply. I still don't know where she's going with this.

"You guys, are so damn lazy, that even for the official car registration papers you can't even spell out the full word 'registration'... you just call it 'rego'... *on the official papers!!*"

Hahaha, I guess she had a point there. I never really thought about it. Yes, in New South Wales at least, and no doubt elsewhere in Australia it's *officially* called car rego (pronounced 'rej-oh'). Say 'registration' to someone and you'd probably get a blank look.

To help foreigners understand us, I've included a list of the most common words that differ from American English (note, people from England understand 'mozzie' and some others, so this is more directed at people that know American English. This list does not include slang as there's too much to include in this book).

Transport

Australian	American
ute	truck
boot	trunk
bonnet	hood
bumper	fender
petrol	gas
servo	gas station
k's	kilometres (these are like miles, but shorter and make more sense)

Clothing

Australian	American
beanie	toque
boardies	boardshorts (men's swim shorts)
sunnies	sunglasses
bondsie	singlet / wife beater
flannie	flannelette shirt
thongs	flip-flops
G-banger / G-string	thong
jumper	sweater

Other

Australian	American
bogan	white-trash
esky	cool box
brekkie	breakfast
smoke-o	short break
Maccas	McDonalds
bubbler	drinking fountain

poppa	fruit box drink
lollies	candy
root	sex
ranga	red head (short for orangutan)
arvo	afternoon
reckon	think
soft drink	soda
Pom	English person
Kiwi	New Zealander
uni	university

Considering that 'root' in Australia means sex, we always find it really funny when Americans innocently ask, "What team are you rooting for?"

In some rural parts of Australia, 'dinner' refers to lunch and 'tea' refers to dinner. Do not try to attempt to understand the logic here.

Another Aussie-ism that we don't realise is an aussie-ism is the use of 'heaps'. This means 'lots' and gets used a huge amount of time.

- This word gets used heaps
- We've still got heaps of time
- I've got heaps of stuff to do before I can go
- How was the party? It was heaps of fun
- The concert was heaps good

Australians also seem to be famous for their liberal use of the word 'cunt'. As it turns out, for most people elsewhere in the world it's not acceptable to say "So, what are you cunts up to today?" however I have a *female* Australian friend that commonly uses this phrase. Best still to avoid using it yourself, but don't be too shocked if you hear an Aussie use the term. If you get called a cunt yourself, don't take offense. There's a saying that Australians call their mates 'cunts' and their enemies 'mate'. It's all about the tone. E.g. "Hey what's up cunt?" is a friendly greeting to a friend but "Listen here, *mate*" is what someone would say shortly before punching you. Of course, if someone calls you 'mate' while smiling then they like you, and if someone calls you a cunt while looking angry, then they probably don't like you. Listen for the tone, ignore the words.

A phrase I like is: "Oh FAR-koff". Literally, 'Oh fuck off' but pronounced 'far-koff', with the 'far' said in a much higher tone. Meaning is the same as 'Shut-up' in the US; that is, 'Wow, that's amazing' or 'I don't believe you'. Interestingly enough, say 'Shut up!' to an Aussie and you'll probably offend them quite a lot, whereas 'fuck off' is totally acceptable. Actually the absolutely biggest insult you can give an Australian is, "You're a joke, mate." Only ever use this is *extreme* circumstances. It is insulting to the bone.

Anyway, this expression can broaden to "Oh far-koff ya did". Maybe this is better explained in an example conversation:

"I rooted Sharee last night!"

"FAR-koff."

"True story!"

"Oh far-koff ya did."

"Yeah nah, I really did!"

Translated would be:

"I slept with Sharee last night."

"I don't believe you."

"It is true."

"I really don't believe you."

"I honestly did."

Note too, "yeah nah", translated as "yes no" is perfectly acceptable in conversation. It is used whenever there is doubt, such as the subjunctive tense in Spanish, and can mean either the affirmative, or negative.

"How was the party?"

"Yeah nah it was heaps good!!"

Other Language Differences

There are a few other differences I've picked up that are specific to England or the USA.

Say to an Australian or American 'pants and a vest', and they'll envision a person dressed for the cold, wearing jeans and a sleeveless jacket. To an English person however, they'll think you're talking about sitting around in your underpants and a singlet. 'Pants' in England means your underpants. Asking whether you should wear pants can draw some strange looks.

In the US, 'entree' refers to the main course, not the entree. They call the entree the 'appetizer'. It can be pretty confusing to go to the USA and only see entrees on the menu and think: "Shit, the entrees are expensive!" and "Where are the mains?!?"

Chapter Summary

• When travelling in a foreign country with a non-Latin alphabet, check the name of the place you're going to and record it in your phone. This will help immensely at the bus or train station

• Don't ask the bus driver, "Are you going to XXXXX?", instead ask, "Where are you going?" This will give you proper confirmation it's going to the right place, instead of just a 'yes'. Learn to say this in the local language

• Try to learn the language as you will get a much richer and deeper experience by being able to intermingle with the locals

• As a minimum learn the basic phrases but not the swear words

• Consider buying a language book or program. As a minimum download a language app on your phone to learn things throughout the day. Best to uninstall other games you may have to avoid the distraction and force yourself to do it. Even better is to take classes in the country you're going to. You will learn at a much faster rate doing this

• If you approach someone of the opposite sex and they say "I don't speak English", it's not necessarily rejection. It could be true and they could like you too. Have a go at it!

• Do the 'Choose my side' trick with Dutch girls for a good laugh

• Australians use a huge amount of slang, but don't even realise it's slang – they think it's proper English. Learn a few of the Aussie words to better understand this strange race

• Pants and a vest in the US and Australia is long pants and a sleeveless jacket, but underpants and a singlet in the UK

Chapter 11: Sickness

Fortunately I've never been properly injured, but have had a broken nose in Thailand, suspect pneumonia and a possible fractured spine in Japan, suspect pneumonia in China, de-nerve-erated bicep in Malaysia, salmonella in Guatemala, giardia in Fiji, Nicaragua and the Philippines, and other intestinal infections in Thailand, Bali, China, Mexico, Honduras and Morocco. Most weren't fun. Actually... they all sucked.

I'm no doctor, so don't take this following chapter as medical advice, but based on my own personal experience I've got a much better idea what to do these days.

Preparation

These days I always travel with a medi-kit, as described in Chapter 2 and a Bit. You might think I'm a nancy for travelling with a medi-kit, but after having stomach bugs in eight countries the novelty factor has worn off a bit for me. Like a scout, Be Prepared.

Also make sure to get all your vaccinations up to date before leaving home.

Prevention

In small poor towns, never eat pork or beef. Always go for chicken or fish if you want meat. The problem with pork and beef is that it is much more expensive for the locals, plus they're a bigger animal. Chickens can be raised at anyone's house or even the restaurant too for that matter. It is much harder to raise a pig or a cow. This makes them more expensive. In addition, they are much bigger. This makes them take longer to consume. The locals won't be eating it as it's too expensive; only the tourists will be. This means if you order pork or beef, you may be eating *very* old meat. Do not be surprised if you get violent food poisoning, as did a friend I was travelling with in the Philippines. With chicken being cheaper, more common and smaller, you can expect it to generally be quite fresh.

When buying drinks in glass bottles; such as soft drink or beer, make sure to give the neck a good wipe. In many third world countries they reuse the glass bottles (makes sense, right. So-called first world countries think we're being awesomely environmentally friendly when we get glass bottles, smash them up, melt them down, then reform them in the same shape. Just bloody refill it!!). Anyway, problem is often they're not properly washed and cleaned as well as we'd like. If you wipe the neck of a reused bottle, expect the serviette to come back black. Best off just to pour it in a glass or drink it with a straw.

Food Poisoning

Food poisoning is a violent reaction when you've eaten something you shouldn't have. Based on my friends' experiences, it will strike 20 mins to 2hrs after eating the offending food, where you will start vomiting so much you think you'll start vomiting your lungs up. Fortunately I've never had it. There's nothing you can do about it. It's just your body trying to get rid of the bad stuff. Let it do its thing. The important thing is to try and replace your lost fluids, although you may find it very difficult to drink. Get a Gatorade if you can.

Stomach (Intestinal) Bugs

Everyone calls them stomach bugs, but that's a bad name as the bug is in your intestines, not your stomach. This is what I always seem to get. This is where you feel generally sick and have to poop a lot. Most I've ever done is 24 in a 24 hour period. That's not a personal record I'm trying to beat.

These bugs come in all sorts of fun types, which get dealt with in different ways. If diarrhoea comes on without feeling deathly sick, let it be for a couple of days. Just like vomiting, it's your body trying to get rid of the parasites. Let it have a go first. The only exception to this is if you have to travel the next day. I was in the Sahara Desert where I got diarrhoea and was catching a 14hr bus ride the next day, with no toilets on board. Fortunately I managed to get some anti-diarrhoea tablets off someone to prevent sitting in my own shit for a day on a hot, packed bus. As it was, I still had to go a lot. The problem was that I didn't speak any French or Arabic so I couldn't communicate with the bus driver. We'd stop at little towns all the time; sometimes for two minutes, sometimes for an hour, however there was no way of knowing how long it would be for. Stopping in a town I'd make a guess, try and signal to the driver, then run to the toilets, shoot out what I could, then return before the bus left. Doesn't sound too bad, but the sad reality is that many Moroccans are total arseholes (of course not all, I have some great Moroccan friends). I highly doubt the bus would wait for me if it came to it (particularly as I don't speak French (my fault) and couldn't properly communicate to him). Problem was I had my pack and all my belongings on board, my travel card was completely empty and I had the equivalent of 30c with me. If the bus left, I would have been, in the nicest possible way, absolutely fucked.

Therefore, *make sure* that you travel with some Loperamide (sold as Gastro-stop) to get you through those tough times. The Loperamide is a 'stopper' that essentially plugs you up for a few hours. Great for emergencies when you're catching transport, but only use it when you have to as all it's doing is treating the symptoms, and more importantly, it's keeping the infection inside you.

If your condition doesn't improve, then self medicate or see a doctor. The doctor is of course the preferred option but if this is not possible delve into your medi-kit. Fortunately my medi-kit contains an appropriately worded diarrhoea 'flow-chart' to help diagnose what you have. Not being a doctor and considering all the arseholes around these days that want to sue people, I can't include the rest of the medical advice in this. I can however share some of my experiences, as well as refer you to the great website, www.traveldoctor.co.uk.

I do recommend taking antibiotics when required, but don't discount natural cures when you only have a mild case of something. For some reason I seem to regularly get giardia before a massive party (I've had it days before New Year's Eve three times in a row!!). The problem with giardia is that the medication reacts strongly with alcohol and you cannot drink any alcohol for the next few days after taking the medication. This is a problem right before

New Year's! After getting a small case of it in Colombia just before New Year's, I didn't want to be in the position of not being able to drink, nor did I want to be partying feeling sick. I decided to try the natural cure of ground-up papaya seeds. Fortunately this is very easy in Central and South America as you can get fresh smoothies everywhere at the side of the road. The girl working there was a little surprised that I wanted all the seeds in, but after drinking that, the symptoms all went away and I could enjoy my NYE!

Different Symptoms

Experience isn't necessarily something you can rely on when it comes to sickness. Something you have once can affect you in a totally different way the next time. For example, in the Philippines I got giardia (verified by tests) in which I felt really sick and dizzy, had lots of diarrhoea, was unable to eat, no energy, etc. It came on fast and the effects were very strong (I was in bed before 9pm on New Year's Eve!). After battling with it for a week I found a doctor, got some Tinidazole and was fortunately better in a few days.

Eight months later I was in Fiji. After about a week there I had a cappuccino one evening, and 2hrs later I was full of gas, feeling super bloated and burping every few seconds, as well as feeling really sick. What's that about?! The same thing happened again the next time I had some milk.

"Oh no!!" I realised, "I'm lactose intolerant!!" From having giardia before, I knew that it could cause lactose intolerance. Mine just seemed to have been eight months delayed. I'd feel 100% normal during the day, but would feel really sick and bloated from just the tiniest amount of diary. I'm talking so sensitive that even if I ate a meal that had a dash of milk added, like a sauce or bread, etc I'd get sick. I put up with it for the next three months, avoiding all forms of dairy, but still regularly feeling sick after a meal. This continued on, gradually getting worse until it got to the stage of feeling sick with anything I ate and then regular throwing up for a few days. I went to the doctor and he says straight away: "You have giardia." What? This is nothing like what it was last time! I was sceptical as it was so different to last time, but by now I was feeling so sick that I had to take his advice. As it was, I already had anti-giardia tablets in my medi-kit (that I had been carrying around with me for the past three months), so I just popped one single dose of four tablets, and 24 hours later I'm feeling great, and can have dairy again. I can't believe I went three months with giardia, while carrying the medicine around with me the whole time!

Don't Be Scared Off

Reading the above you could be scared into thinking you'll get horrible food poisoning from anywhere other than five-star hotels. Well actually funnily enough, the vast majority of food poisoning stories I've heard were from people eating at five-star hotels. So many times I hear, "I was eating street food the whole time without ever being sick, then I treated myself to dinner at a fancy restaurant and got violently sick." Oh no, I've probably made you even more worried now!! It's more to say that you can get sick anywhere so there's no reason to avoid street vendors. As mentioned later in this book, they tend to have more customers and therefore higher turnover of food and therefore generally sufficiently fresh food. If you think you'll get sick, you probably will, if you go with the mindset that it's fine, you'll probably be fine.

Funny Experiences

Bali Belly

Skip this story if poo stories gross you out.

I was in Bali once where I made friends with two English guys. One of them was nice, the other was a total arsehole, but really funny, so it kind of made up for it. One day we're at a restaurant where I wolfed down my meal but Austin (the funny arsehole) had barely touched his fish. He can see I'm still hungry, so he offers me some fish. I eagerly take a large mouthful, as he watches me expressionless. He continues to watch me in a creepy expressionless way, then gets a huge amount of delight when my face contorts and I start gagging on what is clearly some very rotten fish. I mean slimy rotten fish. Not good at all. He, of course, knew the fish was rotten thus why he offered it to me. Soon afterwards my insides liquefy. This would continue for seven days.

The following night, I'm pooping so much (every hour) that I pop a sleeping tablet and try to sleep sitting on the broken toilet seat. Not very comfortable. Almost zero sleep. The next day we're travelling to the Gili Islands. There are two options – the fast boat and the cheaper 'slow boat'. The fast boat does the whole trip surprisingly fast, but costs more. How much slower could the slow boat be? As it turned out, *very* much slower. We are only 105km from the Gili Islands as the crow flies, but this trip takes a staggering 14hours; much more than the four we were expecting. First it starts off by a pickup from our hotel at 6am. This is annoying as all hotels include free breakfast starting 1hr later, at 7:00am. The minibus then goes around picking up a few other hungry and sleepy backpackers, before dropping us off at his mate's restaurant at the wharf. Turns out the boat doesn't leave for another two hours or more, thereby forcing us all to eat at the overpriced restaurant instead of getting our free hotel breakfast. Finally, after sleepily waiting around we board the dilapidated barge. The barge is the local transport which is pretty much flakes of rust holding hands, doused in diesel fumes. This is where the fun started. We get a seat, then put up with all the hawkers trying to sell you all sorts of shit you don't want. This goes on for a good half hour, and just when you think you can't take any more, a 'band' comes on playing the most horrific, ear-assaulting music you've ever heard, and then they want money for it!! I'd gladly pay them to piss off!!

The ropes get cast off and we chug away at literally a crawls pace. I make the mistake of thinking this will just be while they're in the harbour, but a few miles later I realise this is top speed. Before long I need to do a poo again, necessitating use of the dodgy ships toilet. "Augh, gaaw, ergh!" It's a piss-covered toilet seat with a plastic reservoir directly underneath. This doesn't sound too bad, but just like if you quickly move a bucket of water side-to-side, the rocking of the ship is causing the water to slosh around and eject ancient watery shit out of the toilet every few seconds, which incidentally is also what's covering the floor. I'm about to poo myself, so there's no stopping this one. I wince as I sit down, and get greeted with raw sewerage shooting up my bum every few seconds. This is not the exchange I was hoping for. To make matters even worse, there was no paper or hose either, so wiping meant getting a bucket of water and pouring that down your crack to somehow try and clean yourself up. Physics does not work in your favour here.

Unfortunately, even though we were only crossing 8km water, we were going at a crawls pace, so this meant a number of hours, and a resulting number of visits back to the HIV-inducing toilet.

Finally arriving at the dock, we get hassled again by lots of people trying to sell us other shit we don't want, until we find the bus we're meant to catch. This is meant to take us straight across Lombok to the next port, then it's meant to be just a short boat ride to Gili Trawangan. Yay! We're disappointed to discover however that the bus goes via a tourist agency half way along. Oh man you've got to be friggin kidding me! I've been woken up early, paid for a breakfast that I should have had for free, had other people's poo go up my arse and we still don't seem to be getting much closer. None of us want to go to this bloody tourist agency, but our bus stops here so we pretty much have to go in. Inside the guys are trying to convince us to sign up to a volcano hike. I have a fascination with volcanoes so at first I take interest, until I see their photos which are many years old and obviously there's no lava to be seen now. The guy is adamant but I'm not interested. This doesn't mean we can leave. We have to stay at this fricken place for about two hours until enough people have signed up for their stupid volcano tour before we can leave. They also try to make us eat at their friends' overpriced restaurant for lunch, so we find some other street food instead. *Finally* we leave, and make it to the dock. It was actually pretty funny to be going on this mountainous road in an overcrowded bus that was missing the back door, such that Matt physically had to hold on to not be thrown from the bus, plus there were big holes in the floor.

We finally make it to the small dock where every prick there is trying to sell us mosquito repellent 'because the islands are full of mosquitos and they don't sell the repellent there'. I can smell the bullshit a mile off so of course I buy nothing, but most of the other tourists fall for it (there are no mosquitoes on the island, yet if there were, guaranteed they would sell the repellent there too). It's now sundown, so we catch the small 10-person boat there which was actually really nice; going on this small boat under the sunset on beautiful water, although it's well and truly nighttime by the time we arrive. It's been too long since my last defecation, so upon arriving at shore I hobble down the street looking for a hotel, sweat pouring from my face. We're not far off, but I know I'm not going to make it, so I dash off into the ocean for an aqua-turd. Phew.

Looking for a hotel, there's unfortunately no place that sleeps three people (myself, Austin and Matt). This means two of us have to share a bed. I'm quite sure that sharing a bed with a guy doesn't make you gay and I'm pretty confident that I'm not going to get the urge to touch, so I volunteer to share with Austin. This is all well and good, until halfway through the night I see the silly bugger sleeping on the floor. What the fuck's he doing on the floor? Oh well I don't care, so I continue on sleeping. Come morning when we awake I ask the question:

"Austin, why are you on the floor you idiot?"

"Because I shit the bed."

Oh you gotta be fucking kidding me. I now notice that right in the middle of the bed is a big watery shit that Austin neglected to tell me about, hoping I would roll into it during the night. What a prick. What sort of person purposely shits the bed in the hope that I roll in it? What's even more annoying, is that he only has diarrhoea for one day; just enough to shit the bed that I was sharing with him. Remember too, that it was Austin that purposely fed me the rotten fish too that made me sick in the first place.

Come next morning we go for a walk to the beach in front of the hotel. Here I realise the place that I did the aqua-turd on arrival last night is in the most pristine water, with lots of children bathing in it. That's a sea cucumber you do not want to eat!

On the beautiful island there aren't many activities I can do as I'm still going to the toilet every hour, but after a few days it's feeling slightly better so I take the chance of going scuba diving. All well and good at first, but bloody hell everyone is mucking around, wasting valuable time. We go for the dive but the inevitable is coming on. The water is super clear so I really don't want to aqua turd through the wetsuit with people scuba diving right behind me. That's just rude, huh. I grit my teeth and finish the dive, then sit in the boat in agony while everyone swims around for the next 20 mins. I'm sweating profusely now. We finally make it back to shore where I run out of the boat, but the arseholes yell out, "Oi! Help out! Grab a tank!" Fark, fark, fark! I run back, grab some gear and run back to the dive shop, but right in the middle of the road: "Uh-oh".

I just shit myself in the middle of the road.

I go back into the sea and try to wash myself out a bit, with limited success. I'm still wearing the wetsuit, and wetsuits are designed to keep water out, which also means they keep water in too. Dammit. I waddle back to the dive shop, wearing a wetsuit full of watery poo. I take a shower and try to clean it but I'm not doing a great job. This needs further attention. I put my clothes back on and go to ask the dive guys. Problem is they're having an argument and they're not interested in whatever I have to say, so seeing me with a wetsuit in my hands, they grab it, quickly dunk it in the wash-off water and hang it up. "Ummmm.... Never mind."

Finally after a week of putting up with hourly shits, I finally go to the doctor who straight away pulls out some tablets, and sets me on the mend straight away. Why the hell didn't I go there a week ago?!?

Chillies in Thailand

After getting sick in Thailand (within hours of arriving) and losing 6kg in four days, I was in the boring (couples and kids) place of Koh Samui. Riding my motorbike I got to the other side of the island where, upon using the internet, found that I misunderstood the ability to withdraw emergency funds from my empty account and was feeling very alone with zero money; not even enough for the $3 of petrol I needed to get back. There, feeling very sorry for myself, two girls go past on a motorbike yelling and waving at me. No idea who they were. Probably two girls just having fun on a bike. They stop. They walk up to me. No fucking way!! It's the girls that I met on the plane from Melbourne to Thailand! Going from having nothing, they put petrol in my bike and invite me to their hotel where there's a big banquet on tonight. I have no money at all so they cover me. Awesome! We get back to theirs, where there's a huge banquet on with all sorts of food. I haven't eaten in four days so I'm a bit apprehensive about what I can eat. i.e. I should really be starting on yoghurt and bananas or something light. This however is Thailand, so there's nothing like that. I look around, but everything is spicy looking and not ideal for an empty, fragile stomach. I finally settle on the bean salad. Now I'm a bit of a pig when I eat, in that I eat near twice as fast as normal people. This did not go in my favour today. There, with a very vulnerable stomach, I start shovelling fork after fork of the beans into my mouth like there's no tomorrow. Chew a bit, shove some more in there. Chew a bit more... ooohhhhh faaaarrrrrkkkkkk! There, in that small moment I come to the sudden and horrifying realisation... it's not a bean salad... they're chillies!!

Now, I hate chillies at the best of times, so to eat a few mouthfuls on a completely empty stomach was... just... horrible. Within seconds of swallowing, the effect was so intense; I felt drunk, lost all my balance and physically fell over. I picked myself up, tried to walk but just kept on falling over. It was just horrible.

Lesson learned: if you hate chillies, don't eat mouthfuls of them as your first bit of food in four days.

Day After Hawaiian Luau – Fish Feeding

The day after the epically big Hawaiian Luau with Dad and my brother (see Pickpocketing/Theft section), we are, unfortunately, booked to do a Manta Ray tour. Note in the story we drank the bar dry of super-low quality Mai Tai's. Well today they would have their revenge.

We wake up late and I'm feeling the sickest I've felt in my life. We really don't want to do the manta ray snorkelling tour but it was expensive and we've already paid for it. Dammit. We drive towards the dive shop, get lost and drive around in circles till we find it, park, get out, realise we're at the wrong dive shop, realise we're already late, remember they said they leave on the dot and don't wait for people, then try and run to the right dive shop. That run was definitely more like a drunken, painful, sickly, out-of-breath waddle. Covering a few blocks, feeling like we're going to die, we make it. Phew!

Our group consists of us and two nice families (what we thought we were too, until last night). We're still all feeling terribly sick but make the bus trip to the dock. Ergh, not feeling great. We then catch the boat out to the dive site and now I'm feeling absolutely *terrible*! We set anchor and try to put on our wetsuits, but with the boat rocking, my stomach is feeling shocking. They give us a big long pre-snorkel spiel reserved for retards, which drives me nuts as I just need to get off this rocking boat and into the relaxing water. Finally we get to go in the water, where I realise the bobbing around makes me feel even more sick. Ah jeez dammit. I start swimming to shore, but the snorkelling guide yells at me – it's a military airbase and even going near the shore will get you in jail. Hmmm. I ponder it for a while as I really am feeling that sick that jail might be a better option. I swim closer, stop again as she keeps yelling, then decide perhaps it's a bad idea. I swim back to the boat, try and lie down… then just start spewing everywhere. There's the nice family still snorkelling around next to the boat, and I'm heaving up last night's luau right next to them. This draws lots of fish, so I like to think I was helping them out, but the expression on their faces told me otherwise. Oh well, they'll finish up soon and then we'll get the boat back. We've paid the extra to do the double dive – a snorkel in the morning, then another at nighttime when the manta rays come out. At this point I really don't give a fudge about swimming with the manta's anymore, so I just want to get the boat back and go to bed. I ask the captain how much longer till we leave? "About five hours."

"*What?!?!?!?*"

Turns out I misunderstood. It's not a case of go out for a morning snorkel, return home, then go again at night... we have to stay on this friggin boat until night. Sounds like I'm over exaggerating, but hearing those were some of the most horrifying words I've heard in my life. The fish were happy though, as I continued to feed them last night's luau for the next few hours. Finally night came and we all went snorkelling looking for manta rays... but saw none. Finally getting off the boat at the dock was the best feeling ever.

Chapter Summary

• Take a medi-kit – this is further described in the packing chapter (Chapter 2 and a Bit)

• Avoid pork or beef. Likely it will be quite old

• Wipe the neck of bottles before drinking, or better yet, pour it into a glass

• If you have food poisoning with profuse vomiting; embrace it – it's your body getting rid of the parasites. Drink a Gatorade and replace your fluids afterwards

• If you have diarrhoea, let it be for a day or so to let your body have a chance of fighting it off first

• Check the advice on www.traveldoctor.co.uk

• Try ground-up papaya and pumpkin seeds for a natural way to fight parasites

• The same sickness can have markedly different symptoms different times. As such it's best to see a doctor rather than self-diagnose

• Don't be scared of eating street food

• Don't leave it too long before seeing the doctor if you're sick

Chapter 12: Taking Chances, Scams and Beggars

Taking chances. Ahhh yes… the essence of travel. The angel and devil on each shoulder arguing it out. It's pretty much the unwritten law of travel that the most fun you have is when you take a chance; although this is also the same thing that causes most bad situations too. So what do you do? How do you know if that invite from that person you met five minutes ago will end up being the most fun you've ever had… or the last few minutes of your life? Tricky, tricky. Keep in mind too that scam artists are professionals – this is their full-time job, so they know how to manipulate people. Making that decision gets tougher, huh.

I'll share a few stories below first and then give my thoughts on the subject later.

Taking Chances

Morocco

I was at a restaurant in Fez (Morocco) one evening where I met a few other backpackers. Eating at the same restaurant were a few other Moroccans too. Before long we're all chatting together and getting on well. The Moroccans invite us to their house for some shisha (flavoured tobacco). "Why not!" we think, and follow them through the narrow confusing streets of the town to their typical three storey mudbrick house and climb up a ladder through a hole leading to the roof. We smoke a bit of shisha, have a chat, and accept some tea that they offer us too. I get a bit bored after a while as the local is basically just showing us some boring photos on his computer. I get up to go, and the arseholes come out with a bill; a lot more expensive than it would have been in a restaurant. Cheeky bastards! I'm not in too much of a position to argue, so I pay up and go to leave. I climb down the ladder, where at the bottom, a Berber desert-man dressed in full tunic and turban, complete with tattooed face yells at me in Arabic, pulls out his sword (yes, a sword, not a knife) and runs towards me! He rushes up to me and holds the sword to my throat while yelling at me in Arabic. Shit scary for the average person, but for some reason I remain eerily calm in a crisis, quite possibly because I haven't grasped what's happening yet. He yells at me some more, then reaches out and touches my chest, feeling my heartbeat. It's still just going at a normal 60 beats per minute. Bumb-bumb.... bumb-bumb.... bumb-bump. Expecting my heart to be racing, he steps back in total shock, puts away his sword and says in heavily-accented English "Very brave man", steps to the side and motions for me to leave.

I have no idea what that was all about.

San Pedro Sula; Murder Capital of the World

In Guatemala I made friends with two young European guys that had just come up from Honduras. Getting to Guatemala means going via San Pedro Sula, which is the official murder capital of the world (outside of war zones). This is the place where you arrive, go straight to your hostel and don't leave till morning where you get straight on the next bus out. Expect to hear gunshots outside your hostel at night. It's pretty common for buses to be held up at gunpoint too, as happened to someone else I know.

My friends did something a little different.

On the bus to San Pedro Sula they got chatting to an American/Honduran guy on board. When they arrived they went to get a taxi to their hotel, but the Honduran guy said, "No need for a taxi – I have a car; I can drive you there." "Sweet as!" they think. They follow him to his car that turns out to be an absolute shitbox. He had a friend waiting for him in the car, stoned off his brain. They jump in and go searching for the hostel; stoned guy at the wheel. After 1hr of driving around with no luck, the Honduran guy says, "You know what, I have a house here. You can just stay at mine." Ummmmm, ok, the guys think. They drive onward, into the *really* dodgy area of the city. They are no longer in the main part of the city; they are now in the dodgy, dangerous part of the most dangerous city in the world. They pull up behind a row of abandoned shops and enter a rundown bungalow. They're not feeling so good about this. They enter regardless, at which point the dude pulls out a few shopping bags full of marijuana. Oh bugger. Yep, they're at a drug dealer's house in the most dangerous drug-run city in the world.

The Honduran guy feels like a nap and so does one of the lads, so they go for a sleep while the other guy lies down but can't sleep as he's (understandably) seriously shitting himself for the next four hours thinking about the situation they're in; thinking they'll get all their stuff stolen… or worse. When the others wake up, he smokes some pot to calm himself down. Problem is this is some really good quality weed. He gets *super* high. They go out together to buy some food and rum; then it's business time. The Honduran guys start calling all their regular customers to make some sales and use the young English guy as the selling point saying, "Look at this gringo – this is how high this stuff will get you!"

They then head to the local bar, with the driver now both stoned and drunk. They make it there ok and the Hondurans buy the lads some drinks and they have a great old time smoking the pot in the bar and continuing to sell it there too. They then get back in the car, and not 10 seconds after leaving, a police car sees them, puts the lights and siren on and speeds straight towards them. Oooooh crap. The driver does a U-turn and speeds off in the opposite direction; stoned and drunk driver trying to outrun the cops in a car full of drugs. Obviously one of the guys is shitting himself thinking he's about to end up in a Honduran prison where severe beatings and murders among prisoners are rife. The other guy just starts getting the giggles! Fortunately they manage to evade the police and head back to the house where they continue the deals. One of the guys then decides he wants to deal himself 'to tick it off the bucket list' and heads off with the Hondurans to do his own drug deal, in the city famous for having the absolute highest murder rate in the world; all drug related. Fortunately this all goes fine.

They pass out at 1:30am, then get woken up at 3:30am by the Honduran guy as they have a bus out organised at 4am. The Honduran guy has also kindly organised them a taxi and has arranged a good deal on the price too. He then sends them on their way, ending the best ever night spent with the nicest Honduran drug dealers ever!

Very. Lucky. That could have gone so far the other way. Not recommended to try and emulate this adventure!!

Fire Jump in Thailand

While in Bangkok looking in vain for clothes I could buy that included a receipt, it seemed all the tourists had some part of their body wrapped in bandages. When asked why, the response would always, without fail, be "Motorbike accident, Koh Samui," or "Fire jump, Koh Phangan". Considering the amount of injuries I saw, this was a pretty easy decision; no motorbikes in Koh Samui and no fire jumping in Koh Phangan.

Pffft!

After making the mistake of seeing a travel agent in Bangkok while very sick and booking her recommendation, I found myself in Koh Samui in the most boring paradise ever. Some people would find it paradise, I thought it was hellish. There was a beautiful beach lined with coconut palms and clear water, with the bungalows on the beach. Beautiful… but boring as hell. The only other people there were two girls that all they wanted to do was to sun bake on the beach all day. Ergh. I had to get out, but we were in a secluded location away from everything else. Bugger. I started to walk, then saw a sign: Motorbikes, $4 for 24 hours. Easy choice, even though my previous experience with a motorbike wasn't that great. Yes, the last time (also the first time) I was on a bike I hit a telegraph pole at considerable speed while completely out of control, destroying the bike in the process. On this bike the brakes didn't work and the handlebars were loose. Oddly (fortunately) enough nothing happened.

Koh Phangan wouldn't be so lucky.

Arriving in other nearby island, Koh Phangan, I was finally found. Cool people and a cool place. Going to the place at Had Rin (site of the famed full moon parties) it was a cool vibe with just a few people partying on the beach with DJ's and fire twirlers. Soon enough the fire jumping starts. That is, they get a ring 1m in diameter set fire to it, then hold it via ropes two feet off the ground, like those hoops of fire that tigers jump through. Not being one to knock back something stupid when the chance arises, I do it lots of times, jumping through like Superman; all done easily enough. I then go for another attempt, running forward, but two steps before I get there, the pricks suddenly raise the ring so the bottom is about four feet off the ground.

Everything goes in slow-motion.

I've got two steps left, running full speed. The thought goes through my mind, "I can't 'Superman' that – it's too high up!" This left one option – jump high with knees into chest and cannonball through. As I jump into the air, I ponder the physics; I'm 182cm tall and this ring is 100cm across. This ain't gonna work. I make my head through, my right arm through, my right leg through, not really my left arm, and definitely not my left leg. Colliding with the burning ring I land in a firing heap and roll away. "Wooohoooooo! That was *awesome*!!" I yell out. It was great fun and it didn't hurt at all. I've now had enough of the fire jumping for now, so I go for a walk. After walking for a minute, I get this smell in my nose, "Yuck, ergh, what's that smell?? It's disgusting. It smells, like… burning flesh or something. Ergh!"

The smell was everywhere.

I continue walking some more. The whole friggin beach smells like burning flesh. This goes on for almost five minutes. I'm wondering "Why does this whole bloody beach smell like burning fle….. …..oooh shiiit." Yep, suddenly it made sense now. Not wanting to, I slowly raise my arm up for a look. "Ah shyiiit." It's all black. I knew however that my leg copped it a lot worse. Slowly I take a peek at my leg. "Oh no." The lower half of my leg was all black, except for my shin, where all the skin has all molten away, leaving a yucky looking mess. Shit. I go into the sea water to cool it down, which doesn't help much in Thailand where the sea temperature is 28C. I then get some ice out of a drink, then think ice probably isn't going to be the miracle cure I'm looking for. I bang on the door of a 24hr doctor and am greeted by the sight of a very grumpy looking doctor; pissed off that I woke her up. I'm expecting she's going to get some soothing burn cream for me, maybe some soothing menthol and an icepack? Nup, the bitch went into her cupboard and pulled out some medicinal alcohol and before I could run away she started pouring it all over my fresh burn. Fuck. That. Hurt. I'm no doctor, but is pure alcohol really the best thing to put on a burn?!?

Of course the next thing she says is, "No swim, three weeks!" Stuff this; I'm on a tropical island. I'll deal with it when I get home!!

Thai Kickboxing

Three days after the incident of the burn to my leg (and in the meantime getting the absolute worst sunburn in my life on my back), I find myself on the beautiful island of Koh Phi-Phi. It's almost the end of my trip and I'm a bit bummed that I haven't seen any of the famous Thai Kickboxing yet. As luck would have it, that night I meet an English girl who's telling me about a Thai Kickboxing stadium on the island there. The way she describes it, it sounds really cool. Also, she continues, they invite tourists to fight too, and if you fight three rounds with someone you get a free drink! People just go there to have a bit of fun with their mates and if it gets a bit rough, the referee steps in, so it's all good. Girls do it and all.

Sounds awesome!

We head to the place and the moment we walk in they put on the song 'Eye of the Tiger' (ya know "DA!.... dededede DA DA DA... dededede DA DA DAAAAAAAR!) and hold up a sign saying, "Fight 3 Rounds, Get a Free Drink!" Well with a combination of the energetic song and my stupidity I immediately put my hand up, not 15 seconds after walking into the arena. Perhaps I would have been better off to observe for a few rounds first? Pffft. Knowing what you're getting yourself in for is for pussies. The referee gets me to jump into the ring. He needs a challenger for me. He asks the audience. No one moves. He asks again. A rather huge looking dude puts his hand up. Oh shit, he doesn't look fun to fight. Oh well, it'll be fine… right?

Wrong.

There are some people on before us, so I get out of the ring and go over to the dude for a chat. At this point I'd never boxed in my life and had never seen it on TV either. I approach the guy and realise shit, this guy's fucking huge!!! I'm starting to second-guess my decision. Not having had any experience boxing, I ask the guy:

"So what are the rules of boxing? Where are you allowed to hit the person? Guessing you can't hit below the belly button, right?"

"You bullshit."

"Huh?"

"You bullshit."

"What? No. I've never done this before – I'm just here for some fun. So what's the objective? I know you're meant to hit the other person, but how do you know if you've won?"

"You bullshit. You've done this before."

"What? Nah. Seriously mate, I just here for some fun. What are the rules?"

"You bullshit."

At this point, I realise that apart from being absolutely huge, this guy is a total tosser too. I'm feeling less happy about my decision to fight this guy. I realise we're not getting anywhere in the conversation so I just say "Righto, but just watch my leg because it's covered in burns, and my back too from the sunburn."

No response.

By now, the guys before us have started their match. They are two Swedish guys and they are kicking the absolute *shit* out of each other. I've never seen anything like it. This is full on! They successfully beat the living shit out of each other for the three rounds, then leave battered and bruised. Next up are the Thai guys. Fuckin' 'ell! These guys looked like they were trying to kill each other!! At one point one guy had the other on the ground and was repetitively kicking the shit out of him while he's on the ground. The ref mustn't have liked this as he picked up a large metal plate and *whacked* this down with all his might over the head of the guy dealing out the beating. The guy dropped unconscious immediately. That sort of thing could easily kill a person… and that's from the referee!

"What the bloody hell have I got myself into?!?"

The bout finishes so it's my turn. I sure as shit don't want to be here, but hey, I'm in it now. They give me a head protector thing and gloves. No mouthguard. Bugger. I'm standing there gingerly; a leg wrapped in bandages from the second-degree burns, the worst ever sunburn on my back and looking extremely frail due to the 6kg I'd lost from the food poisoning. There are a few hundred people in the arena and everyone is chatting, as you do. The other guy steps in. People continue chatting. He takes off his t-shirt.

Sudden silence.

This guy is fucking *ripped*. To date, he is still probably one of the most muscular people I have ever seen in my life. I'm not exaggerating. HE WAS

FUCKING HUGE!!! Here we have this absolute monster, then there's me who's never boxed in his life and in the worst health I've ever been in. If there was any doubt before whether or not I wanted to be here, it was pretty certain now. I really, *really* didn't want to be in the ring now. Oh well, I'm in it now. Can't back out now! Anyway, he knows I've never boxed before, so he'll go soft… right?

Wrong.

The round starts. Donnnggg. He immediately runs to me and hits me with a combo to my face followed by a huge right-hander that sends my head backwards almost level with my shoulders, knocking me to the ground. The ref counts. I pick myself up. The ref keeps counting. In retrospect I'm pretty sure he was trying to stop the fight, but I'm one determined son-of-a-bitch with more pride than brains. I get up only to be followed by another volley of blows to the face. It doesn't stop with punches. Next up I'm getting powerful kicks to the face, roundhouse kicks, jumping back kicks, flying sidekicks; all to the face. I haven't yet hit him once. First round ends. I go to my corner, feeling very much worse for wear. Someone gives me some advice, "Doesn't matter what you do, *just keep your guard up.*" 30 second break is over.

Round two.

He gets straight into it again, using me as a human punching bag. I remember the advice yet my arms hang at my sides, my face taking the full beating. *Does this arsehole not realise by now that I wasn't joking about never having boxed?!?* The round continues in this fashion; me just getting the absolute shit kicked out of me. My face is nicely smashed up and I'm spitting out blood.

Come third round I haven't touched him once and I think I should probably hit him. I know this means moving forward towards him, but my brain won't allow me to do this. I want to get away from this prick, not get closer! Well if I can't step in closer to him, I need to just jump into him. I wait till he's back away from me, then with all my courage I run towards him, jump majestically into the air and sail towards him with my fist extended; hoping to connect with him. He's unfazed by this and just holds his ground and punches out as I come down, his fist spectacularly connecting with my flying face. The fight ended with me not touching him a single time. Even without knowing the rules I could make the assumption that he won, not me. I ended up with two black eyes, smashed up lips and a broken nose. I can only hope that his knuckles were sore! As it turned out, my nose continued to have a constant slow bleed for the next three years; constantly filling my nose with dry blood that I'd have to pick out every two hours, plus it also had a slow leak into the back of my throat; causing me to cough up blood regularly throughout the day for the following three years. Fortunately that's now stopped!

Anyway I got my free drink, but had a headache from hell so I couldn't drink it anyway. Not one to hold a grudge I go over to the dude to have a chat with him, but the prick had already left with his girlfriend. What an arsehole!

I don't want this all to get in the way of a good night, so I clean all the blood off my face and go out feeling like quite a loser. Walking down the street lots of people came up to me saying;

"You're the guy from the kickboxing, right?!?"

"Yeeahhh..." I'd reply, embarrassed and dejected.

"That was *awesome*!!"

"What?? *Really*???"

After a few such comments from various people, I recognised one of the Swedish guys from the early fight approach me. He comes up to me and says:

"Can I have the honour of shaking your hand?"

"Um, yeah... *but why*?"

"Because you are the absolute bravest person I've ever met. That was just unbelievable."

"Well not really... I'm not much of a fighter – I didn't hit him once!"

"Do you know who that was?

"No."

"That was the heavy-weight Tae-Kwon do champion of Sweden."

"Oh."

"He's a total arsehole. I can't believe he did that to you. We want to teach him a lesson but no one will fight him. I'm a *professional fighter* and there's no way I'd fight him. …but you…. you just went in there! I couldn't believe it! That's the bravest thing I've ever seen!!"

Hearing those words made that the proudest moment of my life. 61kg and in a frail state, with no fighting experience fighting a 90kg+ guy that even a crazy-fuck professional fighter wouldn't fight.

Getting some more swing in my step after hearing that, I continue my night and have a fun night out. Come 3am I'm sitting on the beach with a few hippies in a circle playing guitar and singing Kumbaya. After a while, I see a guy approaching in the dark. I realise 'oh, it's the guy from the fight'. I go to invite him over, because for some strange bloody reason I don't have a grudge against him, but when he sees me, he gets panic in his eyes, turns around and sprints up the beach in the opposite direction, trips over a rope, scrambles up again and continues sprinting away. WTF?!? Did this guy think the hippies would gang up on him? Total Class A1 fuckwit. Still, it made for the proudest moment in my life.

Fireworks in The Philippines

Fireworks are totally illegal in Australia, so when Aussies see them for sale overseas, we go nuts! Doing a road trip around the Philippines with some friends, we see fireworks for sale at the side of the road and pretty much fill the car up with various fireworks and rockets. That night we arrive at a hotel and are keen to set them off, but have no real idea how to, or how big they will be. We figure (hope) the hotel would like a free fireworks show, so we make a makeshift launcher and set off a rocket in the hotel grounds directly next to the main building. Ffffssssssscchhhh…. boom! Woo, that was awesome! We set off a few more big rockets, then light the 50 shot pack. That is; it's a set that shoots off 50 fireworks, one after the other. We're happily setting off fireworks, until suddenly the cops rock up, lights flashing and all and drive right up to where we are. Shit, shit! It's a bit hard to stand there and look innocent while guiltily grinning ear to ear and holding a large rocket while you have a 50 shot set sending fireworks off every second behind you. We try to look innocent but it's no use, so we go to apologise instead. The cops laugh and say, "Oh no, you're not in trouble – we're here to see the fireworks!!" I can only imagine them being on patrol, seeing the fireworks being set off then turning on their lights and siren and racing through the traffic to get to us in time before we finished!

The trip was then pretty much drive for an hour, stop, set off some rockets, continue. This stopping to let off fireworks became a bit tedious so here came the great idea to shoot small fireworks out of the car window while on the highway. Worked great for a few, then one came back in the car and burnt a small hole in the seat. Was a bit scary (particularly as the back seat was full of fireworks), so we put a stop to that.

Later on this escalated to shooting roman candles out of restaurant windows in the next town. Filled the restaurant with smoke, but we had fun. Next came New Years Eve where we let off most of the fireworks, getting very worried by all these young kids taking all our rockets and lighting them while standing above it. Scary! We all survived New Years, but on our last day, we still have our biggest rocket left, almost the size of a child's arm. What do we do with that? We do what any boys would – tape the GoPro camera to it and make a Rocket Cam! We drive till we find a suitable launch pad – a dry creek bed. We walk through head-high dry grass to get to the creek bed and set up the rocket and construct a makeshift launch pad. We light it and it sets off beautifully – launches up and makes a graceful arc in the sky and explodes brilliantly... ...and sets off a grass fire. Yes, when fireworks explode low to the ground they shoot off white-hot particles that, believe it or not, can set fire to dry grass. Problem is it's not just any grass – it's head high and next to a small village. Shiiit! We're slapping it with our thongs and do a pretty good job, then fortunately a fire truck arrives and puts it out... while we scurry to the car and speed off. Phew!!

Having nearly burnt down a Filipino village we decide that's enough fireworks for us on this trip... which also means we return our rental car to the airport with a boot containing 50 rockets in it. Pretty sure you're not mean to bring explosives to the airport! The car rental place was pretty pissed off about it too! Oh well, we had fun.

Scams

The best scam artists I've come across were in China. Generally there is very little scamming in China, but in People's Square in Shanghai it is rife. These guys are brilliant. The first encounter I had was the first time I was in Shanghai. I got off the metro in People's Square where a group of Chinese asked me to take a photo for them. I took the photo and then the guy started crapping about how he's from Shanghai and his friends are up from Beijing, so they're in town for a few days. They invite me out somewhere, but this dude is really annoying and won't shut up. I certainly don't want to hang out with him, so I decline. As it happened, at that point too, some tourist walked past and said, "Watch out buddy, it's a scam!"

As it turns out they use the camera ploy as a natural way to start a conversation with people, then they invite you to some teahouse where they charge you a huge amount for trying some tea. Following this encounter, I saw this trick repeated at The Bund; the other big tourist area in Shanghai. If someone asks you to take a photo of them, make sure after you take the photo to go back through their other photos. If there are other photos of the same scene, you know they're trying to scam you. If so, it's lots of fun to run away with their camera for a while, then hand it back.

Some weeks later I was near People's Park where a tourist asked me for directions. I told him where to go then warned him about the scam in the area, giving a full description. He thanked me and left. Two minutes later I'm walking through People's Park with my wolf beanie on as it was cold. A Chinese girl with a group of friends walking by sees my hat, laughs and starts chatting to me; as commonly happens when you wear a cute, funny hat in Asia. Her friends walk two metres past and are standing there looking impatient as she chats with me. They look very much like they want her to finish the conversation so they can all go wherever they're headed. Their body language says it all; they are standing 2m further in the direction they are going, feet pointed away, arms crossed, heads turned in the direction they were going. Much to their annoyance, I continue to chat with the girl who later invites me to some event. It sounds interesting, and the adventurer in me wants to do something with the locals, but I'm really tired and don't really feel like it today. Feeling like I'm letting myself down, I politely decline. I then walk away and suddenly realise: "Shit! I just nearly got scammed minutes after warning someone about the scams here!" I know for sure that it would have been a scam, but these guys were just brilliant. The initiation of the conversation was very normal and her friends seemed impatient, wanting to go. Masters. Total masters. I later found out that a Chinese co-worker of mine, who is from Shanghai, got scammed himself just a month beforehand. He went to the tea ceremony with another co-worker and ended paying $150 to try some teas!! Even so, he didn't realise he was scammed until afterwards. Amazing.

One trick I've never fallen for, but plenty of friends have, is the 'drinks for bar girls' scam. This is where you go to a bar where attractive girls (hired by the bar) ask you to buy drinks for them, then at the end of the night they come out with the bill; drinks for girls cost 5x the price. Expect a bill of hundreds of dollars and a door blocked by a mafia-type bouncer. Pay up or get beaten up.

Make sure never to take the advice of a taxi driver as to which club to go to. Know where you want to go and make sure they take you there. Many taxi drivers are involved in the scams and will take you to 'a really great club they know' and take you to the scam bar.

Similarly, in Thailand it's a similar story with the tuk-tuk drivers. Often when you ask to go somewhere, they'll go via a gem store or suit tailors where the shopkeepers sell their items at over-inflated prices. Often they won't let you go until you buy something. As Thailand was my first trip I was not yet street smart so I got scammed too. I got a tuk-tuk for a day to find some replacement clothes (as my pack was still in Melbourne). The driver was a pretty nice guy and he mentioned how he gets paid by the suit store to take people there. He seemed to be an honestly genuine guy – basically saying go in, pretend to have a look around then come back out. Well it seemed reasonable to me, so I went in, but bloody hell the salesmen there were good. I'm going with the excuse that it was my first trip, plus I was really sick so my mind wasn't working so well… but I bought a suit. They lied about the exchange rate too, which I stupidly believed and before long I'd parted with about $350 hard earned cash. When the suit came it was nothing like what I wanted. I've never actually worn it!

More information about buying from tailors is in Chapter 13.

How to Tell if it's a Scam or Not?

As above you can see that taking a chance can result in a great unique time or be a big scam. So do you take the chance or not? After a lot of thought on the subject, I have a few ideas of how to tell if it's a genuine offer or a scam.

First: how do you meet the person? Generally the only sure-fire way to know if they're legit is if someone else you know vouches for them, particularly hostel staff. If someone approaches you speaking good English, it's almost

100% guaranteed to be a scam. Why would they approach you, and why do they speak such good English? They may use the tactic that they want to practise English with you, and that's fine, but I wouldn't leave the place you currently are. If they want you to come with them to a restaurant or someplace else, politely decline.

It's very difficult to give it a straight-out 'no' based on both not wanting to sound rude, as well as thinking that it may be genuine and lead to a super awesome experience. I think the best way to play it safe is to say you're busy today, but you'd be keen for tomorrow and ask for their number. If they refuse to give you their number and insist that you should come now, you can be pretty sure it's a scam. Think about it, when you're home, how keen would you be for some tourists to join you for something? How would you react? Most likely you'd like them to come to show off your local culture, but wouldn't be too fussed if they didn't make it. More than likely though, if they were cool enough you'd trade numbers.

This is where I recommend Couchsurfing as you can get the awesome local experience without questioning if something is a scam or not. Of course there are a few shady characters on Couchsurfing too, but the majority are fine. Also, as by nature of the business, you know where they live so it is unlikely that they will try to pull tricks on you.

Beggars

This is a touchy subject in which I've changed my thoughts a lot on over the years. I used to give to beggars all the time, thinking a dollar doesn't mean too much to me, but is a lot to them. Based on better wages in Australia you feel very selfish not to give. I used to meet people in my travels who wouldn't give to beggars and I didn't understand why. My heart goes out to the beggars on the street and I feel terrible walking past.

It was only after living in China when I began to see the dark side of begging. China really is amazing as there're very, very few people begging. Instead, everywhere you see people selling things, be it in train stations, overpasses, side of the road, etc. They're all there with their mat selling various items. They are trying to make their living. Beggars however are only found in the tourist areas, particularly outside the bars. Let's be honest, if you spend $40 on a night out then refuse to give $1 to an old haggard woman, you feel pretty bad. Therefore, when I went out I often did give to them. This act abruptly stopped when I was walking through the area during the day and went into a shop for some good quality takeaway food. I exited the store holding my food in the bag, untouched. Outside was a beggar asking for money. Of course I went and gave her my hot, fresh food but she refused; demanding money instead. I couldn't believe it!! What sort of person would knock back free, untouched food? I wouldn't even do that. Free food is free food! I was infuriated and stormed off. It was after this that I heard numerous stories of people taking a beggar into a bakery to get them something, and the beggar would say "No!" and point to the most expensive luxury item. I would hear of other stories of how people would give to a particular disabled person each day, then one day saw them *walking* home after their 'shift'. When I found out the wage of the average non-skilled worker, I realised that these beggars were making *much* more money than someone working an honest job.

I made another observation in San Pedro, Guatemala where I lived for a few months. There were never any beggars in the market, yet when the annual fair was on, there was a beggar with a bandage around his leg sitting in the absolute most inconvenient place possible, where thousands of people would literally have step over him each day. He was never there before the fair, and he was gone as soon as it was over. Clearly he was from elsewhere, just going to the fair to capitalise on all the extra people walking around with extra money in their pockets. Guaranteed there was nothing wrong with him either.

Through later observation, particularly in the USA, I noticed that there are two types of people; those that beg, and those that go through bins. Since starting my observation I've never seen someone that goes through bins ask money from people and I've never seen someone that begs go through a bin. Those that go through bins look determined; they won't even try to make eye contact – they go through one bin, then without a moment's pause, they're off on a fast walk to the next.

All the above is not to say that I never give to beggars – I still do on occasion, but I make an assessment of the situation. If they are obviously disabled, like missing their legs, then I typically do give. Note however that there are lots of tricks they can do to make themselves look disabled when in fact they're not. For all others, the first thing I look for is smell. If it's difficult to stand near them due to the smell, then chances are they're a legitimate beggar. This can be of course from smelly clothes they are wearing, so observe their skin, particularly their hands and feet. Look for dirty nails and dry, cracked, calloused skin. More than anything though, sit down and have a chat to them. In a kind way, sit down and ask them why they ended up in the streets. Don't be interrogative; be kind about it. Often the best thing you can give is your love. If they're not interested to talk, they're not worth your money. If they do want to talk, you will probably make their week.

The other type of beggars are the people that walk up to you asking for money and won't go away. These are typically children. Often they will be very persistent and not go away. They are often successful as people feel sorry for a child saying they're hungry. Fair enough. What I do however is to say, "Ok sure… but what will you do for me? It's not fair otherwise." For sure they will straight away walk away. Often it's been the case that they were hassling people around me for ages then they tried with me. After asking what they would do for me they walked/ran away and I had to chase after them, saying I'd give the money if they would give me something in return. For sure all the other tourists will be wondering how it is that you're following beggars not the other way around. If they were genuinely hungry, they would think of something to make the exchange.

I know what you're probably thinking as that's what I used to think too; who cares if they're a real beggar or not – it's still only loose change for me! The issue is that it creates a problem. Charity only seems to work when there's an emergency situation or when it's part of a sustainable project. If it's just giving it can set up a culture that they think everything should just be given to them. As they say, buy a man a fish and he will eat for a day. Teach a man to fish and he'll never be hungry again. I strongly believe that if someone asks you for money, you should ask what they will do for you. This will quickly sort out those that just want to ask for money and those that want to take an opportunity to earn money. The problems that charity can generate was further proven to me in San Marcos, Guatemala. In the neighbouring towns of San Pedro and San Juan there were no beggars. Walking through the town, locals would walk past, smile and say hello, but just 4km away in San Marcos you were just seen as a walking wallet. Everyone seemed to be following you asking for money; almost demanding it in fact. I was surprised why there was such a difference. As I stayed there for a further two months, I learned from various sources that there's been a history of charity services in San Marcos, which seems to have set up some sort of feeling that they should receive charity donations all the time. For example, much of their cooking is done by burning sticks under a metal plate. This is inefficient and costs them a lot of money for the wood. Someone from a charity organisation developed a more efficient stove that drastically cut down the fuel required, thus it would save them money as well as reduce smoke in the house. Fantastic idea. The deal went out – pay half and the charity will pay for the other half. The wood saved would pay itself off quickly. Response: "No thanks; we'll just wait for a different charity to give it to us for free." If there wasn't the prior history of receiving charity donations, then I believe there would have been a different response. I definitely do believe that you should help out those less fortunate than yourself, but helping is better in the long run than giving. It's a complicated subject and I don't really know what the answer is.

It doesn't always have to be about money either. I was once in Panajachel in Guatemala where people everywhere are trying to sell you shit you don't want, with everything 1.5x the price of elsewhere. Even at a restaurant there's someone coming over every two minutes trying to sell you something. Gets pretty annoying pretty quickly. Instead of telling them to piss off however, when this 11-year-old kid came up selling pens, I obviously wasn't interested in buying his pens, but the guy had a lot of character and was a pretty cool dude. We ended up just laughing and chatting for a good 15 mins. This kid was super cool hey! Really funny, total character. Total highlight of my day. I finished off by giving him the rest of my lunch and some water and teaching him some magic tricks. I'd normally never give away the secret, but I figured he might be able to make some money doing tricks for tourists. Remember if someone is trying to sell you something you don't want, you can still give back to them in other ways, and guess what; you can have a ton of fun doing it too!!

Chapter Summary

Taking Chances
• Taking chances can leave you having the time of your life, or fighting for your life. Either way, it will be an experience!

Scams
• If someone asks you to take a photo of them in a touristic area, take the photo then go through their photos to see if there're lots of the same photo. If so, it's probably a ploy for a scam

• Be very wary of bars that operate on a tab system. If they do certainly don't buy drinks for girls as they may be multiple times the price of a normal drink

• Never take the recommendation of a bar from a person on the street or a taxi driver. They are probably in on the scam. Ask at your hostel which bar to go to

• If you've just arrived in a country, never believe the exchange rate someone tells you when buying something

• If someone approaches you talking about some sort of party or event say you'll think about it and ask for their number. If they are too pushy, it's probably a scam

• Never accept the invite of a stranger to go to a bar or restaurant. You're probably about to get scammed. Say you want to go somewhere else and gauge their reaction and how keen they are for you to stay

Beggars
• Many beggars are fakes that are making a lot more money than people working honest jobs

• Assess the person – what do they smell like, and observe their skin. Look for cracked, dirty, calloused skin to determine if they are living on the street or not

• Have a chat with them. If you don't want to give them money, give them some time instead

• To get rid of walk-up beggars, ask them what they will do for you. If they need the money they will think of some way to give back. If they are just interested in getting your money without working for it, they will quickly walk away

Chapter 13: General

Cultural Experience

When I was younger, I kind of thought, "Fudge cultural experience, I want night life!!" Though I hate to admit it, I seem to have matured a bit since then. This is why I recommend following what I wrote in the chapter 'Where to go When'. Nightlife you'll forget unless it was a truly epic night, cultural moments will stick by… well, only if they're epic too I suppose!

If there's some local fest on, *go to it!* Below are a few highlights I've had.

Only Foreigners in a 2000 Person Cuban Concert

While in Cuba, I went to the small but awesome town of Trinidad. Actually, it was funny on the way there, passing towns with funny names, such as Moron and Colon. That kept me entertained for a while, imagining signs such as 'Moron Police', 'Moron Council', 'Moron School', etc. I giggled to myself a while about this, until I thought about what the entry sign to Colon must be and had a much bigger laugh…. just imagine the big welcome sign at the city limit's stating: *"You are now entering Colon."* Advice probably more suited to a gay porn movie. Also, is a person who was born in Colon then moved elsewhere; is he a Semi-Colon? I wonder too what people say about Moron, such as 'you can take the boy out of Moron, but you can't take the Moron out of the boy'? I do imagine though that the Colon Hospital must be one of the best digestive disorder hospitals, and surely a damn sight better place to get surgery done than the Moron Hospital.

Anyway, jokes aside, as it turned out, I happened to be in Trinidad for their 500 year anniversary. Timing, huh! They had to wait 180,000 days for this and I just had to wait two!

There was a cultural show in the main square that in typical Central American style started more than an hour late, and to be honest, when it finally did start it was pretty darn boring; just some arty movements depicting their history. We feel like we're being uncultured leaving early but really we can't stay any longer. Surprisingly enough, while leaving I bump into a Canadian girl and her brother that I met the night beforehand and we head to another plaza; where we buy a bottle of rum for $2. Yes please. The Canadian girl has heard that there's meant to be some event here, but after a while the crowd whittles down till it's mainly 12-year-olds. Not too keen on partying with 12-year-olds, we go for a walk and see a street where lots of people seem to be heading out of town. Looks like there's something on, so we follow the crowd for a few blocks out of town to be greeted by a fantastic sight – out here in the middle of nowhere is a large stage and what must be almost a couple of thousand locals dancing to the Cuban live band on stage. I would not be surprised if we were the only tourists there. It was absolutely fantastic to be in the middle of this huge crowd of Cuban locals dancing the night away. Unfortunately the average age seemed to be 40, 50 or more, but we still have a great time dancing with the locals. Everyone is saying hello to us, shaking our hands and taking us for a dance. Everyone is very warm and very happy to have us here joining their concert. Later we realised we really were the only non-Cubans there, and the locals were all genuinely happy to have us there, with them all offering us their rum too. Very generous. Of course I did the trick of only taking a small swig of theirs, then offering them ours such that we could accept their generosity yet ensure they got more rum out of it too.

We move through the crowd for a while meeting lots of the locals, then head off to the side where I see a bar where cocktails range in price from 20c to 40c. We splashed out on a 40c mojito each then decide to call it a night, having had a fantastic night sharing in this small town's grand fiesta.

Swiss National Day, Switzerland

On part of my Contiki trip through Europe, we were lucky enough to be in the absolutely stunning town of Lauterbraunen (Switzerland) for the Swiss National Day celebrations. It was awesome! Imagine being in a really small town in a valley between two large cliffs, with glaciers and snow in clear view, wearing all red and joining the parade down the main street at night, then watching yodelling and a bonfire, followed by a great fireworks show against the cliff face; the booming sound echoing through the valley. Awesome.

La Féria, San Pedro, Guatemala

I made sure to stick around San Pedro to be there for the annual town fair. San Pedro is an indigenous Mayan town in Guatemala, home to 9,000 people. This is the place I stayed in for over two months learning Spanish. Wages here are typically $42 per week for an English teacher, to down as low as 70c per hour for farm labourers. Therefore, the fair wasn't as top-end as those in first-world countries, but what it lacked in moderness, it made up for in awesomeness. Take the Ferris wheel for example – this was one of the scariest rides I've been on in any theme park… Ever.

In safety conscious Australia, the Ferris wheel in the fairs are normally the quaint, tranquil ride that you take your date on, in the hope of getting a kiss when you reach the top. In Guatemala, the Ferris wheel is a heart-pounding adrenaline rush that tries to kill you. Multiple times.

Let's start with the setup. When your town is on the side of a volcano there's not much flat ground. There are no big sports fields or parks or anything like that. This means the fair is all on the narrow streets. Try sticking a full-size Ferris wheel on a street with room to walk past. It's difficult. That's why it's off to one side… underneath the powerlines. Yes, the big metal construction is sitting directly between the powerlines; parting the cables such that they're touching each side of the Ferris wheel. For now the insulation is intact, but get a break in the insulation and the whole thing would be connected to 11,000 volts. Oddly enough, that's just the amusing part, not the scary part.

This Ferris wheel does not just rotate slowly and leisurely – it's connected to a truck engine which they speed up to full revs. The speed is controlled by a guy sitting on the truck engine, using a foot-operated accelerator. It's so fast that it's quite windy standing next to it. There's also no guarding or barriers anywhere around it. It's also ridiculously crowded around it, with everyone in line standing shoulder to shoulder. I saw some people inadvertently take a few steps backward and nearly had their heads taken off by the ride. Yes, if they took two more steps backward they probably would have been killed. Not exaggerating. No one seems to be fussed though as the staff walk between the Ferris wheel upright supports and the very fast spinning inner wheel. Shoulder-width gap. Breach the gap and you lose a body part.

Come your turn, you physically have to run on as they try to fill it up as quickly as possible. You throw them your very reasonable 70c ticket price as it moves to the next seat. In the space of two minutes it's all been filled.

You tentatively sit down on the basic bench and rest your arm on the side. The Ferris wheel starts moving and you realise that if you'd have kept your arm there, *it would be taken off*. There's no guarding between the moving parts of the bench and the wheel. The guy floors the accelerator and soon you're spinning around the wheel much faster than you're comfortable with. The high speed also means that the seats (with not much to hold onto) swing backwards and forwards as you go around, sometimes going almost horizontal.

We survived it and walked off grinning ear to ear. What made it all the more fun was that I was doing it with my local Mayan friends. Felt so good to be part of it!

Fire Safety

Fire safety is a subject I never gave a second thought... until a friend of mine was in a hostel that burned to the ground one night. Fortunately she was ok as she was in a cabana next to the two that burnt down. Once I saw her and saw that she was ok, I knew we had to get her things out of her room, or else it'll be stolen by morning no doubt. We went to her room, but with the power out and all the smoke it was very, very difficult to see. It made me think that if you were in a large building filled with smoke and no lights, plus the panic, it would be a very scary situation. Therefore, I believe it is a good idea when you check in to a multi-storey building to see what secondary stairs there are if the fire stops you going down the main stairs. Once you have corridors filled with smoke and no lights, finding a backup plan is not much of an option.

If that wasn't enough for the poor girl, there was a small earthquake less than one hour later! With the Fire and Earth, I was half expecting the Wind and Water to strike in the next hour!

Pickpocketing/Theft

I was going to start this chapter by saying I haven't had that much stuff stolen while travelling... then I realised otherwise:

- 2 x surfboards (in separate incidents)
- 2 x backpacks (in separate incidents)
- 3 x cameras (in separate incidents)
- 2 x pairs of thongs (in separate incidents)
- Small amount of cash
- All my underpants
- Phone

This sounds like a lot, but then again, this is during the space of over 1200 nights in hostels. A number of the incidents were quite funny too! Let's be honest, having two surfboards stolen isn't much fun at all, but some of the other incidents were pretty amusing, as below.

Lumix

I had a trip booked to go to Bali (Indonesia) then on to Europe. My camera at the time was a Panasonic Lumix compact camera. Problem was I got some sand in the lens, so the lens would often get stuck. It was a great camera however, so I bought another identical one before starting my trip; taking both with me. After two weeks in Bali, the broken camera got even worse and got to the point where it basically wasn't working at all. i.e. you had to smash it on a table to get it to turn on. It probably had about five photos left in it before it was totally stuffed. One night I was about to go out, and stood paused for a few moments deliberating which camera to take; should I take the stuffed one, in which I probably won't be able to take any photos, or the new one which I may well lose once I've had a few drinkies? I ponder this for a while, then go for the broken one.

Good choice.

Someone pickpocketed me that night. I thought it was pretty funny actually – someone stealing a camera that doesn't work! Fortunately I had copied my photos off it before I went out so it was no loss to me. It was then time to start using the new camera. Seeing as I'd killed about four cameras in the past due to sand, I vowed sand would not cause the loss of my new camera.

I would be wrong.

I take the utmost care of this camera; not taking it to the beach at all and it survived the rest of my Bali trip. It then makes it to Europe where it survives Iceland too. Months later I'm in Germany for Oktoberfest, 300km from the beach. Surely it would be safe here? Wrong. Coming back from a huge party I'm playing around on the swing set in my campground with a girl, then go to my tent. I take everything out of my pockets and realise…. Shit… where's my camera? I go back to the swing set, sift through sand, and yes, buried deep in the sand is my camera, and yes, it's no longer working properly either. Bugger!

I continue travelling with it, where its function deteriorates over time. By the time I get to Barcelona (Spain) it's totally stuffed. I decide tomorrow I'll buy a new camera, and take my camera out for one last time. Funniest thing; my camera gets pickpocketed. Mwahahahaha! That's two non-working cameras in a row that have been pickpocketed from me now! It was a truly epic night out that night so I'm disappointed I couldn't have those photos, but still funny!

Single Use Camera

Another funny story was when I was in Hawaii with my Dad and brother (we flew there for free – see Chapter 15). I needed a new camera so I went to a shop and saw a nice masculine-looking black camera there. I bought it, went back to the hotel and opened my new purchase. "Oh man you gotta be bloody kidding me!!" It's not the black camera that was on display – it's the same camera but in a bright sparkly pink version. Faark. It's too far to go back to the store, so I have to keep it. Dad and my brother are in hysterics. Dad's laughing so much he can barely breathe. They both find this highly amusing and pretend they care by saying things like, "Oh well at least no one's going to steal it!" and "It's so bright there's no way you can lose it!" followed by lots of laughs.

They would both be wrong; I would lose my camera the very first time I use it!

50 hours later I'm with my Dad and brother at a Hawaiian Luau. This is a cultural event where they put on lots of amazing food and showcase Hawaiian dances and culture. It also includes one free drink. This 'one free drink' would become something akin to the famous "I'm only going to have a quiet one tonight". That is, a night of epic proportions.

As it turns out, most of the people at the 150 or so person event don't drink. This leaves a heck of a lot of spare Mai Tai's that, as Australians, we feel obliged to consume. These sugary drinks are of course expertly created using the lowest quality ingredients possible. Hangover from hell will be coming up, but a few drinks in this is not something we're thinking about. We then befriend the camp barman and get lots more. We are now royally tanked. Note, until this point I've never seen my dad have more than a single glass of wine. We're now the stereotypical loud rowdy Aussies at the cultural event that we no longer seem to care much about. Once that finishes we spill over into a nearby bar and continue the shenanigans. What happens after that is anyone's guess, but needless to say my night ends with me losing my two-day-old 'non-losable' camera!

Backpack of Dirty Undies

Once at a hostel in Australia I was sharing a room with some other guy who seemed nice and normal enough… until one day I came back to see that he had left, stealing my backpack and all my dirty underpants. WTF?!? The backpack I can understand, but seriously, my *dirty underpant*s?? Urgh, I can only imagine him sitting somewhere, sniffing my undies and having a bat. Ergh! Fortunately someone dropped off my backpack at the hostel a month later. The underpants he kept. Weird; though not something I wanted back either!

Preventing Pickpocketing

Certain places in the world are infamous for pickpocketing. Barcelona is one of them. Almost everyone I know that's been to Barcelona has been pickpocketed. I vowed this would not be me. I even knew the tactic – a group of people will approach you pretending to be drunk and give you a drunken hug and in doing so, take your phone/wallet/camera. I knew the tactic so I vowed that this would not happen to me. First night out, I've had a few drinkies and feeling pretty happy, so of course I wanted to give the friendly guys a hug too. Moments after they walk off; think, "Oh no," check pockets; "Fuck! Arseholes!"

I've also had my phone stolen in Guatemala. This was during the town's annual fair, so lots of outsiders were there, including a few unscrupulous people. Walking down the street it wasn't very crowded at all, except for a small section of about 10m where a tuk-tuk was stopped on the road, forcing people to squeeze by. If the whole place were crowded for sure I would have kept my items in my hands, but it was only this small section. I started to go through, but the crowd wasn't moving, so I decided just to back out, however someone was standing their ground not letting me go backwards. "What the hell?!?" I'm thinking, as there was no need for that. I then immediately realise, and check my pockets. Ah, what a prick. Phone gone. Even realising immediately afterwards, there's nothing you can do as it could be any one of ten or so people and you can't realistically go around shaking everyone. Best move to make is to try and borrow someone's phone as soon as possible and call your phone. Just listen for your ringtone, or look for the person trying to stop a phone ringing.

If you do get something stolen, make sure to tell the authorities and get a police report within 24 hours of the incident happening. All insurers have a clause requiring this. Don't get the report within 24 hours and you're not covered. Make sure to have a good read of your insurance Policy Wording to see exactly what you're covered for, and what you need to do for a claim to be accepted. You're generally covered for a lot fewer things than you think you might be too. As an example, some friends of mine booked a sailing trip from Panama to Colombia. Pickup was at 4am. The group of four of them were waiting in the lobby of the hostel, which was deserted other than the old man at reception. When their shuttle came, they first chucked their packs in, then went back inside to get their daypacks. One of the girls sees her daypack zip open, but thinks nothing of it. Hours later, she realises that the $800 she had in there for the boat trip had been stolen in the short time it took to put their packs in the shuttle bus. As the bags were not on her body at the time, she was not covered. Considering the sacrifices in comfort you make just to save $5 travelling, to lose $800 from one quick lapse of guard totally sucks, especially when you can't get it back! Even if it were stolen from her person, her top-level super-expensive insurance only would have covered a maximum of $200 cash. Know what you're covered for!

Border Crossings

Border crossings are generally pretty easy and hassle free-ish. Just make sure not to have any drugs with you; particularly if they are someone else's. No shit you would say, but it's not always that easy. I have some friends that were travelling from Cambodia to Laos, in which they rode in a tuk-tuk a few hours to get to the border. Halfway along they needed to pee. They went to get their packs to take in with them, but the tuk-tuk driver says he'll look after them, and against better judgement but not wanting to appear rude they went to the toilet while he stayed with the packs. Coming out, they guy was still there, so they were happy he didn't run off with their stuff. They continue on and cross through the border, then on the other side when they open their packs they discover a bag of white powder. Shit!! They immediately threw it away and got the hell out of there. Although they were extremely lucky not to get caught at the border (could have been a seriously long jail term), the just-as-scary thought is that the tuk-tuk driver has no doubt called ahead to his friends in Laos saying to expect two tall blonde Dutch girls with the drugs on them. The value of these drugs in Laos would be a *huge* amount considering the local wage and people may be willing to do anything to get it off them. They got out of the town as quickly as possible and fortunately no one found them.

Thoroughly check your bag when you pack up at your hostel, lock your bags and don't let them out of your sight as much as possible.

When Shit Goes Down

It's not a backpacking trip unless some shit goes down; be it running out of money, losing your passport, getting stranded somewhere, getting in trouble with the police, getting injured or sick, kidnapped or something like that. Definitely not something you plan on happening, but if and when it does, it can easily feel like there's no way out. Deep down you know you'll get out of it, but you still are stuck, very distressed wondering how the hell you're going to get out of it. This is where you just have to rely on Providence. You know that no matter how bad it seems, you will always get out of it. This is all that matters. The 'how' is not so important. As impossible as it seems, it *will* work out… somehow. Positive attitude really helps. Through numerous random encounters I happen to personally know quite well six multi-millionaire CEO's (one was the director of a company worth *billions*). These are people that are all extremely pragmatic and certainly not tree-hugging, pot-smoking, LSD taking hippies. Interestingly enough however, when I asked them what the number one rule in business was, they all said the same thing… visualise. Yes. All six of them said the number one rule in business is simply to visualise your goals. Don't just think about it though; you really have to imagine it all; imagine signing that contract; the type of pen you're using, what people are wearing, the feel of the paper, the sound the pen makes, the feeling of the air-conditioned office, the smell of the new carpet, the feeling of the handshake. The path will work itself out. Just make the intention and the rest will work itself out. How this relates to backpacking is that when you're in the shit, imagine yourself with money again, or healthy again, back with your family again, etc. Really *paint* the picture and set the energies to manifest your goal.

As briefly mentioned previously, within a few short days of my trip to Thailand, I was in a location I didn't like, still very sick, on the other side of the island, realising I had a completely empty bank account with *zero* money. I also had an almost empty petrol tank in my motorbike; and didn't even have enough money to put the $3 worth of fuel I needed to get back to my hostel. I was completely alone physically and felt just so much more alone mentally. I remember knowing it would work out, but for the life of me had no idea how. After having my bags left in Australia, getting food poisoning, getting my other bank card and cash stolen, getting totally ripped off on a suit and being in a place so totally alone, then completely out of money as well; I was right on the verge of just breaking down and having a good old cry. I'd never been this down in my life. I was walking away from the ATM with a feeling of despair, when two girls went past on motorbikes yelling and waving at me. Probably just some random girls screaming, having a good time I thought. Then they stopped. Still yelling and waving, they walked up to me and gave me a big hug. Damn; it was the two Aussie girls I met at the front of the plane on the way from Melbourne to Bangkok. If I hadn't gone to the effort to walk around the plane chatting to all sorts of people, this wouldn't have happened. I told them my story and in an instant I went from being in a state of total despair to being a happy traveller. They paid for petrol for my bike and we went to the beach for a great swim together, then they paid for dinner for me as well. One of them told me how when she was in China she accidently crashed her bike into some old lady and had to spend three days in jail, not knowing how long she'd be there for. Hearing that made my misfortune pale in comparison.

The very next morning, my backpack from Australia finally arrived, and going through it, I found a bag of money which I thought was stolen from me on my first night out (turns out I just split my money and cards before I left Australia, putting half in my backpack). I then took the next ferry to Koh Phangan where it changed from being a really, really shitty trip, to a fun trip (albeit with a few more mishaps). The cash in my pack was enough to tie me through until the bank transfer was complete and I had money again. There's none of that that I could have planned; it just worked out.

Another time (as mentioned previously) I was in the outskirts of the Sahara Desert with just enough money for my bus ticket, with just 30c spare. This is in the desert, so there's no power and sure as hell no ATM. As it was, my travel card was empty too, so that wouldn't have helped either. Fortunately I made the 14hr bus journey into Fez; obviously not buying anything along the way. Arriving in Fez I tried using my other credit card, but this wasn't working either. Shit. I checked into a hotel, and with a stroke of luck they didn't require the money upfront, unlike every single other place on my trip. Winning so far! I then checked into my room and was *highly* surprised to see that the person in the room directly next to mine was none other than a girl I made friends with in Marrakech (on the other side of Morocco) days beforehand. She lent me some money and we went out for dinner. The next day I found a different ATM that accepted my spare card and I'm all good. Phew!

My travel card also ran out in Munich, Germany, but fortunately I had juuuust enough money to catch the train to see my aunt (€37 for the train and I had €38), and the three days there was enough for the funds transfer on my card.

If you believe it will work out (even if you have to lie to yourself), it will work out. I think you can also see why I say never to get a pre-paid travel card!

Changing Location

Changing location is often the most likely place where stuff will go wrong, but you can minimise a lot of hassle by following a few simple steps, as outlined in the checklist below. I recommend saving a copy on your phone to use as a checklist whenever you change location. Here's the checklist I use:

- Hostel booked, directions and hostel phone number saved to your phone
    - *Record how much you should pay on arrival*
- Transport booked
    - *Ensure you have recorded the name of the transport company you're using*
    - *Download map of new location in phone (if not on a data plan). See the 'Know Where You Are' section in Chapter 1 on how to do this*
    - *"Star" location of hostel in maps on phone*

- If doing a border crossing:
  - *Exchange rate recorded*
  - *Time zone difference checked*
  - *Border fee (if applicable) checked. Ensure you have enough cash with you for this*
  - *Have printout of ticket exiting country (where required)*
  - *Have passport handy*
  - *Emergency and reverse call numbers of new country recorded*
- Email your family with new location so in case you go missing they have some lead
- Ensure your phone and laptop are charged so you have some entertainment on the journey
- Check you've packed up *all* your things:
  - *Phone and camera chargers*
  - *Sunglasses*
  - *Camera*
  - *Pillow*
  - *Toiletries (shampoo often gets left in the shower)*
  - *Massage poster (if applicable)*
  - *Towel or any clothes that you've hung out to dry*
  - *Everything removed from locker*
  - *Didgeridoo (this probably doesn't relate to most people!)*
- Get key deposit back
  - *If you have an early morning departure, get the deposit back the night before. Make sure to pack all your bags the night beforehand too*
- Make sure to lock your bags and never let them out of your sight, especially if doing a border crossing

Everything in the above list is fairly obvious, but at the same time, easily forgettable. Before I wrote this list, I had to go from Guatemala to Mexico for a few days for a visa-run. After a few days there, I had booked to do a tour one morning. I got up in time and sat down to a leisurely breakfast, until the hostel owner yelled out to me that my pickup was there. Huh? I was confused as hell as I wasn't expecting it for another hour! I scurried onto the bus; where I later realised that there's a one-hour time zone difference between Guatemala and Mexico! I can't believe it took me three days to realise this! A previous time in Australia, I had to fly to Adelaide for a job interview. I arrived on time yet the boss seemed a little pissed off, as if I was late or something. The interview went fine, but for the rest of the day, everything was happening at bizarre times – all the buses seemed to be running at the wrong time, and even flying out, the plane left half an hour early too. It was only when the announcement came on the plane while arriving back into Sydney that it all make sense, "Make sure to set your clock half an hour forward." Oh shit. So there's a half-hour time zone difference between the states of New South Wales and South Australia, huh!

Yeah, I didn't get the job. Make sure to check if there's a time zone difference before crossing borders!

Trying Different Food

Trying different food is one of the best ways to truly gain the experience of a foreign country. I tend to avoid as much as possible places with an English menu. Generally too, the dodgier the place looks, the better the food. If the building is about to fall down, it has a dirt floor and you eat sitting on milk crates… it's probably the best meal in town. Conversely if it's modern looking, in the tourist area and has English menus, it's almost guaranteed to be expensive and crap. Think about it… the places for tourists only need to look good to draw customers. If the meal is shit, it doesn't matter as there'll be more stupid tourists the next day. The shitty looking places however rely on local, regular customers. The food has to be good for them to stay in business.

I eat a huge amount of street food. Many people are scared of eating it as they think they'll get sick from it, but just look at how busy they all are; there's a constant stream of customers, so you know that the food is reasonably fresh and hasn't been sitting around long. Conversely, many restaurants look like they only get five customers a day, so I'd be very wary of them.

Try new things too. If there's something with an obscure name, try it! That's half the fun. Sticking with things you know is boring. Some things you may be surprised by… although many things that sound shit, taste shit too. At least you get an experience from it though!

Some of the stranger things that I've tried are:

- Hákarl (buried rotten shark); Iceland
- Sheep balls; Greece
- Frogs legs; Indonesia
- Snails; France

- Camel udder; Morocco
- Horse; Japan
- Fresh (still beating) snakes heart taken with a shot of snake blood; China
- Jellyfish, sea urchin, sea cucumber, yak, deep-fried goose head, pigs intestine, bull frog, chickens feet, snake; China
- Snake whiskey; China
- Crickets, cactus, chocolate-coated ants; Mexico
- Pigs foot; Ireland
- Pork knuckle; Germany
- Kangaroo, crocodile, snake; Australia
- Rabbit; Cuba and El Salvador
- Chicken heart, cow stomach soup; Colombia
- Live termites (straight from the nest); Nicaragua

Frog's legs, snails, rabbit, chicken heart and yak are absolutely delicious. Yak is easily the best meat I've ever had, hands down, with frogs legs as my second favourite. Far better than a steak. Absolutely delicious. Snails are great too. Crocodile is good too; a cross between chicken and fish. Kangaroo isn't odd at all in Australia – it's quite common. Very high in protein and very low in fat. Good eating. Anything pig is good. Pig's foot and pork knuckle are fantastic, even pigs intestine is surprisingly good. Horse is tasty. Crickets and ants aren't too bad, but not something I'd feel the craving for. Bullfrog tastes pretty good, but is so full of bones that it's not really worth eating. Termites are pretty good too; they taste like herbs.

Now the not so good bits. Sheep balls look really good – looks like really tender chicken, but damn, it doesn't taste like it. I had them with a bunch of girls that actually quite liked them, but hey, probably not the first time they've had balls in their mouth. Camel udder was really bad too. I mean come on; it's the boob of a camel. Basically just sloppy fat. I suppose though, it's not the first time I've had a boob in my mouth either, so I've kind of lost my sheep's balls excuse. Jellyfish is better, though still not that great. You need a lot of vinegar sauce to give it some flavour. It's just like tough flavourless jelly. Sea cucumber isn't too bad. It's not *bad*, but it's not good either, yet in China you can easily pay more than $3,000 per kilo. They look slightly like a penis so the Chinese reckon it's good for your dick and charge ridiculous amounts for it. Do grapefruits grow your tits? No? Then sea cucumber probably isn't going to grow your dick either.

Sea urchin is terrible. Imagine a big spiky thing sitting 10cm above your plate, looking like a naval mine or one of those alien ships from War of the Worlds. Inside is a green paste with the taste and consistency of snot. Solution: fill it with soy sauce and wasabi and try and swallow it. Deep-fried goose head isn't that great either, nor is chicken feet.

This all pales however to the experience of Hákarl in Iceland. It is said to be the most disgusting food on this planet, and with good reason. If fermented, ammonia-filled, poisonous rotten fish does not appeal to you, then you probably won't like Hákarl either. Essentially it is the Greenland Shark, which is so poisonous that eating enough can cause death. To neutralise the poison, after catching the shark they bury it in the ground for three months until it goes rotten and decomposed. This action breaks down the poison. After this, the soggy, putrid rotten shark is hung up to dry a few more months. End result is rotten fish with a huge ammonia content; smelling like bleach mixed with foul-smelling urine. Standard response to putting some in your mouth is to vomit. What made it even worse for me, is that I had some bad Hákarl. Yes, some people in the hostel bought some and left it in the fridge for a few days until a rotten yellow crust started to form. Even just opening the container stunk out the entire three-storey hostel. While dry-retching, I gingerly fished a piece out, screwed my eyes shut, and tried to swallow it, but just vomited it out the window. The putrid rotten shark sadly wasn't for me.

The snake heart was an experience too. I remember years ago seeing the movie 'The Beach' where good old Leonardo Di Caprio takes a shot of snake blood, thinking I would *never* do that; however after seeing it on offer in a hostel in China some years later, I couldn't resist! We pre-ordered the night before so the old Chinese lady could catch the snakes. Come the night, we get greeted by the sight of an old weathered Chinese woman clutching a moving hessian bag of live snakes. She reaches in, pulls one writhing snake out and cuts its head off with a pair of scissors, then holding it by the tail, wrings it down, squeezing its blood into a shot glass. What the fuck!! This freaks me out a bit and I'm starting to shit myself. She then repeats this with another five snakes, and soon we have a table consisting of six snake heads, six shot glasses full of warm snake blood mixed with Baijiu (strong Chinese whiskey) and six headless snake bodies slithering around everywhere on the table. Faaark. The intense in-your-face visuals have got my heart pumping and adrenaline surging. I'm shitting myself. She then gets the scissors and starts cutting up the belly of one of the snakes and pulls out the heart; still beating. Faaaaarrrrkkk! The visuals were just getting a bit intense! I stick the heart on my tongue, feeling it still beat, take the shot and…. Hmmmm… actually not too bad. The whole preparation in front of your face really freaks you out, but the heart and the blood weren't bad at all actually! She later cooked up the snakes too and we had a good dinner. It may seem mean doing that to the snakes, but at least we were eating the full snake, unlike in Western societies where they would baulk at the thought of eating anything other than good cuts of beef generally.

The snake whiskey was pretty full on too. Going to a restaurant for lunch, I see on the counter large glass vats containing all sorts of spices, as well as a bunch of large coiled up dangerous looking snakes, topped up with Baijiu whiskey. Well it may be lunch time, but this is something I have to try! Bloody strong I'll tell you that, though altogether not too bad.

I say try all you can, but always make sure you're not eating something unethical or endangered.

Getting Tailor-Made Clothing

You can definitely get some great tailor-made clothes overseas, but make sure to do it right. As mentioned previously, don't go to a shop that a local takes you to as it will be overpriced. There should generally be some sort of market area full of tailors. Go for a walk around and check out the suits made for other people there. Sit around for a while and observe the reactions of people when they try on the clothes made for them. How does it look on them? The sample suits aren't a great way to get a feel for the quality, as obviously they'd make these the best possible. Best to observe the customers in coming for their pickup.

Never get a suit made up based on the description given by the salespersons. If they describe a suit, it will probably be shit (this is what I experienced in Thailand). Ideally try on a sample suit that they have and get it custom made for you. Other option is to select a suit from a catalogue. This can be a risk, but can work out great too. In China I had a wool overcoat made from a catalogue and it was just damn brilliant! I followed up with buying another 15 business shirts and a few pairs of trousers. My advice when buying tailor-made clothes is just to get a shirt made up first. These are cheap, and will be the best indicator of quality and tailor skill. If the shirt hangs badly, chances are the suit will look bad too. Conversely, if the shirt suits you perfectly, you can be confident it will be worth your while to use the same people for a suit too. Once again, even if you want five shirts or so, just get one made up first to ensure they get the cut the way you want. Also make sure you are in town for plenty of time. It will always take longer than they say. If you don't have much time it may either not be ready in time, or if it is ready, it won't leave time for alterations.

Avoid places that try to 'sell' you a suit. If they keep saying how brilliant it looks on you, you know they are better salespersons than tailors. If, however you try something on and they look uncertain, then you know they are more likely to be trying to make you look good in a quality suit as opposed to just trying to get money out of you.

Photography

Travelling around, I realise just how little people know about their cameras, even those people lugging around big SLR's. Most people, it appears, put their camera on the Auto function, point the camera in the general direction and fire off a few shots. That still works of course, but you can improve your photos with a few simple tricks.

As quite a photography enthusiast, I believe I should add some valuable information in here, however I still *highly* recommend the books by Scott Kelby. His books are a whole other level of awesomeness. It's not pages and pages of complicated stuff; rather it is straight to the point and just tells you only what you need to know. It's brilliant, and even if you have a crap camera, probably still worth getting. Below however are my main tips that can typically be used with crap Point and Shoot cameras too.

Photography with a Crap Camera

There's typically not too much you can change with a point and shoot (P&S) camera, but the one thing you should definitely learn how to change is the White Balance. This can make a huge difference as this is what controls the 'temperature' of the colour. That is, if it's a warm brown or a cool blue. This is particularly useful for moody clouds, vibrant sunsets or making people look browner. In fact, even though I have top-end professional camera gear some of my best shots I took with a 5 megapixel credit-sized camera just because I chose the right white balance. So which do you choose? 90% of the time the 'Cloudy' setting will be best, giving you warmer, more vivid photos. Try it. Note, if your camera is on Full Auto you may not be able to change the white balance. If this is the case, change the dial to 'P' or 'Program'. This is essentially Auto, but allows you to change a few things such as white balance, flash mode and so on.

Want to take a photo of a flower or person with the background out of focus? Zoom in. The more zoom you use the more the background will be out of focus. Zoom your camera all the way in, then walk backwards until it is framed right. Make sure too that the background is as far away as possible from the subject too; if the person is in front of a wall this will not work. The more zoom a camera has the better the effect will be, but expect some loss of quality at past 10x zoom or so. Also, only use this much zoom if there's good light as more zoom equals more camera shake. Experiment with it.

You may find that the camera will just focus on the background, not the subject in the foreground. If this is the case, put the subject in the middle of the frame, hold the shutter button halfway (to lock the focus on the person/flower), then recompose (frame the picture how you want) and press the button the rest of the way. If this still doesn't work, go to the camera menu and change the autofocus option to 'Centre point'.

Want a great night shot? Don't use any zoom. With no zoom, the camera is more sensitive to light and will make better photos. Set the camera on something solid and set the self-timer to 2 seconds. Put your hand through the camera strap (so you don't lose it off a railing or something) but don't hold the camera. Point it in the right direction then press the shutter button and let go. By having the two second timer it means it's not getting any shake from when you press the shutter button.

For the tripod I highly recommend the tiny travel Gorilapod's. These are small, lightweight flexible tripods (length of a spoon) that you can use to grab onto tree branches, handrails, etc. You can find them in your camera store or Amazon. Buy the real one, don't settle for cheaper variations.

They say you're not meant to have electronics on during takeoff and landing when flying, but what a load of crap. Taking a photo will not send the plane spiralling out of the sky. Does your camera stuff up your car GPS? If you make a phone call does your GPS go haywire? No. This rule is just in place so people aren't distracted if there's an emergency. Just turn off the sound on the camera so you don't freak out the other passengers when taking pictures.

Photography with a Camera Including Manual Control

If you have an 'M', 'S', or 'A' function on your camera, you have manual control. Embrace it. It's not as scary as it sounds and you can produce *much* better photos.

In addition to the tips above, I've added the extra functionality that you can do here.

Background out of focus: Set the camera to 'A' and adjust it to its lowest value (generally about 2 or so). Follow the rest of the directions above.

Night shot: I've lost count of how many times I see people take a night photo and show me excitedly the photo on the back of the camera thinking it's a great photo. Sorry, but generally they're really, really crap each time. A photo that looks great on your small camera screen may look terrible on the computer. A few quick bits of advice and then they're taking much better photos. You should see how excited they become then!

Photography is a mix of aperture, ISO (sensor sensitivity) and speed. For night shots, select M and *always* set the aperture to the lowest value possible. This leaves just ISO and speed. Generally you want no more than ISO 400 or so or else the shot will be very grainy. Therefore, start at ISO 400 and adjust the shutter speed until the exposure is correct. You should see a bar at the bottom of your screen that says when the exposure is correct. Put your camera on a tripod or hard surface, select the 2 second timer and take the photo. If there's lots of light so the shutter open time is short, you can reduce the ISO, however if there's not much light, or it's windy so the photo is blurred (either from the camera moving, or trees in the photo moving), select a higher ISO and quicker shutter speed. It's that simple.

You can use the speed to be creative too. For shots of the sea or lakes, I like to experiment. A longer shutter speed will make the water look smoother and more mysterious. If there are waves, you may want a shorter shutter speed to capture the action of the wave.

For shots through an aeroplane window, use the 'A' mode, select the lowest value and hold the camera right up to the window. The lens should be right on the window to reduce background reflection. Even if the window is very dirty you can still get a very clean shot. Laws of optics! I have a photo of the peak of a snow-capped volcano poking through the clouds in Mexico that everyone thinks I must have taken from a higher mountain. I just snapped it through the aeroplane window, but I'm happy to let people think I'm actually a hard-core mountain climber!

Waterfalls: We've all seen those great photos of small streams and waterfalls where the water looks more like soft clouds. If you have a simple camera with manual control, you may be able to do that too, to some degree. This is most easily done by selecting the 'S' mode ('T' on some cameras) and using the longest shutter time possible without the photo overexposing (going white and washed out). A bit of overexposure is fine as you can darken it in a graphics program, but make sure it's not clipped (too overexposed). If you're outside in the sun there will be so much light that you can probably get a photo at only 1/8 second or so. There will be some movement in the photo, but not much. Professionals use 'Neutral Density' filters to reduce the amount of light, but you can do more or less the same by putting your sunglasses in front of the camera. By reducing the amount of light seen by the camera, you can have a longer exposure and therefore softer looking water. The closer you hold your sunglasses to the camera lens the better. Other option is to go in the morning or evening when there's less light. Of course, make sure to use a tripod or sit the camera on a rock or something.

After taking a photo that looks really great, zoom into the picture and check what it *really* looks like. Often photos will look great on your camera screen, until you zoom in and realise it's out of focus or blurry.

Photo Editing

Now most people are more than happy just to take photos on their iPhone, slap on an Instagram filter and call it a day; and there's nothing wrong with that. If you're willing to put a bit more time in however, you can end up with *much* better photos for little extra effort. I have a friend in Guatemala that was interested in photography but only had a really poor quality camera phone. I got him a copy of a certain graphics program, and now he's posting up images that look like they were taken by a professional with professional camera gear. That graphics program my friends, is called Lightroom. It's freakin' awesome! The great thing about it is that unlike Photoshop, you don't have to open and edit individual photos. Instead, you just import your entire photo album folder into the program, in which you can view and edit all your photos easily using highly powerful tools. The best thing is that you can copy a preset to all your photos. I've developed a certain preset that works for 95% of landscape photos. That is, I just select all the photos, hit the button to apply the preset, and they're all *substantially* improved. The remaining 5% I tweak, and job done. Sure you could just use Instragram, but this is only designed for viewing photos on a small screen. *Everything* looks good on a small screen. Get that same awesome-looking Instragram photo on a full size screen and it will look like total crap. Lightroom really is worthwhile.

There are of course people that don't want to edit their photos on the basis of not wanting to alter nature's natural beauty, but remember there's not a single photo in modern National Geographic that has not been edited. Even the best camera in the world does not have the same dynamic range as the human eye. That is, when we look at a scene of high contrast, such as dark trees with bright sky behind them, we can see detail in the sky as well as detail and colour of the trees, yet a camera will just see a white sky and black detail-less trees. Using editing software allows you to get your photos to how you actually saw it… plus a bit extra of course! At the time of writing the cost is $149 for the full license. Sounds like a fair bit, but if you get 5,000 photos substantially improved out of it, then the cost per photo is 3c. Stuff all.

If you like, you can view some of my photos on my website, www.LiveTheAdventureLife.com. If you have any questions about how I've taken any of the photos or if you'd like more info on the presets I use, feel free to send me an email through the Contact page.

Fun with Photography

Here's a trick I do very nearly every time someone asks me to take their photo. It happens exactly the same way every time. Someone approaches you to take their photo. They give you the camera then they turn around and walk back to where they want their photo. No one *ever* walks backwards watching you. This means there's always time to pull a stupid face and snap a selfie while they're walking back, then look natural by the time they turn around. I've done this a good 40 times and never once been caught… at the time! Once while in Seville (in Spain), a 60-year-old Australian couple asked me to take their photo. Of course I did my trick. Funny thing was a few days later when they saw me again and said, laughing, "Hahaha, we found a *very peculiar* photo in our camera!!" and we all had a good laugh about it.

The other trick I like to do when someone gives me their camera to take a photo of them, is to instead turn the camera around and take a serious looking photo of myself. Keeping a totally straight face I then give them the camera back and say 'No problem', and go to walk off like the job is done. The expression on their faces is always priceless. I pretend to note the confusion on their faces, then feign surprise and say "Oh… you want me to take a photo of *you*? That's a little vein, don't you think?"

I kind of like messing with people!

Not Being the Idiot that Loses all their Photos

Of all the stupid things I've done while travelling, losing my photos is not one of them. I hear so many stories of people that travel around with their camera snapping away, just keeping the photos on their SD card, then on the last day getting their camera stolen, and being left with zero photos from a four month trip. If you're one of those people, I feel bad for you, but I still think you're an idiot. Even if you're not travelling with a laptop, there are plenty of things you can do. Simplest is to go to an internet cafe and copy your photos to Cloud and a USB stick. Do this every week or so, or whatever you feel like.

If you have a laptop it's easier. Just copy the photos to your laptop on your One Drive so it's stored on both your laptop and Cloud. This means it's stored locally on your computer so you can access it offline like normal, but is also automatically backed up to the internet. If you lose your laptop, you just need to logon to the net to retrieve all your files. Brilliant. Microsoft One Drive includes 15GB for free, or you can upgrade to 100GB for $2/month (at the time of writing). Bloody well worth it I reckon!

Tropics

As mentioned in the Packing section, bring your own sunscreen. From my experience, Thai sunscreen is pretty useless; certainly not the SPF value it advertises. I'm sure this holds true for many other obscure brands in other third world countries. Stick with the brands that you know.

In humid areas, it is quite possible to get chaff, particularly if you've been swimming and don't get changed out of your wet clothes. In Thailand I had it so bad that it took a layer of skin off my balls. Yep. Just the slight rubbing of balls against leg was enough to turn it into a putrid, smelly, damp mess. Hurt so much I basically couldn't walk... but still had to walk around with my pack and all. Not fun at all. Solution is to use baby powder, or if that's not available, get a huge wad of toilet paper and stick that in your underpants around your tackle. Change paper frequently. It will dry them out and get them on the way to healing.

In the tropics, get a big straw hat. The bigger the better. I bought a huge one in Mexico and was the jealousy of people everywhere. In Cuba I had no less than 20 people ask if they could buy it from me. Large hats are awesome for a variety of reasons. First is protection. With a big hat like that, you don't need sunscreen anywhere on your body – everything is covered! Shade over your whole body helps keep you cool on hot days too. The other benefit that most people don't realise is it functions as an awesome hands-free umbrella! I've been in tropical downpours and stayed dry just because of my hat. This is particularly useful in the wet season where it rains every day. The other benefit of course, is sex appeal! (Well, that's what I like to tell myself at least!) It does actually work though as, as mentioned in the Party chapter, it draws attention and gives the other party a reason to approach you and start a conversation. I became well known on the island of Caye Caulker, Belize because of my hat. The only downside of course is that more street hawkers will approach you too.

Note, when I say a huge hat, I don't mean the stereotypical Mexican sombrero as you'll just look like a stupid western tourist. Better to get a huge straw hat with its own individual style.

If hiking in mosquito-intested areas in the tropics, make sure to take with you some lightweight hiking pants, preferably the sort that can zip off into shorts. When I did my hike in Guatemala, I needed long pants both because of the mosquitoes, as well as the abrasion on my shins from the gumboots. Problem was I didn't have anything lightweight, so instead I had to wear my thermal pants for six days hiking through a hot, tropical swamp. Not very pleasant. In places of malaria it is probably worth your while to take a lightweight long-sleeved shirt too. There are even some shirts that come impregnated with a mosquito repellent.

If you get a fever in the tropics, go to the doctor right away; it might be malaria. It's a simple test to see if you have it, and the sooner you get it treated, the much better you will be for it.

Respect the Law

It can be easy to 'Go Troppo' overseas, particularly in third world countries; that is, to do things you normally wouldn't do at home. While it seems that there's a lot less safety, fewer rules and cops are often corrupt, don't take this to be a free ticket to your unbound fun. Foreign countries have their own justice system that can seem very unfair compared to that in your own country. Penalties can be very harsh too; including execution. Most people don't realise just how harsh the US 'justice' system is. You can be put in prison for things that you probably wouldn't even get fined for in Australia.

I was in St Simons Island, Georgia (USA) for a huge beach party, where there happened to be two other Aussies there too (we were probably the only Aussies the town had seen in years!). We all have a good time until I found out the Aussies ended up in jail. The story goes that there was a small two-man sailboat sitting on the beach. Either they just decided to take it out, or someone said they could, but either way, they went out briefly and came back to cops waiting for them on the beach with handcuffs. I gotta say I couldn't stop laughing when I first found out. "Hahaha, oh jeez, that's *such* an Aussie thing to do, hahaha!" My American friends didn't think it was so funny. While that act in Australia would result in nothing more than the owner of the boat yelling at you for a bit, you apologising, and that being it, things are different in the US. They got charged for a felony, which is the name given to a major crime, like grand theft auto, rape, etc. A felony attracts a *minimum sentence of one year in jail.* I don't know what happened to them. Hopefully they got out of it.

Another time I was in Japan in the ski resort town of Hakuba. I made friends with an Aussie guy at the hostel and we took a bus a few kilometres across town to the only pub (appropriately named 'The Pub') for the New Year's Eve celebration. It was a huge venue and a pretty epic night, but the problem was it was a ski town with deep snow everywhere and a temperature of minus whatever it was. Come 2 a.m. when we're ready to leave, there's no bus so we're shitting ourselves, wondering how to get home. There's no way we could walk as we'd probably die of cold on the way home. Here comes the bright solution; steal a mini-bus. We find one with the door unlocked, so he hops in and starts trying to pull wires out to start it. I'm sitting in the passenger seat as it's just so damn cold and I need to get home. He's trying for a while, then common sense then comes over me. "Dude. Don't mate. This is Japan; penalties are *harsh*. It's not like Australia. You'd go to prison for a long time for this." He continues. "Mate, we're in a small town… we can't steal a bus and no one find us. What the hell are we going to do with it when we arrive??" He continues. I don't blame him as I'm so damn cold as it is and I'd love a ride home too, so I'm half considering it myself, but no, this is crazy. "Nah mate, sorry I'm out," I say, and get out of the van. I then look up to see the public bus to take us home has just arrived. Phew!!

I really do think it's particularly an Aussie thing to make use of something when you need it, then apologise the next day. Where's the crime in that, right? I didn't steal it, I only borrowed it. Sorry, but that's not how most other countries see it.

If you do get caught doing something by the police (whether you are guilty or not), I've been advised to say: "Is there any way we can settle this?" which is a way of opening up for a bribe without directly saying so. You don't want to be going balls in asking directly if you can pay them off. Be subtle about it and with a bit of luck they'll let your crime go in exchange for some money. Only try this in countries known for police corruption. Still never use this as an invitation for going silly. They may let you off, or you may end up in a third-world prison. Best not to do illegal things in the first place.

Beware of different unknown laws in different countries. For example, Dubai is very strict with, well, everything! Even over-the-counter medicines such as cold and flu tablets containing codeine are illegal. Taking in medicine that you've been prescribed back home can land you in jail in Dubai. Refer to Smart Traveller (www.smarttraveller.gov.au) and http://uae-embassy.ae/Embassies/au/Content/1803. Sure as hell don't take any drugs into the UAE, and don't consume any either, even if taking them in a safe place. The authorities can take blood or urine tests and consider that as possession even if you took it before entering the country.

If that's not enough for you, be aware that sex outside of marriage is illegal. Go with your girlfriend to Dubai, sleep with her and you could be sent to prison. As it is, unless you can prove you're married, you can't even check into the same hotel room! *Make sure* to check out the laws of a country before going there. Once again, check out Smart Traveller. It's an excellent resource.

Napping

While certainly not exclusive to travelling, I think it prudent to include this topic. I'm a huge fan of napping and reckon I must be nearly a black belt in it by now.

While living in China I did a lot of experimentation with napping, varying the duration of my nap, such as sleeping as long as I could, or setting my alarm for short naps. After lots of experimentation, I found the best duration to be 23 minutes. I know what you're thinking; 23 mins?!? That's not enough! I'd find it way too difficult to get up!

That's because you're used to sleeping for longer. Here's the crunch; I realised that if you sleep longer than 30 mins, you'll wake up feeling really groggy and it can take a few hours to feel awake. If you sleep less than half an hour though, you wake up feeling super refreshed and energetic; ready for action straight away.

After all this experimentation myself I then read Tim Ferris's book, The 4 Hr Body, in which he says the exact same thing. He settled on 20 mins. This makes sense why I came up with the magic number of 23; three minutes to fall asleep, 20 minutes sleep time. You see for short sleeps you go into 'emergency sleep' mode; that is, straight into REM sleep which is what makes you rested. Your brain knows you don't have long to sleep so it does away with the other bullshit parts of sleep and goes straight to what you need.

The best I ever did was when I was super tired after work but needed to go straight to Mandarin lessons. I set my alarm for 90 seconds, fell asleep, had all sorts of crazy dreams and woke fully refreshed. All, in 90 seconds.

It seems funny to me that in Western culture everyone drinks coffee when they're tired. Erm, if you're tired, you need to rest. Interestingly enough, in China where napping is common there's no coffee or caffeinated tea in the offices. You should see the expression of the Aussie businessmen when they hear this!!

How all this relates to backpacking is that no doubt you will get tired during the day from exploring and what not, and no doubt want to party again at night. Just jump in bed, stick in your earplugs, set your alarm for 23 mins and wake up ready for ak-shun!!

Feeling Lonely

Of course when you're backpacking you're putting up on Facebook pictures of amazing landscapes and photos of great nights out and posts of the awesome things you've been up to, but a large part of backpacking is feeling alone. These are the bits you tend to leave off Facebook. Compared to life back home, guaranteed you will have a lot more ups and downs with higher highs and lower lows. Of course this depends on a few factors; namely where you're going and if you're travelling with a friend or not.

If you're in a first world country with a friend, it's a fairly flat level high and conversely if you're alone in a third world country it can swing wildly between high highs and low lows. Lower lows equate to higher highs. For sure the lowest points of my life were overseas, yet the simple act of meeting a cool person can make you swing from being in despair to being super happy and elated. These days I travel smarter so I'm in far fewer difficult situations, however there can still be many lonely times. You may be in a place full of awesome people and have the time of your life, then you part ways, going different directions and then you're alone again, going to some unknown destination. It can suck too to have an epic trip, but as all those times were with different people, you have no single person to reminisce about that whole epic trip with. I once wrote a bit on Facebook about the loneliness of travelling. It was something that I put off writing for a few months as I felt it was important but I didn't want to admit to feeling lonely. As soon as I hit 'send', I felt that sense of dread.... that feeling of admitting to be weak, the feeling that people will think less of you. ...but the opposite become true. I had so many people replying to me, congratulating me on my post and saying how they felt the same way, yet never wanted to admit to it. There's nothing to be ashamed about. This is not meant to be a depressing statement that everyone is lonely when they travel – it's meant to be an uplifting comment that it's normal to have sad times. You are not the strange person if you feel lonely. If you're feeling lonely, chances are people around you may be feeling the same way too. Have a chat to them!

Chapter Summary

Cultural Experience
• Try all the local things. If you get the chance to experience a foreign cultural event, go for it!

Fire Safety
• If checking into a multistorey hostel, check where the fire exits are

Pickpocketing / Theft
• Watch out for people trying to give you a hug when drinking – they can easily pickpocket you in the process, as the feel of the hug distracts you from the feel of them removing your wallet

• Even in small crowds keep your possessions in your hands, not just in your pockets, or walk around with your hands in your pockets holding onto your possessions

• If your phone is stolen try and borrow someone else's phone as soon as possible and call your phone. Try and listen for your ringtone, or someone trying to stop a phone ringing

Border Crossings
• Thoroughly check your bags the day of doing a border crossing, lock them, and don't let them out of your sight (as much as is possible)

When Shit Goes Down
• Have faith that bad situations will work out, even if you have no idea how. Just believe

• Use the power of visualisation and positive thinking. Set the intention strongly enough and it will happen

Changing Location
• Refer to the Changing Location checklist located in the Appendix

Trying Different Food
• Avoid nice looking places with an English menu – the best meals will generally be from the worst looking place in town. Look for a place that has locals eating in it

• Try street food and obscure things on restaurant menus. Just don't eat unethical food

Tailor-Made Clothing

• Don't go to a shop that someone 'recommends'

• Stay in the shop for a while and observe people coming in to pick up their suit. Are they happy with it? Does it fit them well?

• Never buy a suit based on the description by the sales people. Ideally try on a sample suit there that you like and get them to tailor-make the same suit for your particular dimensions

• It is best to start with ordering a business shirt off them. This will be of low cost, but will demonstrate their tailor skill and material/stitching quality

• Make sure you're in the town long enough – it will always take longer than they say, plus you need time for a fitting and alterations too

• If they keep saying how great the suit will be, it will probably be really bad. Conversely, if they look uncertain as you try on samples, then they are probably trying to make you a proper good looking suit

Photography

• Check out the photography books by Scott Kelby

• Set your White Balance to 'cloudy' for warmer, more vibrant shots

• Zoom in to make the background out of focus when taking photos of people of flowers for example

• If you can't get the right focus, centre the subject in the middle of the frame, hold the shutter release halfway to lock the focus, then recompose and press the button the rest of the way to take the photo

• Don't use zoom for a night shot. This will make the picture more grainy

• Buy a Gorillapod for a small lightweight mini tripod

• If you have a camera with manual control:
  – *To make the background blurry, set it to A mode and select the lowest value. Use this same setting if taking photos through a window. Ensure to hold the camera right up to the glass to prevent background reflection*
  – *For night shots:*
    • *Select the lowest aperture value*
    • *Set the ISO to 400 to start off with*
    • *Adjust the time until the exposure is correct*
    • *If there's a lot of light you can reduce the ISO and therefore result in a longer exposure*
    • *If there's too much movement in the shot or it's very dark, you can increase the ISO to therefore reduce the shutter speed, however more ISO equates to a grainier image*
  – *To take a photo of a waterfall:*
    • *Set your camera to S or T mode and select the longest value without the camera*

overexposing (a bit of overexposure is fine)
  - *Try putting your sunglasses in front of the lens to darken the scene so you can get a longer exposure. If this doesn't work, go when it's darker (morning, evening or cloudy day)*
  - *Use a tripod, or set your camera on a rock*
- When reviewing your photos, zoom in to ensure they're sharp
- Take a stupid selfie whenever someone gives you their camera to take a photo of them
- Consider a photo editing program. I highly recommend Lightroom
- Backup your photos. This can be done by:
  - *Buying a USB drive and backing up in an internet cafe*
  - *Uploading your photos to Facebook*
  - *Saving them to Cloud*
  - *Copying to your laptop and external hard drive*
  - *Copying to a friend's hard drive*

Tropics
- Bring your own sunscreen to third world countries
- Stick baby powder and/or toilet paper in your dacks to avoid chaff
- Get a big straw hat – the bigger the better (means you don't need sunscreen, protects you from the rain and gives you bucket loads of sex appeal)
- Take lightweight pants and shirt if hiking in malaria/dengue fever areas
- If you get a fever, go to the doctor right away – it could be malaria

Respect the Law
- Penalties can be much harsher overseas
- Taking something without permission (even if you intend to return it) is considered stealing and can result in years of jail time
- Ask, "Is there any way we can settle this?"
- Inform yourself about laws before going to different countries, particularly in Middle Eastern countries. Use the Smart Traveller website

Napping
- Take a 23-minute nap in the afternoons. This will recharge you for the night

Feeling Lonely
- Backpacking is awesome fun, but it's the norm to have lonely times too. Don't feel like you're the only person feeling lonely – it happens to everyone

Chapter 14: Getting your Hippy On

I'm currently writing this chapter from inside my pyramid. Yes, you read that right, and I don't mean a metaphorical pyramid either. An actual pyramid, built to accommodate one person. Next to my bed is an incense burner, a candle and a crystal. I'm also sleeping with my head due East to better facilitate lucid dreaming and astral travelling.

I'm in the hippy town of San Marcos, Guatemala where I'm embracing hippy-stuff as much as possible. I came here just to do a Swedish Massage course, but ended up doing:

- Six-day Swedish Full Body Massage course
- Four-day Indian Head Massage course
- Four-day Reiki course
- Seven-day Pranayama Kriya Breath Therapy course
- Neuro-lymphatic massage
- 'Keith the Cacao Sharman' Cacao Ceremony
- Ecstatic Dance
- Men's Cacao Ceremony
- Acupuncture treatment
- Kambô Frog Ceremony
- Week II of the Full Moon Course
- Holotropic Breathwork session
- Self-Healing course, including Tarot and flower essences
- Energy session using Reiki, drums and cymbals
- Yoga

- Meditation, including things such as Tarot and past life regression
- Sound healing session
- Other things with new-found friends, such as massage swaps, didgeridoo jamming, etc.

Needless to say, I got quite well known in the town for doing so much. Most days would involve doing one course after the other; packing as much as possible into the one day. Pretty soon I would go from a hippy-disliking sceptic to a person where just about all conversations with people would be about chakras, lucid dreaming, astral travelling, auras, meridians, channelled messages, Reiki, energies, frog spirits and so on. I couldn't believe that once in conversation I even used the phrase "Their negative energy really affected me." What the hell happened to me??!

Interestingly enough, a lot of it I was starting to believe. I have intent to write a book entitled 'Hippy Spiritual Stuff for Sceptics', but I'm still a long way off that yet. I believe there are a lot of people out there who are interested in trying out some hippy stuff, but don't know where to begin, and if you start in the wrong place it can totally put you off. I think there's a scale that many things can be put on, from utter crap, plausible, to downright true. Some things definitely worked for me, as described herein.

You may wonder why I'm including this hippy stuff in this book on backpacking… it's because many people say they go backpacking 'to find themselves', yet 99% of the people that say this just go from town to town partying, hiking, exploring, etc, without ever meditating or looking inward. I think backpacking is the perfect opportunity to discover yourself more and undertake such courses. While working, it is too hard to justify taking a week's holidays and paying a sum of money for something that probably doesn't work. As you're making greater sacrifices to do the course, you will probably expect more from it, and ultimately be disappointed. While travelling however, you have all the time in the world, plus you're not affected by work stress. Additionally, it's probably much cheaper to do these courses away from home.

As such, I made sure to sample as much as I could (within reason) in San Marcos. I've included some of my experiences in this book, but as it's not specifically a part of backpacking, I've put this in the Supplementary Material section at the back of the book.

Chapter Summary

• Try different things while overseas. It's a great opportunity to try things you wouldn't normally have the time for back home. You may well find it life-changing

• If interested in yoga, it pays to find someone to do it one-on-one with to properly understand it. It helps to have a skill (such as massage) such you can just do a skill swap instead of paying for it

• If you get the opportunity, participate in a cacao ceremony. If there's none available in your area, you can still order cacao online

• Take a look into breathing techniques such as Pranayama Kriya or Holotropic Breathwork. These should be done guided due to the emotions that can be released

Chapter 15: Making, Saving, Spending Money

Free Flights

Seeing as flights are one of the most expensive parts of a trip, it makes sense to try and do this for free. How? Enter competitions. Be smart about what you enter however; avoid it if you have to pay money, and realise that the harder the competition is, the better. There was once a Jetstar (Australian Airline) competition which involved taking a photo of a specific airbrushed plane and writing about your favourite Jetstar destination on Twitter. This seemed like too much work to me so I ignored it, then thought, "Wait, it *is* too hard… no bastard will enter!" It ended up being a hugely difficult process to enter, so I *knew* I was going to win. I was so confident I was telling people about the competition I was about to win, of which they were quick to shoot me down. Imagine my smiles when a week later I have $5,000 worth of flights!! Ended up being enough for my dad, brother and I to go to Hawaii, my brother and his girlfriend to Fiji and me to Japan. Worth it I reckon.

You can get rewards miles with airlines too, but you have to fly a *huge* amount to get anything out of it. Yes, it's still something for nothing so of course I recommend it, but each flight you make will only give you a miniscule amount of reward, so make sure never to let airline brand affect your flight choice. That is, if you want to fly Paris to New York and there's a flight with another airline that's $50 cheaper than the airline you have the rewards program with, go with the cheaper flight.

Tipping

What tipping is not: a city in China. What tipping is: A standard practice in most of the world of giving extra money to service staff after receiving unexpected exceptional service; or if you're in the USA or Canada, a complicated scheme where managers of service staff severely underpay their staff so that customers have to pay them instead.

Fortunately in most places in the world, tipping remains in its true intended form; that is, if service or the overall experience exceeds your expectations you can give some extra money, or for people on the road with not much change, like cab drivers and pizza delivery drivers it's often a case of 'keep the change', or rounding up to the next dollar. Even so, this isn't always the case as being a previous pizza delivery driver myself; many people did still ask for the 5c back from a $19.95 delivery. For a 6hr shift I'd rarely make more than $5 tips.

In other places however it is much different; particularly the USA and Canada. We all know that the US has an abysmal minimum wage, but it gets much scarier; in professions where tipping is customary, the minimum wage dives down to a paltry $2.13 per hour… for an adult. Yes, if you're at a bar buying drinks all night without tipping the barman, they may end the night with just $15 after working their arse off all night.

Problem is most travellers don't know this.

I mean, let's be honest; we know that 'it's customary to tip in the USA', but unless you go to the effort to check online before you go, no doubt you won't know just how dire it is for the wait staff. I went to Quebec (Canada) knowing nothing of the above thinking 10% was a standard tip. I paid this, and even found this difficult as, for an Australian, if a meal is advertised as $12, then $12 is all you pay. If you're not used to North American culture, then it's a bit of a shock when tax gets added on, then you have to tip as well, and now the meal is more than you thought and out of your budget. Being ingrained with the Australian culture of not needing to tip, it can be tempting to reduce the tip to 5% or so as the understanding is that it's just a 'tip'. I gave the 10% feeling very proud of myself and was surprised to see the waiter look quite angry. I later found out it's meant to be more like 18-20%! No wonder he was unhappy! Without any signs around to say the waiters don't actually get paid and what the tip should be, then how should I know? It's so friggin stupid and the concept really pisses me off. I don't get why it's up to the customers to pay the staff, not the restaurant owner.

It's particularly bad in tourist areas as most people just don't get it (like myself), or just play dumb to get out of paying money that 'they don't have to pay'. If it only says a certain amount on the bill, why pay more, right? Once I was in New York and went on an organised pub crawl. As it was for tourists that don't know about tipping, the ticket said clearly to tip $1 for beers and $2 for cocktails, and the guide told us this too, yet half the group still didn't tip at all. If it weren't for myself and a few other people tipping, the poor barmaid would be working on that crappy $2.13/hr wage.

Once you realise you have to tip, then it becomes confusing… who do you and who don't you tip? Do you tip at McDonalds? What about a normal non-chain fast food place like a kebab shop? What about the barista at Starbucks? I eventually realised it seemed to be a bit of a rule that if you pay upfront (like McDonalds) then you don't tip, but if you get a bill (like a restaurant), then you do tip. Always tip bartenders. This works in your favour too, as you can get a more alcoholic drink and faster service too. Generally it's a minimum of $1 per drink. Add more if it's a cocktail as these take longer to make (just think, in the time it takes to make one mojito they could have sold eight beers; making $8 in tips). Don't tip baristas.

Yay, I learned all this and it (kind of) makes sense now… but imagine my surprise when I found out it doesn't end there. In New York for example, it's *expected* to tip other things like hairdressers, tattoo artists, massage therapists and so on too! Amount is 10-20%. Taxi's 15-20%. Basically the bottom line is that if it's a service, then you should tip.

Best resource to learn about all this madness is the excellent page at Wait but Why: http://waitbutwhy.com/2014/04/everything-Don't-know-tipping.html

To add to the confusion, different countries have different tipping practices. In Mexico for example, you have to tip pretty much everyone. This includes the bagger at the grocery store, the person that 'helps' you park your car even though you don't need them at all, the petrol station attendant and so on. It's only a few pesos though, so it's not going to send you broke. They're always appreciative of the tips too.

Morocco is a different kettle of fish however. *Everyone* is out demanding money. If you give less money than they expect (even if they don't deserve anything at all), don't be surprised if they spit in your face. Fortunately I have not been spat on, but friends have. For an example of how they expect money, I was in the huge market square (Jamaa el Fna) in Marrakech and went to take a general photo of the whole square. Some guy holding a snake sees me with a camera and runs into the frame then demands money because, apparently, I took a photo of his snake. I refused to pay of course but then he started getting super angry, yelling at me, spitting on the ground and so on. I pretty much had to give in and give him some money to avoid being spat on myself. Things like this continued on my trip. The best was on my final day where I had an early morning flight. I left my hotel at 6 a.m. or so and walked to the taxi rank. At this hour, the streets were deserted of people so there were six taxis lined up, waiting for customers. Of course some Moroccan opportunist nearby sees me walking to the taxis with my pack on, so he runs to the front taxi 'waves it down' (the parked taxi in the taxi rank) then demands money from me because he 'flagged down a taxi for me'. What a prick, though I had to laugh at his sheer optimism. Of course he was angrily demanding money (because of course I needed him and he went to so much effort), but fortunately it was my last hour in Morocco and I had lots of coins to get rid of.

Make sure to check on the net where you should tip and how much, and carry around plenty of change. Getting change from a tip can be difficult in some places.

Haggling (Bargaining)

If not familiar with haggling, this is the act of bargaining at markets. You will find that this is standard practice in many countries. It can be very frustrating when you're used to fixed-price items. It's annoying when there's no price tag on anything, so you have to ask them the price of every item that grabs your fancy, yet asking the price sets up the act of negotiation. I was just trying to find out roughly how much it was, and now he's bloody trying to sell it to me!

I'm really not a fan of this as it means you're unable to browse. Asking the price means nothing either, as their first price will be much more than the final price will be. In general, don't ask for the price of an item unless you actually want to buy it.

Haggling is something I used to do very well when I travelled with very little money, but now I don't do it with as much ferocity. You still have to make sure to haggle to some degree though. It can be tempting to think "I make a lot more money than them, so it's no problem to pay more," but if you don't haggle it can be insulting that you're able to pay an absurdly high price without negotiating.

First of all, you should get a rough idea of what a specific item is worth. Try and find a fixed-price store to get an idea of what certain items are worth. These items should be cheaper in the markets. Fixed-price stores can be hard to find in places where you need to haggle, so in these places you're advised to chat with the hostel staff to find out what things should cost, and how ferociously to haggle in general.

Many people say the general rule for a haggling is to start at one-quarter of the starting price and settle on half; however this rule doesn't always hold true, especially outside of tourist areas. Away from tourist areas the original price they offer will be much closer to what it should be. Sometimes the original price they offer will be very good to start off with. In Mexico you would probably only knock 20% off. This is what makes it confusing. If this is the case, just say you'll think about it and go to walk away. If they yell out a lower price then you know it's up for haggling, whereas if they don't say anything then it's probably a reasonable price. Go to another store and ask what their price is. If possible see what the locals are paying. As customs are different in all countries, it is advised to ask the hostel staff what the general etiquette is and what sort of price you should expect to pay for certain items.

Tactics

Note foremost that haggling is not an argument, it's a negotiation. See it as a game, not as them trying to rip you off. These are ancient customs, so play along with it. Treat the seller with respect and have a good-natured haggle. The goal is not to deprive the seller of all their profits, but to reach a mutually agreed final price.

In many third world countries, the word 'luck' is your ticket. For example, if you're in the markets around closing time say, "Last sale, lucky sale! Give it to me for $6!" This also works with things like 'lucky first sale' in the morning, 'lucky Sunday', 'lucky first Monday of the month', etc. You can generally think of some 'lucky' thing about any time or day.

A great phrase to use is: "If you sell it for $10 you'll be happy but I'll be upset. If you sell it for $5 I'll be happy but you'll be upset. Let's both be a little bit happy and a little bit upset and settle on $7."

Of course, the 'walk off' technique is always the most powerful. Get down to a reasonable price, then act on the fence about it for a while, then thank them and say sorry but it's too much and walk off. For sure they'll call out a lower price to you.

Sunglasses from Markets

On the subject of markets, I feel it necessary to include this; don't buy sunglasses from markets, no matter how awesome they look!

The issue is that it's pretty much guaranteed that these sunglasses will offer no UV protection. So what's the issue? No different to not having sunglasses, right? Unfortunately, no; it can actually be very damaging to your eyes. If you're outside in strong light without sunglasses you squint your eyes to reduce the amount of light coming in as much as possible, but with tinted sunnies your pupils dilate more, letting in more UV light. Non-UV-protected sunglasses are damaging your eyes. It's not worth it.

Earning Money

There can be many ways to earn money while travelling. Some are better than others. I met many foreigners in Central America working at hostels or bars earning $1.40/hr, plus free accommodation. This doesn't seem like a good way to me to earn money. It's enough to sustain yourself but nothing more. Good if you're on your last dollar and want to stay overseas as long as possible, but to me it seems better to go back home, save up and come back. Having said this, I have many friends that have worked for months on end in hostels in Central America and absolutely loved it. It's a matter of personal opinion. From my perspective, I lived in a hostel for 2.5 years in Australia while working a normal job. This meant I got to live the backpacker life whilst still making good money. As such when I'm travelling, I like to just travel and not work. Haha, ok, that's not entirely true – while travelling I semi-regularly work 16hr days on book promotion crap and writing new material... but that's different!

Lots of other people make jewellery or baked goods and sell these on the roadside, but I don't agree with this if it's competing with the locals. If you're selling something different and unique that's fine, but if there are already locals selling jewellery or banana bread, then I think it's just rude to compete with them – they need the money to live and raise their kids. If you're selling something unique, then I think that's fine.

If you don't have any craft skills, then a good trick to do is to travel with souvenirs from back home. A great tactic is to buy a bunch of Australian flags for example. Go to a $2 shop back home and buy a bunch of 5ft x 3ft lightweight flags. Out of the packaging they fold down to the size of a golf ball and weigh virtually nothing. Stick them in a compression bag and they take up even less space. Go to a concert, beach party, New Year's Eve celebration, etc and you can be sure to sell them at whatever price you want. Australians in particular like to get wasted at events and run around with an Aussie flag as a superman cape. There'll always be Aussies angry with themselves for not bringing a flag and will pay top dollar for one, no matter how bad the quality. You could make hundreds of dollars in just one night.

Best option however is to learn a skill that backpackers want; namely massage. I learned Swedish full body massage, which is good to learn massage techniques, but is pretty impractical on the trail. For a start, the person needs to be completely naked (which can be difficult in dorms, plus the person may not trust a stranger that it will be a professional massage), you need lots of towels and you pretty much need a massage table. It can be done on the ground or a single bed, but it's still difficult.

Enter Indian Head Massage. Learning this changed my life. The Indian Head Massage is *awesome*! I mean, how often do you hear someone say, "Ergh my neck hurts. Can anyone give me a massage?" The beauty of this massage is that it's done with the person sitting in a normal chair and you need nothing other than some massage oil (can even just use normal cooking oil). Prior to doing a massage course I thought that massage just wasn't for me, as whenever I tried to give a massage to someone I just felt uncoordinated, not in touch with the person and my thumbs hurt within about one minute. After the course however, people were regularly saying it was the best massage they've ever had. It's much easier than you think.

The massage that I do starts on the back and shoulder blades, tops of shoulders, then neck, head and face. Duration is approximately 1hr. Even though the person is sitting outside in a hard chair with flies buzzing around, 90% chance they will fall asleep. Minutes after you finish, they will slowly wake, then take another minute with their eyes closed, then say, "Woooow. That... was... amaaaaazzing!" In general, people won't be able to manage anything more than four-word sentences for the next five minutes. I've had many people say they felt like they'd just smoked pot. It's more of a trip than a massage. For reference, I learned to do this in San Marcos, Guatemala. Cost was approximately $100.

What I did was make a poster on my computer, printed it and had it laminated. It's surprisingly easy to find an internet cafe with a laminator. This means you have a few posters that you keep with you and put up in each hostel you visit. You can use a whiteboard marker to include your phone number or room number in each hostel as it changes.

I generally charge around $15 for one. This might be a bit much for some people so instead, on my poster I say 'By donation. E.g., $15'. This way people know the average price should be $15, but if they can't afford it, then can give me less. Even better than charging money is to do trades. Trade massage with whatever you can; such as other massages, haircuts, jewellery, accommodation; whatever you can manage!

If you're able to make jewellery or are awesome at fire twirling or something like that, you can make money teaching people.

I also recommend taking certain chances once you've weighed up if it sounds dodgy or not. In Madrid (Spain), I was walking down the road and heard someone behind me say, "Speak English?" Expecting it to be a scam, I turned around anyway, and there was a team of three English guys including a photographer with some pretty serious gear. Here came the offer, "Would you be interested in doing a 3hr photo shoot for Sony for €150?" "Jeez yeah, I'd do it for free!!" Unfortunately I had a flight to catch soon, so they negotiated it to a 1hr shoot for €50 (which I would have done for free anyway). All I had to do was go to cafes where'd they pay for my coffee and I'd play the yet-to-be-released 'Sony PSP Go' while they'd take photos. Too easy, and I got the equivalent of $80! I was hoping that after this model shoot that I'd have lots of girls flocking to see me, but alas modelling for a gaming console isn't quite the same as Calvin Klein.

Don't discredit getting sponsored to travel either. A friend of mine from Argentina is currently travelling Asia and getting paid for it. Is she a professional writer? No, it's just a case that not many people from Argentina travel to Asia so many people are interested in it. All she is doing is keeping a blog on Facebook, and has already amassed 6000 followers. She gets paid by occasionally putting in links for businesses.

There are other travel websites that pay travellers for well-written stories too. Just Google it.

Saving Money

Other than making money, you can extend your trip by saving money too, believe it or not. There are so many tricks you can do, but with many of them you have to question, "Is it worth it?"

I met some guys in China that argued with the guy at the entrance to some attraction for about 15 mins to save about 10c. This is just really shit, as for a start, it was cheap as it was, and it was a fixed, signposted price. That's what the Chinese have to pay too. That's just rude and a waste of both your energy and theirs.

I have another friend that walks around with tea bags in his pockets and goes to cafes and asks for a cup of hot water, then leisurely enjoys his tea while sitting at their tables and using their internet. Ok, maybe it's the cafe's fault for not charging him for the cup of hot water, but it's still a bit rude. At Starbucks fair enough, but at independent places it's pushing it a bit.

I know another guy that had to live on $14 for two weeks while in Guatemala (that's $1/day). This involved making friends with people renting houses and sleeping at their house, going to restaurants and eating leftover food, scabbing used teabags and refilling the cup with hot water, etc. It was quite inspiring talking to him actually as he was saying how it was such a great morning and he felt so blessed to get all this stuff.

The above is a bit much for me though. I find the best ways to save money is from the start; getting a good bank card that doesn't charge overseas fees. This can save you a huge amount. Next up is transport as the difference between different flights can be huge. Even better is to use a rideshare service and go by land for shorter distances. And of course, use Couchsurfing for accommodation. Generally to use Couchsurfing you have to give something back, and if you cook for them and buy them drinks, it can soon cost the same amount as a hostel. Therefore it's good to know a few skills such as magic or massage as you can give back without spending a cent. They'll be super happy to receive either as it's something they wouldn't be expecting. You can always clean their house for free too.

Often half people's money is spent on alcohol, so it makes sense to save money here. This of course means staying at places where you can drink your own alcohol, and getting tanked before going out to bars. Even better is to find a cool party hostel and just stay there as you'll save money on transport, plus it's safer too. Make sure to check out the price of the Long Island Ice Teas, as, as mentioned in Chapter 8, this could work out cheaper than beer (alcohol for dollar). Do the 'rum in dark beer bottle' trick I described there too if you're in a hostel which doesn't let you drink your own alcohol.

I always take a deck of cards with me to the bar and do the 'Wanna Bet' trick as described in the Supplementary Material section. Guaranteed to win you a few free drinks. Added bonus is when you do it to a girl, the girl is buying drinks for you, not the other way around. This stops you looking like an 'average chump' and guaranteed you'll have more of a chance with her.

In first-world countries it makes sense to take your own lunch with you. My favourite is flatbread with peanut butter. Easy to travel with, easy to prepare and delicious. In third world countries however, it will probably cost a similar amount to buy lunch as to make your own.

If going to attractions in first-world countries, there's never a need to pay the advertised price. There's always discounts in tourist brochures or online.

Of course, don't forget about saving money back home. It seems crazy how people will forego nice comfortable interstate buses to instead navigate five different crowded and uncomfortable chicken buses taking twice as long just to save $5, yet will gladly spend this on just one beer back home. It's a heck of a lot easier to save money back home, but doing the dodgy things is half the fun. I'm guilty of not spending $1.50 a night for air-con in hot-and-humid Bali just so I could have an ice cream instead, or walking 7km on snow-covered sidewalks in Quebec to save spending $3 on the bus, just to go out that night and spend $40 on drinks. Even in Nicaragua where taxis are only $0.40 to anywhere in the city, I'll still walk to my hostel, struggling with all my bags for 4km in the heat. There's no need to torture yourself for the sake of a dollar, but you're still getting exercise while walking, and catching chicken buses really isn't that bad. Save money where you can, but don't do it if it results in you hating life. Saving money back home is one heck of a lot easier!

Budget

How often do you hear of people coming home from their travel, checking how much money they have left in the bank and absolutely shitting themselves when they realise just how much they've spent. Even worse are the people that realise this while overseas and have to end their trip early, or worse still, don't have enough money to get home.

Best way to avoid this: keep a budget.

Geeky no doubt, but it can be really beneficial. I've tried in the past to note down all expenses in my phone as I go, so I know how much I've spent on accommodation, alcohol, food, transport, etc such that I can see where my expenses are going; but the reality is that it's just too much effort and you can't keep it up. Better to do something simple that you will stick with. All that I do is every few days see how much money I have left. That is, how much is in my bank accounts, and how much cash I have. Note that down every few days and it's pretty simple to see how much you're spending. Because I'm a total nerd, I use all sorts of graphs to track my spending. I originally had a few pages in this book about how I do my budget tracking, then took it out when I realised no one is as nerdy as me. If you're *really* interested in all the different nerdy budget tracking techniques I use, send me a message via my website www.LiveTheAdventureLife.com.

Chapter Summary

Free Flights

• Enter competitions to win free flights, but only if the competition is free. The more difficult the competition is, the better

• Join airline Rewards programs (such as Frequent Flyer), but don't let this affect your decision of which airline to fly (unless the price is the same)

Tipping

• In the USA and Canada bartenders and waitresses may only be getting paid around $2 per hour. Therefore the 'tip' is not a tip; it's their wage. Pay it

• A general tip is 18-20% at restaurants and $1 per beer or $2 for a cocktail or mixed drink in bars

• Don't tip at fast food places

• Other services expect a tip too, such as hairdressers, masseuses, tattoo artists and so on. 10-20%. Taxi's 15-20%

• In Mexico, tip basically everyone

• In Morocco you'll learn quickly enough who you have to tip – they'll soon let you know!!

• Spend the five minutes to research the tipping customs before going to a different country

Haggling

• As annoying as it is, haggling is an ancient tradition so play along with it

• Even if you can afford the first price, you should still negotiate to respect the tradition

• The 'start at one-quarter and finish on half' doesn't always work, particularly in more local markets where you may only knock 20% or so off

• Best to ask at the hostel where you are what the haggling custom is, and how much you should generally pay for a certain item. In the markets feign disinterest and see how much they lower their price, particularly when you walk away

• Use the 'lucky sale' technique and of course the 'walk off' technique

• Don't buy sunglasses from markets as they won't be UV protected and will be damaging to your eyes

Earning Money

• In places you can make money making and selling jewellery or food in the street, but when in third world countries only do this if selling something markedly different to the locals

• Consider taking Aussie flags (or any other country flag) to festivals to sell. These take up very little space and weight yet a dedicated festival-head will pay good money for a flag to wear as a cape. Get the 5ft x 3ft size

• Learn massage, particularly Indian Head Massage

• If you know massage or some other skill you can do or teach, make a poster and have it laminated. Looks professional and you can just use a whiteboard maker to change your details (room number / phone number) as you change hostels

• Consider taking chances after you've weighed it up. It's probably a scam, but you never know!

• See if you can get sponsored to keep a travel blog by going to unusual countries, or doing unusual things

• Check out other travel websites that pay for stories

Saving Money

• Concentrate on the big items;
- *Get a good travel bank card with zero fees*
- *Hunt for cheap flights*
- *Use rideshare for transport*
- *Use Couchsurfing (and learn some skill to pay them back, or just clean their house)*
- *Drink your own alcohol before going out to pubs/clubs. Ensure you stay at hostels where you're allowed to drink your own*
- *Check the price of Long Island Ice Teas. In some countries it works out cheaper than beer for the alcohol content*
- *Take playing cards out with you and do the 'Wanna Bet' trick*
- *Take lunch with you on day trips*
- *If going to attractions search online or in a tourist information place for discount coupons*
- *Keep a budget to know how much you're spending per day. Don't leave this till you get home!*

Chapter 2 and a Bit:

Packing... the rest of it

General Considerations

First of all, where are you going, when are you going and what are you doing? Sounds pretty obvious huh…. though often you don't know what you'll be doing. I mean, I once took 23kg of paragliding gear to China and only used it once in the nine months I was there. It was still worth it as it was one of my most enjoyable flights ever, but yes, it did suck to carry 70kg of luggage through the airport, when combined with all my other crap I accumulated while there.

Here are some thoughts:

If you're going to Europe, pack light. Most budget airlines only allow 15kg luggage. Keep it under this. In my experience, most other places in the world are more liberal with luggage allowance, except when using small airplanes to fly to remote areas or islands.

Europe tends to be more about the cities, so you're probably not going to be hiking much, and therefore probably wont need hiking books. Best to get some shoes that are comfortable to walk a 10km hike in, yet look good in a club. Always go for black – it goes with everything and doesn't show the dirt. Get leather so you're not uncomfortably sweating when walking in the heat. Getting a bit nerdy here, but try to get shoes where the sole is stitched, not just glued. I started a five-month trip to the US and Central America without shoes, only thongs. I thought I could just buy some there… until I realised the US doesn't generally have pedestrian malls where you can shop. If you don't have a car, you're pretty much stuffed when it comes to shopping. I then went to an upmarket mall in Mexico City (Mexico) and bought some great shoes from the Lacoste store. Super comfy and looked great – the perfect clubbing/hiking shoe. Problem was the first time I wore them was to climb a 4500m volcano. After just one (very strenuous) day, they were pretty much destroyed. Possibly they were fakes, but it was in a ritzy mall so you'd expect them to be real. Perhaps they just weren't designed for climbing volcanoes? When climbing a mountain you're climbing very steep angles which bends the shoe a lot more than walking on the street. If that strip joining the sole to the shoe isn't stitched, it's likely it will come apart.

For places that are more about the outdoors, I definitely recommend taking some hiking boots with you. I've been on some great multi-day hikes in Australia and the Americas where I was glad to have the boots with me. Makes it easier on the knees when descending and they are a lot more durable than sneakers.

My advice – get all your shoes before you leave home. You know where the cool shoe stores are in your own town. Going shopping in a foreign place can be quite difficult unless the place is known for its shopping.

As it was, for my Euro trip, I needed new shoes halfway through, but Europe is *expensive*! Even some *second-hand* Adidas shoes were €70 ($110). I didn't want to delve into my beer money, so I settled on buying some crap second-hand shoes for €10 in Amsterdam, complete with holes in them. Those holes really sucked when walking around Iceland, just 40km from the Arctic Circle. More in the story later!

The above goes for all items. If there's something you need, buy it before you leave home. People always say, "There are shops where you're going," but the reality is that things can be hard to find in foreign towns.

For brand name electronic items, such as cameras, it can be a natural thought to think, "I'm going to a cheap country – I'll buy the camera there." Problem is it's almost guaranteed to cost you more. In third world countries fewer people can afford such luxuries, thus there's less demand and therefore less competition. Cheapest places for camera gear are the USA and Hong Kong. In my experience, you're best to buy off the net from a dealer based in your country that procures their cameras from Hong Kong.

Tourist Refund Scheme

In Australia (possibly other countries too) there exists a government scheme called the Tourist Refund Scheme (TRS). This is implemented to encourage people heading overseas to buy items here in Oz, not overseas. How this works is if you have items (and receipts) from the one seller totalling more than $300 from the past 60 days then you can get the tax back in the airport. Note it must be from the one seller. If it's on separate receipts it's fine, but if you have $300 of stuff from five different shops it doesn't count. This means if you have to buy stuff for your trip, it's best to leave it until the 60 days before you leave. If you buy a $250 pack and also need some boots, compression bags or something, you're best to buy it from the same shop unless it's much cheaper elsewhere.

Note *you must have the items with you*. As the TRS office is inside the terminal, ensure you take these items in your carryon, not in checked in luggage. Keep in mind too that when returning to Australia you're meant to declare products bought duty free with a value more than $900. That is, if you buy a $1000 camera before you leave Australia and get the tax back on that, by rights, you're meant to pay the tax back on it on your return. Whether you do or not is a different thing!

Best to refer to the scheme details at
http://www.customs.gov.au/site/page4263.asp

When Packing Light Sucks

On a Euro trip, I decided to go to Iceland, knowing absolutely nothing about it, other than it's probably fairly cold. Knowing is one thing, acting is another.

I made the bold decision before I left to buy an $8 jacket of questionable quality, which I unfortunately lost on the first night out in Reykjavík during one of the greatest nights out in my life. Nightlife in Reykjavík is *freaking amazing*, but that's another story.

I met a fellow traveller in the hostel with the same intents as me – get a 4x4 and go on the adventure of our lives. We get an amazingly good deal on a Ford Escape 4x4 and set off. Having lost my jacket, I'm now in Iceland with no thermals, no beanie, no scarf and no jacket. In fact, all I had was one pair of jeans, a few t-shirts, a thin jumper with almost zero warmth and shoes with holes in them. Here came the bright idea that I would just wear all my t-shirts… because that's like a warm jumper, right?

Wrong.

The first day we set off on our adventure, find a 4x4 trail, and continue on until 2am when we reach the top of a mountain, and park 10m from a glacier. We know it's going to be a damn cold sleep, but the sunrise will make it worthwhile… right?

Wrong.

I climb into my $30 super-low quality travel sleeping bag that's cold even when used indoors in summer. Actually not too bad it appears. Five minutes later however, after the engine (and corresponding heater) has stopped…."hhhrrrrrrrrrrrrrrr… hhhhhhhrrrrrrrrrr…. faaaaaaarrrrrrkkkkkk…. iiiitttssss c-c-c-cooollldd!!!!"

It was *unbelievably* cold. I put on all my t-shirts and come to the horrifying realisation… it makes absolutely no difference. Five t-shirts are just as cold as one! We're hours drive from any civilisation so we're forced to tough it out. We wake up the next morning to totally overcast sky – not even a sunrise! I make myself warm by tying some socks together to use as a scarf and put socks on my hands and ears too. When you're walking around with socks on your ears, you know you've gone wrong somewhere in life.

We proceeded to do this for the next five days, doing 2000km four-wheel driving across Iceland, sleeping in the car each night. Of course everything in Iceland was too expensive for me, so saving grace came in the form of a single pair of thick Angora socks which near saved my life. When a single pair of socks makes all the difference to your warmth, you know you're near your limit. The other mod we did was to go to a shop and get all their cardboard boxes which we used to line the back of the car. A bit hobo-like, but the cardboard insulation made a big difference!

Part of the journey included crossing about 20 rivers in the absolutely middle of BF nowhere, which we did with zero prior river crossing or even any 4x4 driving experience at all for that matter. At each river we'd stop, get out of the car and estimate how deep the river was, then drive through. Stopping at each river gets a bit tedious after a while, so here came the bright idea of, "Fuck it, let's just plow through all of them!" Of course the very next river was so deep that the bow wave went all the way over the roof of the car! The water was going all the way over the windscreen so I couldn't see a thing. Scary when you're in the absolute middle nowhere, it's freezing cold and you're crossing a river so deep that all you can see through the windshield is water, and then the car slows down and nearly stalls. Very nearly got stuck there, in the middle of nowhere. Luckily we made it through, though we cracked the front bumper bar (fender) and cracked the windscreen too. I hate to think what would have happened if we got stuck. Possibly my new socks wouldn't even have been enough to save us!

By the last day I was really sick from all the cold, but was smiling ear to ear from an epic journey of a lifetime.

Lesson learned: It's called *Ice*land for a reason. Take some frikken thermals!

My Packing List

Note, I include a lot of brands in this section. I'm not endorsed at all by any of these companies, though I wish I were. I'm just giving a list of products that I felt were best that were available to me.

Packs

Backpack

I find getting a good backpack essential, and the money spent is a worthwhile investment. I'd rather carry a comfortable 20kg backpack than a 10kg crappy backpack. The amount of pockets it has, attachment points and how cool it looks is nothing if it's not comfortable.

The other major consideration is the type of pack. There are three main types:

1. Hiking pack
2. Travel pack
3. Wheelie travel pack

Get 2, or 3. Don't get the hiking pack. The difference with the hiking pack is that's it's made for durability and waterproofness. What this really means it that it doesn't have any zippers. Instead there's just one hole at the top with a cover that clips over the top. As there are no zippers it's a bit more waterproof, but would be a right bloody pain in the arse to travel with as you cannot open it all up. E.g. if you need something at the bottom of your pack, you have to pull everything out. Impossible to organise and you will just hate it. Trust me, every person I've seen with one of these packs was swearing about it. The other problem is that as there're no zips you generally can't lock them either. The only benefit I see of the Hiking Pack is they tend to come with a better harness and will be the most comfortable.

A Travel pack is a similar construction to the hiking pack, but with a full-length opening zipper and generally a lesser quality harness. They will often also include an airport cover, which is a flap that zips over the harness to prevent it getting caught on the airport conveyer belt systems. These packs are the most popular as they have almost the comfort of a hiking pack, yet they open up completely so you can access all your things without pulling everything out.

The Wheelie travel packs are a hybrid of a very basic pack plus wheels and a retractable handle. The wheels are included at the expense of a lesser quality harness. They tend to weigh more too. These would be good if you're mainly travelling around cities where you would be mainly wheeling it along, with the occasional need to carry it where the ground is unsuitable for the wheels. They are not designed for hiking.

There is another fourth sub-category – Hybrid packs. These are Travel packs, but with a Hiking pack harness. This means you get the convenience of the Travel pack, but with a top-end harness designed for carrying the pack for weeks at a time. This is what I use. These come at the expense of a greater price and a little extra weight; though I find it worthwhile for something that should last close to a lifetime.

My pack is a 65L 'Tom Thumb' Hybrid pack made by One Planet. I spent a full day going around all the outdoor stores in Sydney trying on all packs and this was the clear winner. The packs look like total crap, but the comfort blows all others out of the water. Quality is second to none too. Here are a few things to look for in a pack, with regards to quality:

- Material

- Stitching
- Clips
- Zips

Two packs may look the same until you take a closer look and see the vast differences. I'm yet to see a pack with quality equivalent to One Planet. For the stitching, all stitches are double stitches. That is, for all stitches there are two parallel lines of stitches, not just one. For the load bearing parts, such as handles, 'bar tack' stitches are used (very tight overlapping zigzag, like what is used on seatbelts and rock-climbing gear). I've had my pack for five years now in which it's had a huge amount of use, and other than looking a bit dirty, it's still in perfect condition.

Common materials used for packs are canvas and nylon. Canvas is overkill for backpacking and is really only for hard-core hiking through abrasive scrub. Nylon will suit you fine. The durability of the nylon can generally be checked by its 'denier rating'. This is the weight of the fibre. For comparison, the One Planet packs use 1000 denier nylon. The more the better.

The quality of the waist buckle clip is very important. Try carrying a heavy backpack without the waist strap and you'll quickly see what I mean. This is not something you want to have break on you. Many packs use acetyl buckles that are strong, but brittle. That means if you step on it or move it too much it is likely to break. The One Planet packs use nylon buckles. These you can actually bend 180 degrees backwards on themselves without breaking. Test the quality by seeing how stiff yet flexible the clip is.

For zips, ensure they are a large size YKK zipper, with a hole in the slider to allow the zippers to be locked together with a padlock. Avoid just locking the pull-tabs together as these allow a gap such that someone can open the pack enough to slip some drugs inside.

Personally I find mine is too small for me (65L). No doubt the salesperson will say, "Get the small capacity pack – if you get a big pack you'll just take more stuff." What getting a smaller pack really means is that you can't fit all the stuff you want in it, and end up having to put things in your daypack which is much much harder to carry. Get the bigger pack and just don't fill it. It's that simple.

Of course 65L is fine for most trips, but packs should last a lifetime and no doubt there'll be times where you want a bigger pack, particularly when going on ski holidays.

I believe that how it looks has some degree of importance; the crapper the better. If you were to steal someone's pack would you take the brand new expensive-looking one, or the crappy used-looking one? That's another bonus about the One Planet bags – they look like shit!! I purposely settled for the beige colour, plus even rubbed a bit of dirt into it. Of course, only put the dirt on the front of it, not the harness where it'll rub off on your back! The more it looks like a hippie's 30-year-old hessian bag, the better.

Daypack

Many backpacks come with a daypack. My feeling; get rid of it. They're too small and basic to function as an organisation pack and there are better options for a daypack. In addition, when attached to your main pack they tend to add little extra storage room as the pack will press into the daypack; halving its capacity.

What I do is carry a separate daypack, like a school bag. This is what I use to carry all my important/expensive items. It's the bag I don't leave out of sight. These will have a number of compartments that I use to organise all my small things. Considerations to look out for are:

- Quality (particularly shoulder straps and zippers)
- Laptop/hydration pack compartment
- Attachment points on the shoulder straps

Quality is important, as finding a replacement quality bag in a third world country can be extremely difficult. Having bought a daypack in Thailand that lasted 2hrs before the shoulder strap came off, then deteriorated even more over the next three days, this is not something you want to experience.

As I travel with a laptop, a laptop compartment is quite useful to me. It gives it extra protection and makes it easy to remove your laptop for airport security checks.

One of the main considerations for me however is whether it has attachment points on the shoulder straps. If ever you've carried a backpack on your back and a daypack on your front, you'll no doubt agree that the 5kg daypack will wear you out more than the 20kg backpack. Bags are designed to hang on your back, not your front. Putting a daypack on your front pulls your shoulders forward and tires you out very quickly. Instead I've devised a great trick that greatly reduces the discomfort, and all it requires are two S-Biners and a daypack with attachment points on the shoulder straps. All you do is to attach your daypack to the shoulder straps of your backpack and that helps to take the weight off your shoulders and transfer it to your back and hips. Carabiners can be used too of course, but S-Biners are game changers. Carabiners often get stuck (that's the whole idea behind them for rock climbing – you don't want them to open) and are just hard to use, whereas S-Biners are very easy to clip. Just ensure to tape them to your main pack or you may (will) lose them.

The bag I have is made by Mammut and is perfect. It is very lightweight, yet is strong, has a laptop compartment and has attachment points on the shoulder straps. I believe it is best to buy your daypack in an outdoor store as opposed to a sports or surf store (catered for school bags) as the outdoor designed ones will more likely be a better quality and lighter weight.

Golf Ball Size Daypack (Ultra-Sil)

Once you put all your important things in your daypack, it makes it a big pain to use this bag to carry your water bottle and camera when exploring around a town. This is where the golf ball size daypack comes in. Perhaps other brands make them too, but the only ones I've heard of are made by Sea-to-Summit (called Ultra-Sil Daypack). They are a daypack, but they fit into a bag the size of a golf ball. Incredible. Not only that, they are surprisingly strong and the fabric is waterproof. The type that I have is the dry bag sort which is completely air and water tight. Why these are so great is that it takes essentially zero room in your pack (fits in your pocket) yet can be used as a daypack to hold your water bottle, lunch, jumper and camera. Being waterproof too, I use this to carry my camera in when kayaking. By blowing it up before closing it, it will float too. For reference, the day bags weigh 68g and the dry bags weigh 90g. Nothing.

Use your main daypack to carry all your valuables, use your Ultra-Sil day bag as your day bag for exploring.

Clothing

Clothing is personal, so I'll leave that to you but I suggest taking a nice collared shirt with you. Might as well look good when you go out! No need for fancy pants or shoes – just a nice shirt with black jeans. Can even wear a nice collared shirt with shorts and thongs and still look great.

Don't overestimate the dress code in beach places like Bali though. Once I was in Bali with a friend and it was laundry day. He put in the laundry absolutely everything except for one pair of boardshorts. We went out on the town, him with no shirt, not even any shoes – just a pair of shorts and nothing else. I had doubts about getting into clubs as he looked homeless, but walking past a really, really nice lounge bar, all in white leather; the sort of place that would charge $50 entry back home, the bouncers were almost pulling us into the bar; free entry. In Bali there's no need for shoes, or even jeans and certainly not a jumper, other than for the flight. I'd still bring it with you, but don't expect to need it.

Make sure however to take quality clothing. Before going on my two-year-long Central/South America trip I bought a few t-shirts that looked great… but turned out to be really bad quality. Before long they were faded, stretched and had holes in them. Pay a bit more, get something a bit better. Finding cool clothes in third world countries is very difficult. There are lots of locally made hand-woven clothes that look awesome, but tend to be bulky and heavy. Similarly, buying cool clothes in Europe can be insanely expensive if you don't know where to go.

For most places there's no need for a rain jacket, unless hiking or going to tropical countries in wet season – then it's essential. I ended up buying a Gore-Tex travel jacket on a great sale. Rolls up really tightly and fits into a small pouch. Something I've recently discovered too is an umbrella. I put off buying one for the first 28 years of my life, then got one and realised; hey, they're actually quite useful!

I find a lot of value in taking lots of pairs of underpants, as this will normally define when you have to do your laundry. Doing laundry sucks as it can be expensive and means hanging around an area for a day or two. I use bamboo fibre undies as, apart from being really soft and super comfy, they have properties that make them antibacterial… which translates to being able to wear them for a few days if *really* required. I travel with ten pairs of undies. Some practical bamboo sorts, some nicer going out ones. There are the travel underpants made by Ex-Officio but these are expensive and not very comfortable. You could buy a pair to try them out, but I prefer the bamboo. Get these from a cheap camping/outdoor store. Underpants in a travel store will be needlessly overpriced.

For towels, I've finally caved in to getting microfiber; and my word is it worth it. I always like the big beach towels, but the reality is they're heavy and take up a lot of space. When paying for laundry, my towel was often a third of the cost. I think big beach towels are great for a beach holiday as you can enjoy it on the beach, and can probably wash it yourself and know it will dry soon. Also for a beach holiday you will have more room in your pack, so probably no problem. For other trips however I really do recommend microfiber. I'd always only felt horrible, sticky feeling towels that I didn't like, but at one shop I found a nice microfiber towel that was very soft, with a chamois feel (made by Sea to Summit, of course!). I absolutely love it!

If you lose your towel and are really low on space, you can replace your towel with just a tiny microfiber dishcloth. This will be ok for the shower, but a dishcloth won't be much fun to lie on at the beach.

Toiletries

The toiletries are where a significant part of your weight can come from due to all the liquids. This is also the source of many frustrated backpackers after their sunscreen or shampoo goes all through their bag. Fortunately there are a few good tricks to do, as below.

Washing

Discover the awesomeness of shampoo bars. Designed for hippies that don't want to use chemicals in their hair, they're actually super useful for backpacking. It's like a bar of soap, but it's a natural shampoo. It's solid shampoo, so you're not carrying around the extra weight of the liquid as per normal shampoo, plus it's much more compact and can't spill through your bag either. I use a beer shampoo made by Beauty and the Bees. Say wha..? Beer shampoo?? Yes, that's what Catherine Zeta-Jones uses and check out her hair. Beer contains hops which is full of vitamins and all that. One bar will last you near a year, yet it's not much bigger than a box of matches.

People always leave their shampoos and so on in the shower (just go into any hostel shower and see how many bottles people have accidently left in the shower). I find myself sometimes doing the same, but to lessen the blow, I keep big containers in my bag and take small containers into the shower. Go into a $2 store and you'll probably find small containers for sale. Put some of your conditioner and face wash into these bottles, so when you leave it in the shower you'll only lose a bit. For my shampoo bar, I cut it into three sections, leave two sections in the box in my bag, the other section I keep in a small zip lock bag in my toiletries bag.

For my toiletries bag, I use a Sea to Summit Cordura Ultra Sil waterproof bag. These are expensive, but are pretty awesome too though. Being totally waterproof it doesn't matter if something spills in it. Don't buy the older non-Cordura as it can tear reasonably easy. Some sunscreen or exfoliate containers can have sharp edges. I just wrap electrical tape over the corners to stop it poking holes in my bags. I like these bags as you can also hang them from hooks in the shower.

For all the big bottles in my pack however, I just double-bag them in large disposable Zip-lock bags.

For clothes washing detergent, I use Sea to Summit ultra-concentrated detergent. Size of a box of matches, lasts ages.

Deodorant

If you can, buy aerosol cans less than 100mL so you can take it on the plane in your daypack. Guaranteed you'll be sweaty and smelly by the time you arrive at the airport after carrying your pack. Imagine if you're sat next to a beauty on the plane and you smell like BO for 10hrs. Worst comes to worst, if you're in a situation feeling smelly but having no deodorant, go to the toilets, wipe water and soap over your armpits and wipe it dry with toilet paper.

Sunscreen

Bring your own sunscreen from home. My brother went to Thailand for his honeymoon, bought some local factor 30 sunscreen and got totally burnt. You can't trust the brands you don't know. Also, sunscreen will almost certainly be cheaper at home than your destination.

Medication

I highly recommend taking a basic medi-kit with you. Generally you can find doctors anywhere you're going, but to avoid communication difficulties, cost and hassle, it pays to bring your own medications.

This is particularly recommended in China. In China, there are no doctor's surgeries, only hospitals. Go to the local hospital and it's absolute pandemonium. Not a place you want to be, especially when sick. Also don't expect them to speak a word of English. Being a hospital not a doctor's surgery, getting by without English is much more difficult as it's not just a simple doctor and receptionist. Just finding out where to go in the building can be extremely confusing and frustrating, particularly when sick. In some of the bigger cities you have the option of going to an English speaking doctor, but the bills are horrendous. Expect in the vicinity of $180 for a simple consultation.

Other countries are generally a lot more simple, but still can be a hassle and expensive. Also, from personal experience getting diarrhoea in the Sahara Desert with a 14hr bus ride the next day with no toilet on board, *as a minimum take a stopper with you*!!! That was an experience I never want to repeat.

Here is my recommended medi-kit:

- Diarrhoea
  - *Stopper. I believe this to be the single most important thing. It cures nothing, but at least it stops you going to the toilet for a few hours when you need to travel. The active ingredient is called Loperamide, and is often sold under the names of Gastro-stop, Imodium, Dicap and Harmonise.*
  - *Tinidazole. This is used for giardia.*
  - *Norfloxacin. Antibiotic used for general persisting diarrhoea.*
- Nausea
  - *Stemetil. For anti-nausea. Used for motion sickness and after vomiting. Do not use at the first sign of being sick as you need to vomit to get rid of the bad food you have ingested.*
- Eye and ear infections
  - *Soframycin. Used for eye infections such as conjunctivitis and ear infections that may come from swimming in tropical areas.*
- High Altitude
  - *Acetazolamide (Diamox). Used for altitude sickness.*
- Sex
  - *Condoms. These are used for… well, I think you know.*
- Headache/Pain
  - *Ibuprofen, such as Nurofen. You can't get headache tablets in China without a doctor's prescription, so take a few packets with you.*
  - *Anti-inflammatory tablets, such as Voltaren. These are particularly useful when hiking.*
- Bites/Burns
  - *Tea tree oil. Good natural antiseptic used for bites and burns. Very concentrated, so you only need a small amount.*

Bandages are pretty much always included in medi-kits but I generally fail to see the point. Any activity that would necessitate the use of bandages you most likely would do without your pack.

Make sure however that everything you take is legal in the country you're going. Dubai is particularly strict with substances, even things that are common place back home. Check that your prescription medication is allowed there. Refer to the Respect the Law section of Chapter 13.

While certainly not a travel essential and out of the scope of this book, I think it prudent to include my experience with the hair loss product 'Regaine' as it really does work. It's easy to get in denial about hair loss, but if you act you can stop it in its tracks. There're lots of products out there, most of which don't work or others that can cause impotence. I wouldn't touch any of these. The one thing I do use which works wonders is a topical liquid sold under names such as Regaine, Rogaine, Hair-a-Gain, etc. Brand is not important. The active ingredient is called Minoxidil 5% w/w. Put 1mL in your hair in the morning and another in the evening and you will reclaim some of your hairline, get thicker hair and slow down the hairloss process. It really does work.

I think it also goes without saying that you should get all your vaccinations before you leave, particularly yellow fever if travelling through South America. Coming back to Australia from South America without a yellow fever vaccination can mean going straight into quarantine on arrival. Had I not had my yellow fever vaccination before I started my trip it could have meant missing my brother's wedding, which I flew back specifically for.

Sleeping Gear

When I travel, I always take a pillow even just for an overnight trip, and for trips longer than a few weeks; a sleeping bag and thermal liner too.

"Are you kidding me, you travel with your own pillow??! How can you call yourself a backpacker? Man you're soft!!"

That's the sort of reaction you can expect from people, but you'll be the person enjoying a great sleep while they're struggling on their lumpy hostel pillow, trying to avoid the old cum stains on the pillow case.

Years ago I discovered a memory foam travel pillow made by Tontine and that changed my life. It's a travel pillow, so it's about 1/3 the size of a normal pillow, but it's memory foam and is just super comfortable. In fact, this is what I sleep on at home too.

For me, my pillow is probably the second most important thing in my pack, after my camera. Why it's so important is that when travelling you're normally partying till 3am, then up again at 7am to do activities. For my Euro trip I managed an average of an appalling 4hrs sleep per night. Those hours count. If you're travelling fast, chances are you're changing hostels every third night, which means you're probably going from a thin pillow, to a thick pillow, to a lumpy pillow multiple times per week. Guaranteed 80% of your hostel pillows will be uncomfortable and no doubt a petri dish of assorted bacteria's, lice, spooge and bedbugs. By having your own pillow it keeps at least one part of your sleep consistent.

I once did a ten-day meditation course where the bed was too soft for me. No worries – I just slept on the hard floor for ten days. I had a comfortable pillow so I slept great each night. A good pillow really does make all the difference and is a lot more important than the mattress in my opinion.

For long trips I definitely recommend taking a sleeping bag. It has so many uses. Often when travelling (particularly at high altitude) it gets cold at night, so putting the sleeping bag over the blankets keeps me cosy. More importantly though, it lets you go exploring. With your own sleeping bag and pillow you're a lot more welcome when Couchsurfing or staying at friends places. Better than that, you can go camping and really have an adventure. In Mexico I got a $30 Wal-Mart tent and spent five weeks camping in it, including sleeping on a mountain at 3600m. An amazing experience and so worthwhile.

I travel with both a down travel sleeping bag and a thermal liner. This way it gives you three different warmth options. When it's warm, just use the liner, when it's cool, use the sleeping bag, when it's cold, use both. Both take very little room in my pack. I went for down over synthetic as it's more compact. Only real negative of down is that it doesn't keep warmth when wet, but most of the time you'll probably only be using it indoors anyway. Size and weight matter. The thermal liner is made out of polypropylene, like thermals. I use a Mont Hotwire Extender sleeping bag and a Sea to Summit Thermolite Reactor liner.

If I'm planning on hiking or camping I bring thermals too. In Mexico I wasn't originally planning on going hiking so I didn't bring any with me, and had to pay the absurd price of $80 just for some thermal bottoms. Worth it though when you have ice in your tent!

Nowadays when I plan on hiking I take my 'hiking kit' including my two sleeping bags, a few pairs of hiking socks, thermal tops and bottoms, beanie and possum gloves. All this I put in a compression bag which takes up surprisingly little space. All warm stuff is very compressible, so the compression bag makes a big difference.

Hiking Gear

Go into any quality outdoor store and you'll see a wall of awesome looking high-tech Gore-Tex hiking boots. Don't buy them.

But why? Isn't Gore-Tex awesome? Guaranteed to keep you dry™, right? Erm, only if you're in really cold climates. Gore-Tex is a membrane which allows moisture to escape while preventing water entering. Problem is there needs to be temperature differential for this to work; that is, it needs to be cooler outside the boot than inside. In warm climates, Gore-Tex boots function more like non-breathing synthetic boots. It's like wearing plastic shoes – your feet will be hot and sweaty as hell, making them more damp and a lot more uncomfortable than the cheaper non-Gore-Tex shoes.

For my shoes I bought some 'approach' shoes made by the brand 5-10. It looks like a skate shoe on steroids. That is, it's full of comfy padding yet provides mid-length ankle support and one of the grippiest soles on the planet. It's so grippy it actually sticks to tiles and linoleum. This does mean they will wear more quickly, but I only need them to last two years, so I'm not fussed. They are also designed to be able to take crampons for ice climbing. The other great thing about them is that they are really lightweight, and better than anything; they cost 1/3 of any other boots, at just $100. If you can find some 5-10's, definitely try them on.

As listed above, I travel with possum gloves. These are fan-bloody-tastic! They are the same basic design as polypropylene thermal liners in that they're extremely thin and lightweight (takes up not much more space than a pair of business socks), but are made with possum fur fibres blended in with the polypro. Possum fur fibres are hollow, so it makes a great insulator, as well as feeling nicely soft. I had just a pair of these in Quebec in -7°C and my hands were fine. This is particularly impressive for me as my hands get very cold very easily.

If you're planning on hiking in hot, malarial areas I recommend taking lightweight pants and long sleeved shirt, as mentioned in the Tropics section of Chapter 13.

Gadgets and Electronics

As I generally buy electronics online, most items come with a US plug. This means travelling the America's is easy as you already have all the correct plugs. The only non-US device is my laptop as I want to be able to use this in airports in Australia too. Australian-US adaptors will include the earth pin (round pin in middle). Make sure to remove this as most power points don't have an earth plug. Generally you can do this by unscrewing the plug and pin. If you can't unscrew it, a hacksaw works well. Note, I take no responsibility if you do something wrong and electrocute yourself.

In Central America I also bought a 2m extension cord that included three receptacles in the end. This often comes in handy as sometimes the power point is high up and the weight of my laptop adaptor hanging in the air will pull the plug out of the socket. It's the same for cell phones; so often I see people trying to charge their phone, but as the socket is so high up, they have to try and balance their phone on top of the charger, 1.5m above the ground. Good way to end up with a cracked screen! With an extension cord, the adaptor can rest on the floor and the plug will stay in. Of course the three plugs in the end helps too when there's just one power point.

For Europe, I use all my Australian cord items. As I often will want to have a few things on charge at once, I take an Australian power board and just the one adaptor. You should see people's eyes light up in jealousy in hostels when you pull out a power board. *Everyone* wishes they brought one too! It's so useful in hostels where there're just two power points in a four-bed dorm and every person wants to charge their phone, laptop and camera.

Phone

Beware; your mobile phone may work at home, but may not work where you're travelling to. Different countries use different frequencies, and while you will still be able to use it for calls, the internet may not work. Have a look on the box for something like 850/900/1700/1900. Using Wikipedia you can check what frequencies are used in the country you're going to. Unfortunately for me when I went to the US I had to buy a new phone to use the net.

If you are taking your home SIM card with you, make sure to disable mobile internet or at least make sure that international roaming for data is turned off. Otherwise you could be easily up for a bill of thousands of dollars just to check your Facebook.

If intending to buy a SIM card in the country you're travelling to, I recommend researching which company to use before you arrive in the country. Saves mucking around once you're there. That is, check which frequencies they use and whether that's compatible with your phone, check their phone coverage and of course their price.

In terms of the phone itself, I much prefer Android over iPhone for the simple fact that, apart from being a fraction of the price, you can download the entire Google Translate for offline use. That is, you can get the app for both phones, but only with Android can you download the entire language pack to use offline (at the time of writing). You should see iPhone user's faces drop when I tell them I can use Google Translate without an internet connection. It's pretty much essential in non-English speaking countries if you don't speak the language. Even if you have a good grasp of the language, it's still useful to be able to look up certain words on the go.

Another good trick that a lot of people don't know is that you can 'pre-cache' sections of Google Maps. That is, when you have an internet connection you can download an area to use later on. I always pre-cache a new town before I go there so I can find the hostel. In Cuba, as there is no internet, I pre-cached all the towns I was planning on visiting and as such I had maps of everywhere I went. More of this in Chapter 1 ('Know Where You Are' section).

GPS Receiver
The GPS receivers on many phones are low sensitivity receivers that work in tandem with cell phone towers to find your location. This is fine if you're in the one country and have a SIM card, but if you're travelling through many different countries, you probably won't have a cell connection, and therefore you may have very poor GPS functionality. For myself, I carry with me an external stand alone GPS tracking device. This provides a stronger signal. I'm not recommending to rush out and buy one (I only bought mine to track my flight path while paragliding), but they can be handy for tracking where you've been. That is, if you're doing a big hike it can be cool to have a record of how far you've walked and to see the path on Google Maps. I also find it useful for sports as you can record your top speed. In Nicaragua I was trying to break the world record speed for Volcano Boarding, so it was really useful to have the GPS logger with me. Unfortunately I only managed 75km/h; quite a bit short of the current record of 95km/h. The logger I have has

Bluetooth so it can communicate with my phone and provide a strong, accurate GPS signal such that I can see my location on Google Maps.

USB Shaver

I have a full beard now, but at the start of my trip I liked to keep just a few days growth. This is best kept using a beard trimmer. Mine is excellent. It's really small and powerful, but better than anything, it's rechargeable via USB. This means I don't have to carry around any other charger. Mine is made by Remington, but I'm sure lots of other brands have an equivalent.

Headlamp

I travel with a headlamp, and this comes in handy more often than you'd think. Headlamps are much better than torches (flashlights) as you can use them hands-free. Don't get the headlamp from your local two dollar store though – these may advertise to be 9 LED or something like that, but will still be very dim. I cannot recommend enough the website Bang Good (www.banggood.com). Yes, I agree it sounds like a porn site, but instead it's a huge super-cheap Chinese warehouse store. Most of the stuff on the site is total crap, but the headlamps are amazing. Just go to the section Sports and Outdoor --> Cycling --> Headlamps. You can pick up a rechargeable zoomable 1600 lumen headlamp for $20 or so including postage. In comparison, a 1600 Lumen Scurion brand headlamp will cost you over $1100. I'm sure the Bang Good lamps aren't quite the 1600 lumen they claim, but are still *seriously* bright and unbelievably good value. Note, Lumens refers to the light output. The more, the better. I recommend getting the zoomable lamp. That is, so the beam can be adjusted from spotlight to wide flood light. Note, some of the lamps on the site don't come with the batteries or charger. These can also be purchased easily and cheaply on the site too though.

Camera

Having travelled a few times with all my professional camera gear (tripod, full frame body, three lenses (including 1.8kg telephoto lens), flash unit, filters, remote triggers, spare batteries), it's something I'd only ever do for a short trip, certainly no more than three weeks. It really is an absolute bloody pain travelling with all that gear! Fortunately I've now discovered the ultimate camera – a Sony RX100. This is a fixed lens compact camera that fits in your pocket but delivers picture quality very nearly on par with a DSLR. Seriously check it out – it is just superb. The other great thing about this camera is that it charges via USB. This saves bringing another charger, allowing you to use the one charger for phone, beard trimmer and camera.

I prefer this far more over other popular options, such as the bulky bridge cameras or 4/3's cameras and so on (these are the cameras that are halfway in between the size of a normal pocket camera and a DSLR). I really fail to see the point. A bridge camera is too big to fit in your pocket yet doesn't deliver the quality or creative freedom of an SLR. They try to market them as the perfect all-rounder, but the reality really is that they're a bit of a nothing camera, in my opinion. If it's too big to fit in your pocket, chances are you'll take it with you less, and miss out on some good shots.

I previously travelled with a Panasonic Lumix Tough FT3 underwater camera, but the quality was just too bad for my liking. It was fairly heavy too. I was once in Nicaragua thinking, "I wouldn't care if I just lost this camera," and two days later I checked and my camera was missing! No idea where it went. I've now ordered an underwater housing for my camera (the Sony RX100) as this means I will be able to go diving with it, yet have very high quality photos (the image sensor is far superior than any underwater camera available). The additional benefit of the case is that it protects the camera in camera-unfriendly places, such as the beach, waterfalls, hikes where it's muddy and rainy, etc. I bought this off the internet and arranged to have it sent to a friend's house in Colombia. Hopefully it arrives!! (this is another reason to buy all your gear before you leave home!). The cost for this was $150 which is very reasonable and a much better option than buying another underwater camera.

Many people these days (should I say, probably the majority now) seem to travel with a GoPro. I have a GoPro (that I use for extreme sports), but I don't travel with it. Why? The quality sucks. They are good for underwater or sports (what they're designed for), but for taking photos they're really bad. They're made as an action-cam to record video while stuck on a helmet. This means they're made as small as possible and therefore have very basic functions, a clunky menu system and no flash. Group shots look cool, but anything else is total crap. Unless your holiday is primarily extreme sports, I wouldn't bother. In the end what camera you take all comes down to how important picture quality is for you. I'm fussier than most people, so for you a GoPro may be fine; I just wouldn't buy one if you don't regularly do extreme sports.

General

In third world countries I try to avoid brand name sunglasses like Ray Ban as I don't want to be mugged for some sunglasses. I've just recently discovered the brand Otis which look as cool as Ray Bans but don't have the big 'mug me' logo on them. The really cool thing about them though is that the lenses are scratchproof glass. Seriously. I carry them in my bag without any pouch and not a single scratch. What makes them even cooler is that it's some special type of glass that weighs just as much as normal plastic lenses, unlike the other awkward heavy glasses there are. Best sunnies I've ever seen, hands down.

Quality earplugs are a must when staying in hostels, noisy places, aeroplanes, etc. There's a huge difference between good earplugs and bad ones. With good ones you shouldn't be able to hear a thing. Don't settle for the crap ones! Make sure you get plenty – you will lose them for sure. They can be quite difficult to find in third world countries.

Notebook and pens are always useful.

Definitely always get yourself a good pair of thongs before going to a hot third world location. Replacement thongs can be really difficult to find. Even in the super-touristy beach city of Cancun (Mexico) it's surprisingly difficult. After losing my thongs in Caye Caulker (took me five days to realise I lost my thongs as you just walk barefoot everywhere), I was in Cancun to get a flight to Cuba. I was thinking there'd be people selling thongs at the side of the street everywhere, however it was nothing of the sort. According to Google there was only one surf shop in the city, and even this didn't have thongs. You've got to be bloody kidding me!?! Here is a Rip Curl store in one of the most beach-touristy places in the world, and no thongs. After a day of mucking around I finally found some crappy overpriced thongs (which, unfortunately went missing two weeks later). In all other third world locations, it is *much* more difficult to find some thongs. Yes, you can find *something*, but they will always look absolutely ghastly, plus finding larger sizes such as size 10 is near impossible. FFS by now you should know I mean flip-flops when I'm talking about thongs!!

Bring quality thongs from home and *guard them well!* People used to always bang on about Havaianas, but after resisting for years, I finally bought a pair and damn they're good. They really are worth it. You have to guard them well though as I've had a few pairs of thongs stolen while travelling.

If you get a blowout (one of the plugs comes out), there're a few tricks you can do to prolong the life of your thongs. The popular, tried and tested method is the bread clip trick. Just push the plug back where it should be, then stick the bread clip on to hold it in place. The other method is to push down one of the other plugs to expose it, then use string to anchor the bad plug to this one. This will get you a few more weeks, depending on the rubber compound used. I've even fixed a pair of thongs while out in the jungle using only a vine.

Organisation

Zip-lock baggies are awesome. Buy a variety of sizes and bag 'em up. They are strong, light, cheap, and clear so you can see what's inside. These are particularly useful for toiletries, though I recommend double bagging them to prevent spills.

I pack my clothes into a clothes bag. This is a fitted shallow box-shape cloth container the size of a folded t-shirt. These are great as you can fold your clothes up, stick it in the bag and they will stay folded no matter how you jam it in your pack.

I also carry a stuff bag to put my dirty clothes in. Zip-Lock bags are not suitable as they will break. Keep your dirty laundry in one place and it makes laundry days much easier and saves you having to sniff-test each of your undies to see if it's clean or dirty before you meet up with that hot Scandinavian that invited you out.

Security

Quality locks for your pack are essential. I strongly recommend *against* using the 'TSA approved' locks on your bags however. If unfamiliar with TSA locks, they are a lock that the security in US airports are able to open with a special master key. This means each one of these locks can be opened by the one special key. Doesn't sound very secure to me! A friend of mine was staying in a hostel in Guatemala and had his passport, cash and professional camera gear locked in a locker with a TSA lock. In the time it took him to go to the toilet, someone went in his room, opened his lock and stole all his stuff.

I also strongly recommend against using key locks. I once went travelling with small compact quality locks, which was great… until one day when I realised my keys were in my pack. Most places this wouldn't be a real issue as you can generally find workmen around somewhere with an angle grinder, or a hardware store with bolt cutters. Unfortunately I was in Cancun for the night. Searching around the crappy, overpriced, fake place of Cancun I managed to find a hacksaw blade at a restaurant, but trying to cut through a quality lock with a handheld hacksaw blade was near impossible. I had to laugh when a local on the street asked:

"Hey man, need anything? I can get you *anything*. Absolutely anything you want, I can get. You want women? Cocaine? Ecstasy?"

"Really? You can get me anything?"

"Si amigo. Anything. *Anything*."

"Oh great! Just the man I need! I need some bolt cutters."

"Oh no, I can't get that."

"Oh."

End result; I had to cut into my $370 pack. Ouch. Get a bunch of quality non-TSA combination locks. Get one or two more than you think you need just in case.

Gifts

I always travel with 20 or so small toy koalas. These are small, lightweight, cheap and quintessentially Australian (even if they're made in China!). It's great to travel with these to give as gifts to Couchsurfing hosts, local kids that you make friends with or super-awesome people you meet along the way.

Chapter Summary

• Pack light in Europe

• Take a pair of shoes that's good for both a 10km hike, yet looks good in a club too. Black to avoid dirt marks, leather for good breathability, stitched soles for durability. Get these before you leave home

• Brand name electronic items (such as cameras or phones) are more expensive in third world countries. Get this before you leave home. Cheapest from USA or Hong Kong

• See if your country has a Tourist Refund Scheme. If so, leave it until the last 60 days to buy all the items you will take with you on the trip. There're a few terms though, so check out the website

• Don't go to semi-arctic countries without warm clothes (duh!)

Pack

• Ensure your pack is comfortable. Comfort and quality are the most important things

• Don't get a top-entry hiking backpack. Get a travel pack with a hiking harness if possible

• Thoroughly observe the quality; material, stitching, clips and zips

— *Nylon is fine. Look for a high denier rating*
— *Look for double stitching and bar tacks on handles*
— *Look for a stiff yet flexible belt buckle*
— *Large size YKK zippers with padlock hole*

• Get the large one. You may not use the full capacity all the time, but it's nice to have the extra capacity for certain occasions

• The worse the pack looks, the better

Daypack

• Daypacks can be handy to organise and carry your essentials

• Daypacks that come with backpacks are often too small and basic to be useful

• I find it better to take along a lightweight school bag style. If purchased in an outdoor store it is more likely to be better quality and lightweight

• Get a golf ball sized Ultra-Sil daypack to carry items such as camera, jumper, water bottle and lunch when exploring during the day

Clothing

• Take a collared shirt

- Take along good quality clothes
- Rain jackets normally aren't needed unless hiking. Umbrellas are cheap and function fine
- Take lots of underpants, particularly those made from bamboo fibre
- For a beach holiday, take a beach towel. For anything else take microfiber
- If you lose your towel you can replace it with a dishcloth temporarily

Toiletries
- Take a solid shampoo bar instead of normal bottle shampoo. So good in so many ways
- Buy small containers to keep your other liquids in (such as face wash). Big containers in the bottom of your back, small containers in your toiletries bag. This way if you leave it in the shower you only lose a small amount
- Use a waterproof bag for your toiletries. I recommend Cordura Ultra Sil bags
- Get deodorant less than 100mL so you can take it on the plane with you
- Take your own sunscreen from home

Medication
- Refer to the Appendix for the contents of my medi-kit

Sleeping Gear
- Take a memory foam travel-size pillow to ensure you get consistent sleep
- Take a compact down sleeping bag and thermal liner. This gives you three warmth options. Having your own sleeping gear allows you to go camping, Couchsurf and keeps you warm in cold hostels

Hiking Gear
- Don't get Gore-Tex books if hiking in a hot climate as they will only breathe if the outside temperature is low
- Consider possum gloves for cold climates. Warm and takes up minimal space
- Take lightweight long pants and long-sleeved shirt if hiking in hot malarial areas

Gadgets and Electronics
- If going to the Americas try to get items with US plugs
- If you can't replace all and need an adaptor, remove the earth plug
- Similarly if you can't replace the plugs, take along a power board

- Check if your phone is compatible in the country you're going to
- For short trips where you take your home SIM with you, ensure to disable mobile internet to avoid a huge bill
- Research which phone company to go with before leaving home
- Android phones allow you to download the full language packs of Google Translate for offline use
- Pre-cache the map of the place you're going to with Google Maps on your phone
- If your phone has poor GPS, consider getting a stand-alone GPS tracker. This will give you a much stronger signal, plus it can be cool to track your trip with it too
- For low power electronic items see if you can get them that are rechargeable via USB. This will save having to bring multiple chargers
- Consider taking a headlamp, particularly if planning on hiking. I recommend the website Bang Good
- If you can afford it, a Sony RX100 really is the best travel camera (at the time of writing). Consider getting an underwater housing

General

- Avoid flashing around expensive brands, such as Ray Ban in poor countries
- Bring quality earplugs (multiple pairs)
- Take quality thongs (such as Havaianas and guard them well)
- If you get a blowout on your thongs you can fix it with a bread clip, or by tying string to one of the rear plugs

Organisation

- Take a bunch of various sizes of zip-lock baggies
- Get a cloth bag for dirty laundry
- Take a fitted bag to store clothes in (allows shirts to stay folded)

Security

- Don't use TSA locks. Recommend to take quality combination locks. Much better than key locks to avoid locking your keys in your bag

Gifts

- Take something small from home. For Australians, I highly recommend the small koalas that you get at the $2 stores, or in the airport if you forget

Chapter 16: End of the Journey

Friends and Family Back Home

Phew! What a trip! You've just had all the most amazing experiences of your life, and now it's time to return home. Crikey, you realise just how much you've changed in that time, and you're returning as a much mentally stronger and streetwise person with many amazing experiences. You might return home expecting a hero's welcome; with everyone intrigued to hear all your stories, like some brave explorer from the 16th Century. This, however will almost certainly not be the case. When catching up with friends and family, don't expect them to ask how your trip was. When they say, "How was it?" they'll probably expect an answer like, "Yeah, it was great," even though you did so many amazing things you could talk about it for days. The only thing is; no one cares. No wait, that's not quite true; no one can *relate*. Unless they're a traveller too, they have no idea what you're talking about. Saying you went to Chang Mai or Siam Reap will mean nothing to them. Even with seasoned travellers, if you go somewhere that they haven't been or don't know about, they'll be quickly lost too. Typically while travelling, I can realistically only take in information about the next country or two. If I'm in Honduras and someone's talking about a certain place in Panama, I can't relate unless they explain it while showing me a map so I know where these places are that they're talking about.

Your family and friends probably are interested, but find it too hard to relate to it. Therefore, make it easier for them. When you show them your photos, show where it is on the map. When you talk about going places, show them where it is on a map. This will really help put things into context.

Make sure too that when you show them the photos that you have whittled them down to just the best. Show someone your best 20 photos and they'll be fascinated. Show them 500 and they'll be super bored. No one needs to see five different angles of the same thing.

Chapter Summary

• Don't expect friends and family back home to ask too much about your trip. They are probably still interested, but can't relate to what you're talking about

• Make it easier and more interesting by showing them your travels on a map when showing them photos or explaining where you went

• Sort out your best photos before showing people

Supplementary material

In the following pages I have included some extra material that isn't necessarily specific enough to backpacking to keep in the main section, but I still considered important or interesting enough to include in the book. Read on and enjoy!

Getting Time Off

There're two things you need to travel; time and money. Ok, so you can do it with very little of either, but the more of each, the better. Getting time off can be difficult, but with a bit of word smithery and bullshit, you can get time off and make yourself look good at the same time.

After graduating uni and working for a bit over a year, I had money saved and wanted to do a five-month euro trip. Problem is how do you ask for five months off after you've only been working for not much more than a year? Fortunately (for me) the Global Financial Crisis started, and people were losing their jobs left, right and centre. Of course I therefore said to my boss, "Bruce, I can see the company's struggling and people are losing their jobs. I'd hate to see another person get sacked that's trying to support their family, so, tell you what, I'll take five months leave without pay if that will keep someone in a job that needs the money more than I." Of course, leave granted, and I looked like a selfless hero out to save the company!

GFC's are hard to plan, so for those other times think of how your travel will 'benefit the company'. Make up some bullshit about increasing your creative skill by learning another language, improving your problem-solving and organisation skills by general travel and so on.

If you've worked for a few years you could also try for a redundancy. After working for five years, I was planning to leave my job to travel Central and South America for a few years. As luck would have it, another financial downturn started and my company offered voluntary redundancies. Yes please! This resulted in a ten-week tax-free payout, plus as I'd cracked the required five year mark by just two weeks I also got a five week Long Service Leave payout. If that wasn't enough, I ensured that payments didn't come until the first week of the next financial year, such that this would be my only income for the whole year, and therefore got all my tax back.

I'm currently still on this trip, and it will end up being a few years between leaving my engineering job and returning back to engineering (if ever I do). Of course, potential employers would question why I haven't been working in my profession for numerous years and would no doubt think that I'm no longer proficient in my job (probably true). You can however turn it around, and as above say that now you're in fact an even better engineer as you've developed all your soft skills, such as your right-brained thinking, problem solving, budgeting, forecasting, critical thinking, decision making skills, etc, to make you even better, and in fact, probably even suited for a management position.

Magic

I have umm'd and ahh'd about this section for months. Magic is a very special and sensitive subject. Before learning magic I never understood the Magician's Code, that is, 'never reveal the secret'. I thought they were just being arseholes keeping the secret to themselves. Now I understand. It is not so much about 'never reveal the secret', it is more 'don't let people know how it is done just to satisfy their curiosity'. I have deliberated a very long time whether I should include the explanation of my favourite tricks in this book or not. Sorry, but I decided no. I will however tell you how you can find out how. This is the fundamental part. Magic is all about effort. If you go to the effort to find out how a trick is done, then you are worthy of it. You should never learn how a trick is done unless you wish to learn it so well that you can perform it yourself. For myself, I never want to know how any stage magic is done as I have no intent to perform it myself. As such I never watch the TV program 'The Masked Magician' or any other show which reveals these sort of magic tricks. Knowing how magic tricks works really, really sucks. I love to be amazed and be completely fooled. Once you know the trick, there is no entertainment. I hate being in the position that often I see magic tricks, but as I know how it's done, or can figure out how it's done; it's no longer entertaining. For this reason, I will not give away the tricks here as it makes it too easy for you. There will be many people without interest in magic who will just read how the trick is done just to satisfy their curiosity but won't do the trick themselves. There's nothing worse than performing a trick for a bunch of people who are enthralled in the magic, only to have it spoiled by some arsehole yelling out how the trick is done; spoiling the trick for everyone. The worst part about this is that now everyone in the audience knows how the trick is done, and probably can't help themselves but to yell it out the next time they see a magic show too. The knock-on effect can be huge. Do not underestimate the damage you do when you reveal a trick to someone. Unless you really want to learn magic to a performance level, then *PLEASE* don't read on.

Seriously! I meant it! Stop reading this unless you really want to learn!

Ok, so for those soon-to-be chick-pulling, hostel-famous, totally legendary magicians, here's how you can be awesome:

In my view, the best book on magic, by far, is 'Magic: The Complete Course' by Joshua Jay. It's available on Kindle, so it's a simple and cheap download. Note too, that you don't need a Kindle to read an e-book – turns out you can download a program for free called Kindle for PC, or for smartphones, tablets, etc. Awesome stuff; though if you're reading the eBook version of this you probably already know this. His book really is amazing. I also recommend 'The Complete Idiots Guide to Magic Tricks' and 'Tricks to Pick up Chicks'. You can learn a lot of tricks on YouTube too, but there is just so much *crap* there, that it takes weeks to sort through all the crap stuff to find the good stuff.

After spending a lot of time finding and learning new tricks (of which most I didn't like), I've compiled a list of my favourites, based on the most 'wow' factor without needing much skill. These are also suited to backpacking as they require minimal props, and half can be done without any props at all, other than knives and napkins in a restaurant, or paper and pen out and about.

My favourite tricks are:

- Sponge Hearts (purchased off eBay or any magic shop)
- Invisible Deck (purchased off eBay or any magic shop)
- Wanna Bet? (MyQuickTricks, YouTube)
- Ashes on Arm (Joshua Jay)
- Bendy Cards (MyQuickTricks, YouTube)
- Messed-Up Cards (MyQuickTricks, YouTube)
- Her Card, Her Name (Joshua Jay)
- Knife Swallowing (FreeMagicLiveVideos, YouTube)
- Arm Twist (ScreamFreakRewind, YouTube)
- Torn and Restored Napkin (The Complete Idiots Guide to Magic Tricks)
- Magic Kissing Trick (YouTube)
- Circled Number (Called 'Nein' in The Complete Idiots Guide to Magic Tricks)
- Magic Square (Joshua Jay)
- PATEO (Joshua Jay)
- Soul Mate (Called 'Math Prediction' in Tricks to Pick up Chicks)
- Napkin Rose (Google)

These can all be done with items that fit in your pocket. I perform quite a few other tricks but these often require props that may not be in the pub and you'd look like a weirdo if you were carrying them around with you (yes even more of a weirdo than a person carrying around sponge hearts and cards!).

The Sponge Hearts you can just buy off eBay. It is one of the most visually astonishing tricks you can do, yet is extremely simple. I always keep a set in the coin pocket in my jeans and shorts (you know that silly little small pocket that you never know what it's for!). Perfect.

Many of the above are classic tricks, though I have added my own twist to them, and in my view, have substantially improved the trick. I have bucket loads of respect for the people that first developed the trick, but magic is all about personalisation to make it suit your personality better. You may read the original and my adaptation and decide which you prefer. If you have no interest in reading the other books I've mentioned, then please do not read this following section. It probably won't make much sense anyway (I've purposely written it this way), but it may get you in a way of thinking that will destroy the magic of other card tricks for you. Please, only read this if you want to learn magic, not just to satisfy your own curiosity.

Invisible Deck

This trick is included in the Joshua Jay book. It uses a special deck of cards that you'll need to buy from a magic shop, but it is well worthwhile. The trick is flawless and absolutely stuns the audience. I've found however another way of doing it that makes the audiences heads explode even more. Start by saying, "Have you ever heard of Derren Brown? You know the guy that can hypnotise people into saying whatever he wants them to, even though they don't feel like they've been hypnotised at all? Would like you like to experience that yourself?"

Get the deck of cards and say, "I have a deck of cards here. I will now turn one solitary card over, upside down." You then turn around out of the audiences view and pretend to flip one solitary card over. You then place the deck of cards in plain view on the table out of arms reach and say, "Ok, I have the deck of cards on the table, with one card flipped over. On the count of three, I want you to name a card." Pause. "Not the card you're thinking of now. The very first card that pops into your head when I get to three." Count to three and they will name a card. Using the trick described in Joshua Jay's book, open the deck and thumb through the deck of cards to reveal them all face up, except for the card they said. They'll be astonished that they've just been 'hypnotised'. This is a great trick as it really solidifies you to be a true, powerful magician. In general you should never repeat a trick, but this is one exception. It is so flawless such that if you do it again they will be even more dumbfounded. I wouldn't do it any more than twice however.

Note too, I arrange the cards differently; pairing odds with evens of the same suit. That is; 2&3, 4&5, 6&7, 8&9, 10 & Jack, Queen & King. This just leaves the Aces by themselves. If someone names an Ace, it will be either an Ace of Hearts, or Ace of Spades. Very rare to be Diamonds or Clubs. Pair the Hearts with the Diamonds and Spades with the Clubs.

Wanna Bet?

This uses the basis of the trick described in MyQuickTricks's video but makes it more effective (in my opinion). Prepare the trick as described in the video, then get the audience member to choose any card, memorise the card, and place it on top of the deck. You then give them the deck and instruct them to break the deck approximately halfway such that their card is now approximately in the middle of the deck, then get them to square up the deck too, so it's not obvious where the break is.

Pick up the deck and say, "Ok, so you've broken the deck approximately half way… actually probably a bit closer to the top. Anyway, I can probably guess the position of your card to within about 1 in 6 cards… so that gives me about a 10% chance of getting it right. I'm going to start flicking the cards over and I'll guess which is your card. Obviously it's not in the top, so I'll go through that quickly."

As you start flicking cards off the top, say, "Now if you do see your card, don't say anything. Take note if I go past your card, but don't say a word."

Continue the trick as explained in the video.

Why I find this a better alternative is that the audience member does everything themselves. It takes out all confusion and makes the trick as simple as possible. The more they've understood what's just happened, the more likely they are to bet. They are the person that's put the card on the top and they are the person that's cut the deck and squared it up. You will get at least 80% of people betting, earning you a free drink. Yahoo!

Her Card, Her Name (renamed to Star Card)

I use the same principle as what is described in Joshua Jay's book, but I don't mark the card. I find this to be more effective for a variety of ways. If you write their name on the card then they know that you've done some fancy shuffling or something like that, whereas my method makes it a bit more mysterious, plus it saves having to write on your cards. This allows you to do this trick with your normal deck of cards, and then use the marked deck solely for the Magic Kissing Trick.

I start by trick-shuffling the deck, then start dealing the cards out and tell them to say stop when they get the feeling, and use a Sid Lorraine force to force my intended card to them. When they say "Stop", I bang the deck on the table (to square the deck up) and put the deck on the table (with the forced card remaining at the bottom of the deck, unseen). This stops the confusion otherwise of why a Sid Lorraine force means they take the next card.

I then say, "You felt that, huh? You felt compelled to say stop at that specific card, didn't you?"

I then follow on by questioning the person, "How many cards in a deck of cards?" Most people will know the answer to be 52. "Correct! And how many weeks are there in a year? …that's right 52 as well. Coincidence? No… no it certainly is not. As it turns out, every person has their own 'star card', similar to astrology and tarot. This all works by your birth-week plus a shift-factor based on the year you were born. When is your birthday please?"

You ask for their year of birth and date. Pretend to muse around it for a while, then triumphantly call out the card that you forced on them. Say, "I know you felt something when you said stop, even if it was a feeling so subtle your conscious didn't even realise. I'm willing to bet that the card you chose is your star card."

You then pick up the deck of cards, showing the bottom card to be their star card. They, of course, will be baffled by this. The great thing is that you can even do a trick shuffle and repeat the trick, them 'stopping' on the same card again.

Magic Kissing Trick

This is one of my favourites for obvious reasons. The trick goes that you have a deck of cards and get a girl to sign a card, or draw a picture on it. You then fold that card and get her to put it in her mouth, held between her teeth.

You then sign the next card and stick that between your teeth, then say some bullshit like, "You know what one of the most powerful forces in the universe is? A kiss. Yes, a kiss can change the world. A kiss can move mountains. A kiss can be everything. This trick will demonstrate that power." You then motion for her to put the card in her mouth, then step forward and give her a quick grandma-type kiss. You step back, motion for her to remove the card, then ask her to very slowly open the card. She will near shit herself when she sees the cards have switched places. This trick is performed using what's called a 'double-lift'. This is the standard trick. The next part is my little addition:

After experiencing 'real magic', they will believe you can do anything. While she's still amazed and everyone is clapping, say, "Whoa, whoa, settle down, save the applause. Believe it or not, the next trick is ten times better. Please, choose either of the cards." Once they choose a card, say, "Ok, now fold that up in your hand and hold that out as far away from me as possible. Check it again to make sure it's still the same." They check it. "Ok, because this trick is 10 times as powerful, the kiss, needs to be, like, five times better." You then go in for a kiss, and 100% guaranteed you will get a great tongue kiss going for a good five seconds until you pull back. "Whoa, I said five times better, not 10!!" you joke, getting some laughs. "Ok, so I didn't touch your hand at all, did I? Ok, I'll stand back here. Very slowly bring your hand forward. Now, very slowly, open your hard." Very slowly, very apprehensively, they open their hand, look for a few seconds not saying anything, then look up a bit confused (nothing has changed). "Yeah, nothing's changed," I say, "… but the kiss was magical!!!" Guaranteed everyone will laugh like they haven't laughed before. I've done this trick countless times and I've never once had a person pissed off at me. As mentioned previously, in Mexico I did it to this absolutely stunning girl. One of the sexiest looking girls I've ever seen in my life. No exaggeration. We had a great ol' tonguing session, although I didn't realise however that she was there with her huge steroid-filled boyfriend, just 1m away watching all of it. Did he punch me in the face? No, he laughed, high-fived me and said, "Dude, that was *awesome*!!" The more people you do it front of, the more fun it is. I've done it numerous times with an audience of 40 or so people and had the audience in stitches.

Make sure however to learn how to do the first, proper trick first. If you just do the second part without learning to do the first, it probably won't work and you'll just look like a tool.

Getting Your Hippy on – Experiences

I mentioned in the main body of the book how travelling is a great time to try some hippy spirituality things that you normally may not consider. I've included some of my experiences below for your interest.

Massage Courses

The massage courses have nothing to do with looking inward, but are *highly* recommended as a skill to learn and can earn you good money while travelling. Refer to Chapter 15 for more information on this.

Reiki

Reiki is something that comes across as total hippy bullshit… but actually seems to work. I'm highly surprised. If you read about it, you will see the story goes that some Japanese bloke 150 years ago wanted to heal people, so he went on a mountain with 21 stones, chucking one away each day. On the last day, after chucking away his last stone, a ray of light came to him and gave him the power of Reiki. Yay! He then passed that power down to other people, and now all Reiki Masters can give someone else the power of Reiki. You don't need any training to be able to give Reiki – a master will just 'attune' you in the matter of a few minutes (after charging you some money of course). You pay the money, then you are able to heal people just by holding your hands above them. If that doesn't sound like bullshit then I'm not sure what is.

Strange thing is, it seems to work.

Before long I would be able to transfer energy to people from a distance of 2ft, and even through thick jumpers. Amazing feeling when you can put your hand up to someone 2ft away and you both can feel a strong heat sensation (and no, there wasn't a candle between us). Similarly, holding my hands a few inches above someone wearing a thick polar fleece jumper, we could both feel heat energy. And no, that's not just warmth from my hands. I experimented holding a hot cup of 90°C coffee and even a candle next to their jumper, which they couldn't feel, yet they could feel the heat from my hands. Pretty cool stuff.

I also tried Reiki session on a girl who said when I was over her stomach, it felt like I was doing surgery inside her. She even looked up to see what the hell I was doing. When she did it to me, I could feel exactly where her hands were on my chest and I could feel them moving, even though there was no contact. At the start of the session I would also do a body scan, where you run your hands over the body, from a foot high, and feel areas of energy blockages, and after the session I could feel their whole body had become even. For someone else she complained of back pain on the left side (where I felt the energy). The more interesting part is that I also felt a strong energy on the left side of her chest, near her shoulder. I mentioned this to her and she looked at me surprised; she said she had problems there for years and had seen many doctors who couldn't diagnose it. It was a shame she was leaving the next day as I would have liked to try a few sessions with her to see if I could fix it.

I know what you're thinking, but remember I'm a sceptical left-brained electrical engineer, not an impressionable hippy. I did all sorts of checks such as ensuring I didn't feel the sense of touch due to a hair sticking up, doing the hot coffee cup test, and getting two Reiki people to scan the one person and individually write down what they felt, then comparing them together (same). I'm still a bit on the fence about it (mainly because I don't really understand it), but I cannot deny the sensations I've felt. Reiki is in fact used in hospitals in Australia, so that's certainly something.

Kambô Frog Ceremony

I made friends with a guy in town who, one day, was sporting some cool looking small tribal burn marks going down his chest. Looked awesome so I asked him about it. Turns out it was from a 'Kambô Frog Ceremony', and there's another coming up if I'm interested. Some weird ceremony that involves toxic frogs and burning holes into your chest; of course I'm up for it!!

I sign up straight away, then later check it out on Google. Sounds very interesting. It's the Ultimate 45 min Detox. Basically the Sharman will burn four or so marks into your chest (using a smouldering stick), then apply the highly toxic poison from the sacred *Phyllomedusa Bicolor* frog, from the Amazon. This frog is so poisonous that it has zero predators, not even snakes. Effects are said to be immediate, being sudden swelling of the face, burning heat all over the body and profuse vomiting and defecating for 45mins as your body excretes all toxins. On the semi-official Kambô Frog website, it said to prepare for the most difficult 45 mins of your life. Apparently it's not unusual to *feel like you are going to die*. Whoa. Afterwards however, you're meant to feel amazing… though I'm sure even having malaria probably feels amazing after experiencing that!

I'm shitting myself about it, but still committed. A few days later the ceremony is on, but the Sharman doesn't show up, so it's cancelled. Somewhat disappointed, somewhat relieved. I wait around for a week, then get a message one morning: "Kambô Frog Ceremony 8am tomorrow." Yiew! By this time I've done some inner work and I feel ready. I spend the day meditating and determining what I want from it. I know I just need to surrender myself to it. Come next morning, I'm prepared and excited. I'm prepared for the worst 45mins of my life and I'm not even scared (well, ok, I am still scared, but not *tooo* much). We go to the Sharman's houses where there're some rugs organised around a smouldering fire, plus some wooden carvings, a vase of feathers and various crystals. The location is awesome, with a view of the volcano seen through the banana plants in his jungle garden. After making our prayers, he does a small ritual on each of us, then uses a pipe to blow tobacco dust up our nose, with so much force it goes up one nostril and out the other. This is to open up our pineal gland. He then does this to the other. Needless to say this hurt, but I was committed for some serious discomfort today. Next up is getting a smouldering stick to apply the burns to our body. I ask for a line down the centre of my chest and close my eyes as he applies the burns. Once finished, I open my eyes to see that instead of a nice neat line, he's put it in the shape of a cock and balls. Great. Instead of an awesome looking tribal line of dots, I have a penis pointing to my face. I don't have long to worry about this as he then comes around with the poison, applying the poison to the burns. The effect is instant; swelling of the head, heat, ringing in ears, then dizziness and vision that goes haywire – bright and blurry. It's like you've been poisoned… strangely enough. I have a lie down, then actually feel pretty good! The uncomfortable part really only lasted probably just one minute. I'm lying down, smiling as I meditate; enjoying the nice tingling in my arms. I'm actually quite enjoying it. The others meanwhile, are all vomiting. The Sharman says I should be vomiting up all the toxins, so he gives me another round of tobacco up the nose which really isn't nice at all, prompting some forced vomiting. He then decides to give me a fifth point of the poison, and reapplies the other four points as well. Not sure if I got the equivalent of a nine-point then? Fingers down the throat and there's more vomiting, but then, well, that's it! It was all over pretty quick. I felt a bit dizzy and unsteady for another 30 minutes… then I felt great! The feeling continued through the day, feeling more energetic and tingly. Towards the end of the day I even had to look at my feet to make sure I was walking not flying, as it felt. I felt pretty great for the next two weeks. I'd definitely do it again. Go the Kambô Frog!

Cacao Ceremonies

The first cacao ceremony I did was with the famous 'Keith the Chocolate Sharman'. Imagine sitting cross-legged on a crowded porch of a 65-year-old white American hippy, complete with long hair and long beard that freely admits to consuming (and selling) copious amounts of all drugs in existence back in his day. The classic hippy from the 60's that's somehow survived. On his porch are an assortment of other young hippies, mainly attractive bra-less girls. Keith the Chocolate Sharman starts off his story about how the Chocolate Spirit came to him to talk to him about how the sacred cacao ceremonies of the Mayan's had stopped and how it needed to be revived. After numerous conversations with the Cacao Spirit, Keith went on a quest around Guatemala to find the best cacao beans with the highest spiritual value. I'm at this point wondering why the Mayan Cacao Spirit chose a white American hippy as opposed to all the indigenous Mayans that populate the area. Not sure. Anyway we each have a cup of cacao (basically a cold hot chocolate), at which point some of the girls start crying, and others are sitting, meditating, and swaying in a trance. What the fuck's going on??? We've just drunk some chocolate and now everyone's crying?!? I'm a bit confused, but I try to stay open and receptive. He's talking, giving advice to people, but I'm just not understanding what he's saying. By now more people have poured in too, so I'm sitting squished cross-legged with people all around too. Far from comfortable. We then do some other meditation exercises but I'm just not getting it, and realising this doesn't seem to be finishing soon, leave after four hours of uncomfortable confusion. As I leave and walk up the road, I think, "Whoa! My legs are just full of *energy*!" I get back to my hostel but just can't sit still. In fact, the energy effects of that one cacao peaked after a full seven hours and continued on for hours more. Wahoo!

For me I just didn't resonate with Keith at all, yet when I caught up with a friend of mine that stayed, she said it was life changing!! She was positively beaming. This would turn out to be standard response from all following people that I saw go to the ceremony. I think the key is that if Keith talks directly to that person then he can understand exactly what they feel, what they need and set them on the right path. Keith didn't speak directly with me so maybe that's why it didn't work for me. Basically everyone says it's life changing. I later went to a Men's Cacao Ceremony a few times run by a different guy, which I really enjoyed. These times I really did feel the effects of the cacao, which really helps you to open up emotionally. It was good just hanging with the guys having a chat.

Looking at how this works, we all know chocolate makes us feel good but this is always heavily processed stuff and is devoid of 90% of the chemical goodies (supposedly; I'm not so sure why). Thereby having raw cacao gives you the full chemical cocktail that is like a mild version of ecstasy. That is, you feel more energetic and open up a lot more emotionally. It definitely works. The reason (that I later found out) why the girls started crying as soon as they had it was because they had done numerous cacao ceremonies beforehand, and this was somewhat akin to Pavlov's Dogs, in that being on Keith's porch brought them back to emotions that they'd experienced previously there. As weird as it was the first time, it's actually totally legit – you just need to resonate with the shaman/counsellor to get the full benefit.

On another occasion I also did the 'Ecstatic Dance'. Imagine a small rave in someone's backyard in the middle of the day, attended by about 10 people, with zero alcohol or drugs. Basically you have a cacao drink (remember this is like a very mild version of ecstasy), then dance like crazy to the DJ. It was actually a lot of fun! No-one's there judging you, so you can do whatever the hell you want. I consider myself a pretty reasonable dancer with a sense of beat, but after a while, I thought – wahoo! It's not about picking up girls so there's no need to look good or even be in time with the music – just have fun! I did all sorts of stupid dance moves I'd normally never do and even went for a roll around on the floor! Fun times!

Yoga

I've always freakin' hated yoga. I even once did the Bikram hot yoga almost every day for a month. Hated it, but still did it. Everyone in the class is just doing all the moves without question, but I'm there wondering what the hell is the purpose of standing on one leg while you try and hold your other foot and extend it all the way out. Here's me jumping up and down on one foot while holding my other foot, with my terrible flexibility only allowing my leg to make it to a right angle, not straight like everyone else. What the hell are we trying to achieve here?!? Is this a balance exercise, or a stretching exercise?? *What are we trying to achieve here?!?*

I forced myself to do a session of yoga as it was included in the Moon course that I did, and as expected, I bloody well hated the whole session, swearing under my breath as I tried to contort my body into unnatural positions. I always think that it's all well and good for people with already good flexibility, but if you're someone like me who can barely touch his knees (I'm not lying), then most moves I can't even do, so I'm not getting a stretch. I had a bitch of a time in the class and decided not to go again.

Of course, that afternoon at the meditation session I started chatting to a girl about my shitty yoga session in the morning and how I hate yoga. She looked like I just insulted her mother – turned out she was a yoga instructor! Oh. Sorry. She then explained a few things to me, and invited me up for a one-on-one session. In just half an hour she explained to me the concept of yoga, the importance of breath and showed me how an unflexible person like me should do the moves and so on. Next day I went to the same yoga session, actually enjoyed it and even felt really energetic afterwards! Turns out yoga can be really good, even if you're totally unflexible. My advice; if you're new to it, see if you can book a private session with a yoga instructor. Yes, it will be expensive, but one or more sessions one-on-one to set yourself straight is much better than straining through sessions, hating it and doing it wrong. Best option is to learn a skill such as massage and just do a skill swap. Learning massage really is amazing – you can swap it for anything!!

Breathwork

My first foray into Breathwork was 'Holotropic breathing'. This really is just a fancy word for 'forced hyperventilation to an extreme level'. That more honest name may however put some people off. This stuff is pretty incredible though! Many people (if not the majority) that do it, say its effects are stronger than magic mushrooms, LSD and even Ayahuasca. …and this is just from breathing. Say whaa??

Basically, you lie down and the guide puts on some tribal fast-paced doof music and you hyperventilate (breathe in and out as deeply and quickly as possible) for one hour. Within minutes you feel your face tingle and start to cramp up, your eyes start vibrating, your whole body feels numb, and you get the worst ever cramps in your hands. Before long I was looking like a spastic (note this is not to be derogatory – this is the correct term for a person with cerebral palsy, where their hands fold tightly inwards towards the forearms). I got to the stage where my hands were up on my chest folded in so tightly that I was in a huge amount of pain. They were absolutely unmovable, like concrete. I was in a lot of pain, but continued on the breathing, wondering if I would ever gain the use of my arms again. After fighting the cramps all this time, I finally gave in and just totally relaxed. Whoooaaa!! As soon as I stopped fighting it, I was washed over in a crazy euphoric feeling unlike any drug. My hands felt like they curled in past my arms, and it was just such an awesome intense feeling sensation. I then just spontaneously started laughing; laughing a huge amount, then started doing a cross between laughing or crying or whatever the hell it was. This went on for a few minutes and damn it felt good. It took another half an hour or more before I could regain any movement in my arms and they hurt for another three days afterwards but it was still worth it, both for the emotional release, as well as the awesome feeling of being disconnected from your body.

Weeks later I did another session, but didn't go as deep. Other people in the session however were laughing and crying hysterically. One girl who was really affected by it was just amazed, saying how she normally feels nothing from drugs and other therapies, yet with this she was crying hysterically; finally expressing years of trauma. It helped her immensely. It definitely goes deep, with many people report releasing trauma of when they were a toddler. I'd be interested to hear a doctor's opinion on it. So far I haven't found enough to say whether to say it's dangerous or not. Worth looking into.

Another Breathwork course I did was Pranayama Kriya Breathing. This was incredible too, while being 100% safe. I found this to be the most effective method for getting rid of past trauma. In my experience, much more powerful than Vipassana, and one helluva lot easier. All this requires you to do is a specific routine of deep breaths in the morning, and again in the afternoon for a period of five days. Each day you also write down all you can from that fifth of your life (that is day 1 is age 0-6, day 2 is 6-12, etc). Our teacher warned us at the start that it makes you super emotionally sensitive, but as a *man*, I knew this didn't include me as well. Just the girls, right?

Wrong.

The first day was great. I did this one hour after the Kambô frog ceremony so I actually felt like I was floating the whole rest of the day. The second day was fine too, but come third day I started the day feeling absolutely super great, just top of the world, but then in the afternoon I was talking about Reiki to someone who was a sceptic, and that slight bit of negativity just killed me. I went from flying in the clouds to depressed from one very small remark. For the next three days I couldn't talk to anyone and shut myself in my room hoping no one would talk to me. Going out for dinner sucked as it meant dealing with people. I was feeling really depressed and wondering if I could ever be happy again. Day six was a pause day to keep the emotions coming, then reprieve finally came on the seventh day where we did a calming breath. By evening of the seventh, I was feeling great, and continued to do so afterwards. I really did feel like I dealt with my issues from the past. Of course I still remember things that pissed me off, but now I can look at things without any anger or sadness. I really can't believe how well it allowed me to deal with past grievances and be ok with it. Amazing!

Ayahuasca

Ayahuasca; it almost seems a waste to mention it without writing a full book. Ayahuasca is still very unknown in the western world, outside of some serious hippy circles. This may well change in the future. Ayahuasca is a sacred plant-based medicine from the Amazon; or if you're a narcotics agent, it's an illegal Schedule I hallucinogenic drug. Ayahuasca is somewhat like the more commonly known 'peyote' from Mexico (which is a powerful hallucinogen extracted from a cactus). Ayahuasca on the other hand is the made by the combination of two plants from the Amazon, in Peru. While Ayahuasca has some extremely strong hallucinogenic effects, it is certainly no 'recreational drug'. As such it is in somewhat of a legal grey area as its use is for medical/spiritual purposes. Ayahuasca is known as the 'God' drug for the visions and insights it purportedly gives its users. Those that take it say it shows them how to be the best person they can be, get in touch with past demons, cure addictions and so on. Some say it to be the absolute best medicine/psychologist/motivator in the world. The phrase '20 years therapy in six hours' seems to be the general descriptor of Ayahuasca. This is not something you take at a party to get high; it is a powerful medicine that works on the mind, not just the body. The controversial point is that it is a powerful hallucinogen, which therefore by definition makes it an illegal drug; however considering the spiritual insights it gives; banning it would be like tearing down the Vatican. This is why no one seems to hide taking it. There are many outspoken university professors on the matter, and it appears the legality is starting to turn around, with some Ayahuasca churches successfully winning Supreme Court cases in getting permission to use it for spiritual purposes. In short, the synthesized active compound DMT is illegal but the plant form is fine.

Interestingly enough, whilst on my travels in Central America, there've been certain individuals that I've been particularly drawn to. They have had some sort of unexplainable good energy that radiates from them and they have been such positive, happy and down-to-earth people. Not coincidently, all these people have tried Ayahuasca. Who could not be tempted by that? I did some reading up on the net in which all reports were that taking it made miraculous changes to people's lives. I, of course, became very interested, and after spending two months of doing inner preparation work in the hippy town of San Marcos in Guatemala, I felt prepared. As luck would have it, an Ayahuasca ceremony was organised for the last week I was there.

This however, would become the single most terrifying and unsettling thing I've ever experienced. Even final-editing this story months later, the thought of it generates a fear in my stomach like no other. Read on to find out more.

I am doing it with some friends and friends-of-friends in the village of San Marcos, Guatemala. We are a group of 10, including the Sharman and his helper. We have organised a Sharman from Honduras and a house to do it in; a huge modern style palapa perched above the lake. It's a round room with a beautiful wooden floor and a very high ceiling. The wall facing the lake is all glass; providing a mesmerizing view of the lake and the three large majestic volcanos just a few kilometres away on the other shore. Absolutely beautiful. We all gather together in the room and at 9pm ceremoniously take a tablespoon of the medicine. Most people were almost gagging as they swallowed but I actually thought it tasted fine – like a tobacco flavoured Hershey's Chocolate Sauce. We wait around for around 40 minutes or so, then have another. He says if we feel we need more later, we can ask for it. We then all have a liedown and wait for it to kick in. Lying down with my eyes closed, I could go into a type of dream state, going into a kaleidoscopic world of rotating patterns. Sometimes it would feel like I was inside some 3D fantasy factory of sorts. With my eyes open however, all was normal. Based on some of the stories I read about the Ayahuasca prior, I was expecting to see blue light dancing around the room, visions of the Ayahuasca spirit and so on. My inner voice started up with dialogue on the lines of, "This so-called 'Sharman' is from Honduras, not Peru. He's not a real Sharman. The stuff he has given us has gone bad during the long bus trip here. It's a sham. I need some more." As I wasn't seeing any blue spirits, I asked for more, and got another two spoonfuls. Now running on double the initial dose I go back to lying down where the kaleidoscope factory continues and gets somewhat better, but my inner dialogue is very strong and keeps distracting me. The rule of the Ayahuasca is not to fight it, just to let it be. It seems the opposite with me; I have to concentrate really, really hard to see the visions, and with any small distraction I snap out of it. If I concentrated really hard I could see some cool things, but generally I'd just keep snapping out of it before getting too deep. The visions are pretty cool however, so I decide I need more to really force the visions upon myself. I approach the Sharman who is quite surprised as everyone else is tripping balls, and he says;

"Really? Do you smoke a lot of pot?"

"No, not at all."

"Amazing. Well, if you wish I will give you more. I have some more potent stuff for you."

He then gives me a spoon of not just the syrup, but a solid paste, somewhat like toffee. This is just solid Ayahuasca, in its concentrated form. I take it down, and sit, practising breathing and meditation, waiting for the blue spirits to start dancing around the room. My inner dialogue is getting stronger. I'm seeing nothing. I go back to closing my eyes and trying to drift off. It got pretty cool in fact. In one part I managed to meet my subconscious in a very abstract way – there were two groups of little red men that met each other for the first time – one representing conscious, the other representing subconscious. Hello Dave! At another point I felt my mind drift out and leave my body and for the first time, I felt a disconnect from the mind to the body. This gave me the realisation that the mind and the body are two separate entities. I realised that me, Dave, is my mind that is currently habituating this body. That was pretty awesome. These visions and sensations did not last long though, and I'd unfortunately snap out of it. This can only mean one thing... I need more. I went back to the Sharman and this time he gives me two tablespoons of the paste. I've now had four spoons of the syrup and three of the concentrated paste. This is now around six times the dose that got the others tripping off their faces.

This was not a good idea. Some time later after that dose, *everything* changed.

The world stopped existing.

Life had boiled down to just my mind-chatter; my inner dialogue. All along I thought that I needed more Ayahuasca to get rid of the mind-chatter so I could reach my subconscious. Now, this was all that existed in the world. I'm talking mind-chatter to the next level, and then some. It became a mental battlefield. And it became scary. Really scary.

I ended up being stuck in limbo for 4-5hrs. I thought I would be there for eternity; and I mean actual eternity, not just my life. I honestly thought that was it and that I'd never get out.

This next section is going to make me sound totally crazy and I'm well aware of that, but remember, I did have a 6x dose of the most powerful drug in existence, so I believe I deserve a little lee-way. Here is what I experienced:

Utter confusion. The inner dialogue battle of history. A battle of logic to the death (of reality). With nothing other than my mind, I pondered the mind; "What *is* the mind?" I came up with the amazing revelation, "The mind is the mind". I later developed and refined it to "The mind is the mind is the mind". At the time it was such a breakthrough and made so much sense. Now I'm not so sure what that means.

I developed the thought that the mind is not so much the brain – the brain is what controls the body; what makes us move and what controls our digestion, heart, etc. The brain is also what makes us think, what makes us have new ideas. The artistic works of Michelangelo, the writing of Charles Dickens, the scientific breakthroughs of Einstein, the philosophical thoughts of Socrates; this is all the brain. The mind is something entirely different. The mind is an energy force working inside the brain. It is not inherently part of the brain; it is a separate entity that typically resides in the brain but can transmutate. This is our spirit. This is also our inner dialogue; our relentless mind-chatter. The body is born with the brain, but the mind is generations old and is an energy force that comes from elsewhere.

After a lot of pondering, I got to the thought – where is my mind? If my body is here and my brain is here, where is my mind?

Bad idea.

I cracked the code. The Matrix crumbled. I took the red pill. Everything that I knew ceased to exist. I am my mind. That is all there is.

One hour prior I was living happily on planet Earth; now I realised it doesn't exist at all. It was all a creation of my mind. I'd always believed in God, and now I had a horrifying realisation; I *am* god.

I remember from age 5, I used to ponder where we came from. Where did earth come from? Where did the universe come from? What made that?!? I clearly remember asking my mum who said "We can't think that far". I was shocked. Age 5 and I realised that parents don't know all, and even more than that, no one in the world apparently knew where we came from.

Now I knew.

From age 15 onwards I often thought that maybe reality is like Dream V2.0. That is, it's just a souped up version of a dream. In dreams you don't know you're dreaming (unless you lucid dream). When you lucid dream, you can see that the detail in a dream is just the same as the detail in real life. It really is fascinating. It's an interesting thought to ponder if life is just this better version of a dream. The difference is that if you're in a dream and ponder whether if it is a dream, you 'wake up' in the dream and become lucid; able to control everything like a superhero or a god. In real life, it's not so easy. Wondering if life is all just a dream is nothing more than an academic exercise – you cannot wake up from it.

Unless you take Ayahuasca.

I woke up. I don't mean I woke from a sleep, I mean I woke from reality. Just like taking the red pill in The Matrix, I woke up from reality and realised that 'reality' is nothing more than a creation of the mind. I burst out laughing. Fuck me, it's all fake!! Anything I do is just a dream!! To cement this fact, the day before the Ayahuasca I spoke with a guy I made friends with in San Marcos, a 20-something-year-old Australian guy. Really nice guy. Turned out he previously lived in Peru where was a helper in Ayahuasca ceremonies, and therefore had taken it a lot. He said, after you take it, you're never the same again. Now I knew what he meant. I had a vision of seeing him the next day and we'd give each other that look; that knowing look. That look that we knew The Truth and no one else did. The world doesn't in fact exist, and this is all just a dream.

The next two spoonfuls kicked in.

If I'm now out of the dream that we call reality, then where am I now? The Control Room. I entered My Mind. My Mind existed in 'actual reality' which was just space with no planets or universe. Just blackness and the energy force of my Mind. Nothing else.

From there I could see that for every (perceived) reality, there were infinite permutations. I was happy in the solace that everything is created by my higher mind and that nothing mattered in reality – if I died in one reality, I'd start life in another. My mind was the entirety of the world. Nothing I did to anyone would matter as they weren't real people – they were just a creation by my higher conscious.

Here is where I had another real epiphany – I was always confused by the term 'higher conscious'. I always thought higher *sub*conscious was a more apt term as what controls the universe would be subconscious, not conscious right? Now I realised that the Control Room, My Mind, was my conscious mind, not my subconscious mind, just on the next level. Therefore 'higher conscious' is indeed the perfect term.

I then had another thought – if The Mind exists out of the body, how can I be having thoughts (mind chatter) while I'm in My Mind? Phfzzzz, boom! That world collapsed to nothing, and I woke up the next level down, in My Mind. Whoa, what a realisation! I realised, yes, this is it! The last world wasn't in fact My Mind, this here was! Then I thought; Wait…. How could I realise that? Where did that thought come from? I then had an epiphany – there must be another level! As soon as I realised that, that world collapsed and I entered My Mind. Yes, I got there! Awesome!! Wait, how can I still have this thought?…

This is where I entered Limbo. An endless, relentless battle of logic, confusion and questioning that would last the next 4 hours. And no, it wasn't as bad as it sounds; it was far worse than it sounds. It was a paradox. Then I'd question the paradox, which would become a paradox of a paradox. Am I starting to lose you? Good. Because I was lost in confusion beyond all belief.

This is where life became scary beyond all imaginable belief. I had gone from leading a reasonably happy, somewhat ignorant life on earth, and now I'd taken the 'red pill' and entered limbo. I wanted nothing more than for it to all go back to how it was, but it's irreversible. I felt extremely lonely.

I would go from happy to despair. I was happy in the solace that all my lives were in fact just controlled by my higher conscious and that nothing mattered – everything was therefore fine. I just kept on laughing, both at the thought that all was just a dream, and laughing at the fact that nothing in life mattered.

It's like waking from a bad dream and laughing how none of your trials or concerns in the dream mattered. The lonely part was that I had woken up from the blissfully ignorant life I was leading in 'reality'. The Control Room sucked. It sounds good in theory to be god, to be the creator and controller of all; but the reality is that it's extremely lonely. If you create all, everything stops existing. Your family isn't real anymore; love ceases to exist. If it's all something that you've created, then you're just imagining someone loving you; it's not real. I then pondered love and family and all that then disappeared too. I couldn't remember the feeling of love, and my family became nothing more than a distant, abstract idea.

Then *everything* ceased to exist. If I was the creator of all, then those 'rules' of feelings and sensation no longer existed.

At this point, the Ceremony officially ended for everyone (as for them, all effects had worn off), however I had just reached my peak. I took my earplugs out, and like a newborn baby, started to eat them. I could have swallowed them, choked and died and not cared, as I knew that life was just one permutation of an infinite amount, and that it was all just an imagination anyway. The idea of death was nothing more than should I wear a blue t-shirt or a green t-shirt today? Luckily however, it was not something I felt like testing.

The guys brought out some fruit. I recognised the fruit as food, but all my previous notions about sensations had been wiped clean. I grabbed the pineapple and started to eat the green spikey bits at the top. Fortunately the others advised me that's not the right part to eat and cut off a slice for me.

I tasted food for the very first time in my life.

Every memory of every feeling and sensation I've ever had had been completely wiped clean. It was like being a newborn baby. It was like going from a black-and-white world to a world of colour. My taste buds had never tasted before until now. I tried an apple as well. Imagine tasting for the very first time in your life. It would be somewhat similar to a person born blind being able to see for the first time. It was just incredible. I then touched my nose. I was the first time I had ever touched my nose; the first time the touch sensors in my nose and fingers had ever been activated, the feelings travelling up my nerves, and firing off neurons in my brain. The sense of touch. I kept touching the end of my nose, playing with it. I then felt my hair. Wow. No doubt I looked crazy touching my nose and running my hands through my hair so much but I didn't care.

Even though I was interacting with the people in the group, I was still deeply off my face, and didn't believe they existed. I thought they were all just people that my mind had created. This could have been dangerous as I still didn't believe in repercussions. I thought it doesn't matter what I do – they are all just creations of my imagination (like a dream) so nothing matters. Luckily I didn't do anything inappropriate.

I was lying down, happy in the knowledge that nothing in life mattered; that everything is fine, but also deeply desperate to get out of My Mind, and back to my 'life'. Remember I'm still going through the constant loop, receding back to one more level of My Mind every few seconds. I tried to find the 'key' to reality – the item or action that would take me back, e.g. holding my necklace, putting my necklace in a bucket, holding an apple, eating an apple, etc. Nothing worked. I knew I had to wait for daylight, but in my mind I created all, including the day. I willed for it to become day, but nothing changed. I then believed that My Mind was in a place that was perpetually night. I thought I would never see day again. The reason it was so scary was that it was my conscious that discovered the world is fake, not my subconscious. Once the Ayahuasca wore off, I would return to my conscious which would be the same, knowing everything was made up.

Eventually as day started to dawn, so too did the effects wear off, and much to my delight I was able to go back to 'reality'. My fears were that I would never feel the same again – knowing that everything was just a creation of My Mind. Thankfully however, by next morning I felt almost the same as I always had, but trying to forget my experience. It was something I never ever wanted to experience and didn't want to know. I tried to forget. I wished I'd never taken the Ayahuasca. I spent the morning chatting with a friend from the ceremony, and that human contact made the Earth feel more real. We sat on the dock, admiring the beautiful lake and the volcanos on the other side. There was just too much for me to create this all. I felt like I was back in the 'real' world. Later that day we walk to meet up with the others to have a review and discussion session. On the way I see Justin, the Australian guy I saw in my visions. The next few minutes would become the most unsettling time of my life. We stopped. He gives me 'that' look. That knowing look. My pulse quickens. I know what's about to come next, but there's no stopping it. Just like my vision, he says the most unsettling words I've heard in my life.

"You saw it, didn't you?"

He then continued to say, "You understand now. I couldn't explain it to you yesterday. You had to experience it yourself. Now you know. I told you you'll never be the same after Ayahuasca. Remember, everything you saw, is real."

The blood drained from my head. "No!" I shouted. "No. No. No, it's not!" and I ran away. Just in that moment, I went from feeling somewhat re-integrated into the world, to having everything crashing away. I found the others and chatted about my experience from last night. I explained all I saw, and they said, "That is exactly what the monks from thousands of years ago said. You've experienced in one night what people devote their entire lives to."

They didn't help by agreeing it was true.

I told them just how much Ayahuasca I took last night and they couldn't believe it. "That amount should have sent you crazy. You must have a very strong mind."

My response: "Perhaps too strong. That was the whole problem."

Three months later, I'm still not sure what I feel about my experience. It was the most terrifying and unsettling thing I've ever experienced, but most people's experience with Ayahuasca is nothing short of absolutely amazing and life changing in a good way. I think I just jumped in way too deep and wasn't prepared for it. As such, I would encourage you to try it if you feel the calling, *but not until you can meditate without a thought.* Also, don't take 6x the dose. That's just dumb.

I wrote more about what I think my experience all meant on my website (www.LiveTheAdventureLife.com), but this falls outside the scope of the book, so I have not included it here. Actually to be honest, it wasn't much more than just some ramblings without conclusion anyway. All I'll say is to remember that life is perfect. The up's and down's is what makes it so perfect. Don't fight it – roll with these, learn from the bad times and let it roll through to the next good experience. Most bad experiences people have ultimately turn into a good thing… eventually. It may not make any sense at the time, but eventually it will. Just trust in that, and remember that nothing in life really matters. It's all just a dream anyway.

Index

No index included. You'll just have to read the whole thing again. Mwahahaha-haaaa!!!

Appendix 1: Packing List Summaries

These packing list summaries are what I use. Your personal requirements may well be different, but I've presented my packing list for interest's sake and to help you think of things you may otherwise forget.

All Items

- Sleeping
    - *Lightweight down sleeping bag*
    - *Thermal liner*
    - *Memory foam travel pillow (small normal-shape type, not the neck pillows)*
- Hiking
    - *Hiking socks*
    - *Possum gloves*
    - *Beanie*
    - *Thermal tops and bottoms*
    - *Zip-off lightweight pants/shorts for mosquito areas*
    - *Long-sleeved lightweight shirt for mosquito areas*
    - *Gore-Tex lightweight rain jacket (for visiting countries in the wet season)*
    - *Lightweight hiking boots (non Gore-Tex for warm countries)*
- Clothing
    - *Nice collared shirt*
    - *Jeans*
    - *Dress shorts*
    - *Boardshorts (for swimming)*
    - *Singlets*
    - *T-shirts*
    - *10x underpants. Mix of bamboo fibre undies and nice going out undies*

- *Socks*
- *Boxer shorts for sleeping in*
• Medi-kit
    - *Loperamide*
    - *Tinidazole*
    - *Norfloxacin*
    - *Stemetil*
    - *Soframycin*
    - *Diamox (only if going to high-altitude)*
    - *Condoms*
    - *Ibuprofen*
    - *Anti-inflammatory tablets*
    - *Tea tree oil (for bites and burns)*
• Electronics
    - *Laptop (an Ultrabook if you can afford it)*
    - *External hard drive*
    - *USB stick*
    - *Camera (recommend Sony RX100)*
    - *USB rechargeable beard trimmer*
    - *Phone (compatible with country you're going to)*
    - *Powerboard*
    - *GPS tracker (not really necessary)*
    - *Headlamp*
• Toiletries
    - *Regaine (only if you suffer from hairloss)*
    - *Toothbrush and toothpaste*
    - *Shampoo bar*
    - *Conditioner*
    - *Face cleanser*
    - *Small bottles for conditioner and face cleanser*
    - *Hair wax*
• Other
    - *Umbrella (purchased overseas – these are always cheap and easy to find in rainy places)*
    - *Gift mementos from home (such as small koalas if you're from Australia)*
    - *Bunch of flags (to sell at festivals)*
    - *Pens*
    - *Small notepad*
    - *Quality sunglasses (UV protected)*
    - *Hat (but you could probably just buy this once overseas)*
    - *Pocket knife*
    - *Spork (combination spoon, knife, fork)*
• Footwear

– *Thongs (Havaianas)*
– *Comfortable black shoes (suitable for both long walks and going out). Leather preferable*
- Organisation
    – *Clothes bag (rectangular shallow box-shape)*
    – *Laundry bag*
    – *Compression bag for hiking gear*
    – *Zip-lock cheap disposable plastic bags for various items (variety of sizes)*
    – *Cordura dry bag for toiletries*
    – *Ultra-Sil daypack*
- Massage Items
    – *Massage oil*
    – *Essential oil*
    – *Shot glass (used to put massage and essential oil into and to apply it to customer)*
    – *Cordura dry bag to put these items into*
    – *Laminated massage poster*
    – *Whiteboard marker to annotate poster as you change hostels*
- Magic Bag
    – *Invisible Deck (Bicycle brand)*
    – *Normal cards (Bicycle brand)*
    – *3 x thin lightweight decks*
    – *Scissors*
    – *String*
    – *Permanent marker*
    – *Lip balm*
    – *Magic gimmick tricks, such as flying saucer, dice in box, etc.*

Airplane Ready-Bag

- Quality in-ear headphones, with an airplane adaptor
- Earplugs (two pairs as you'll probably lose one)
- Laptop. Charger too if flying in an A380
- Notepad and pen
- Book
- Water bottle
- Jumper (sweater)
- Socks
- Saline spray for your nose for long flights if easily affected
- Jeans and all essentials in daypack in overhead bin

Day Trips
- Spork
- Pocket knife
- Water bottle
- Food
- Camera
- Sunglasses
- Sunscreen

Nights Out
- Phone (if you have a SIM card)
- Wallet (cash only, no ATM card. Emergency $50 kept in zip-up section)
- Crap camera
- Magic
    - *Two decks of thin lightweight cards (one normal, one for Magic Kissing Trick)*
    - *Sponge hearts*
    - *Permanent marker*
    - *Lip balm*

Appendix 2: Checklists

Changing Location

- Hostel booked, directions and hostel phone number saved to your phone
  - *Record how much you should pay on arrival*
- Transport booked
  - *Ensure you have recorded the name of the transport company you're using*
- Downloaded map of new location in phone (if not on a data plan). See Chapter 1 for how to do this
- "Starred" location of hostel in maps on phone
- If doing border crossing:
  - *Exchange rate recorded*
  - *Time zone difference checked*
  - *Border fee (if applicable) checked. Ensure you have enough cash with you for this*
  - *Have printout of ticket exiting country (where required)*
  - *Have passport handy*
  - *Emergency and reverse call numbers of new country recorded*
- Email your family with new location so in case you go missing they have some lead
- Ensure your phone and laptop are charged so you have some entertainment on the journey
- Check you've packed up all your things:
  - *Phone and camera chargers*
  - *Sunglasses*
  - *Camera*
  - *Pillow*
  - *Toiletries (shampoo often gets left in the shower)*
  - *Massage poster (if applicable)*
  - *Towel or any clothes that you've hung out to dry*
  - *Everything removed from locker*

– *Didgeridoo (this probably doesn't relate to most people!)*
- Get key deposit back
  – *If you have an early morning departure, get the deposit back the night before. Make sure to pack all your bags the night beforehand too.*
- Make sure to lock your bags and never let them out of your sight, especially if doing a border crossing

Note from the Author

Yay, you made it to the end! I hope you enjoyed reading it as much as I enjoyed writing it! If you got a few laughs and learned a few things, what better way to spread the love around the world other than to let your friends know about it! What would be even more awesome is to write a review on Amazon too! I know writing a review takes effort and sucks to do, but hey, more reviews equals me writing more books so it's good for you too!

Best way to write a review is just to go to the book on Amazon, scroll to the bottom of the reviews section where you'll see the button 'Write a Customer Review'. Honest reviews are always most appreciated. If you have any other comments or feedback, thought it totally sucked or even just feel like a chat, I'd love to know about it! Just send me an email at LiveTheAdventureLife@gmail.com.

I'm pretty sure I'll release a follow-up book soon too (I'm still travelling and doing more stupid things). When it releases, I'll do a 99c promotion for the e-book version for the first week. If you like I can notify you so you can be the first to hear about it and get it cheap! If interested, just send me an email to the above address. Don't worry – I'll only use this to let you know when a new book is out or in other rare circumstances – I'm not going to spam you with all sorts of crap!

Cheers, and travel smart!

David

Notes

Use these pages for scribbling notes, writing down exchange rates and email addresses, and of course, playing Mr Squiggle!!

Mr Squiggle Pad

Mr Squiggle Pad

Notes

Notes

Notes

Notes

Notes

Printed in Great Britain
by Amazon